the Jewish World *365 Days*

דן לכה את המשפט
ועשיתה עלפי התורה אשר יגורו לכה ט הדבר
אשר ואמרו לכה   מספר התורה ויגורו לכה באמת
כי הסוס אשר מבוה לשבץ שמו עלוו ושמרתה לעשות
כטל אשר יגורו ועלם המשפט אשר ואמרו לכה
תעשה לוא תסור מן התורה אשר יגורו לכה ימין
ושמאל והאיש אשר לוא ישמע ויעש בזדון לבלתי
שמוע אל הכוהן העומד ישמור לשרת לפני אואל
ושופטם ומת האיש החוא ובערתה הרע מישראל ונול
העם ושמעו ויראו ולוא יזידו עוד בישראל

כי תבוא אל הארץ אשר אנוכי נתן לכה וירשתה וישבתה
בד ואמרתה אשימה עלי עלי מלך ככול הגואים אשר סביבותי
שם תשים עליכה מלך מקרב אחיכה תשים עליך מלך
לוא תתן עליכה איש נוכרי אשר לוא אחוכה הוא רקלוא
ירבה לו סוס ולוא ישיב את העם מצרים למלחמה למען
הרבות לו סוס וכסף וזהב   ואנוכי אמרתי לכה לוא
תסוף לשוב טרך הזואת עוד ולוא ירבה לו נשים ולוא
יסורו לבבו מאחרי וכסף וזהב לוא ירבה לו מואדה
והיה בשבתו על כסא ממלכתו ונתבו
לו את חרה רח הזואת על ספר מלפני הכוהנים

the Jewish World *365 Days*

from the Collections of The Israel Museum, Jerusalem

Harry N. Abrams, Inc., Publishers

FOREWORD

It is with great pleasure that we welcome the publication of *The Jewish World: 365 Days*, an imaginative book project based on the collections of The Israel Museum, Jerusalem. Its subject is vast and multifaceted—and well served by the visual richness of images drawn from the Museum's holdings.

At the time of its founding in 1965, the Israel Museum already held the nucleus of what would become, over forty years, a unique collection of Jewish ceremonial art and artifacts of material culture. Today, our Departments of Judaica and Jewish Ethnography continue to grow, all the while expanding their holdings and deepening the quality of the research that interprets them. As a consequence, we have been privileged to become the most important repository in the world for art and objects that illustrate Jewish ritual and secular life. At the same time, the Museum is encyclopedic in scope: our archaeological holdings extend from prehistoric times through the medieval period, and they include some of the greatest finds in biblical archaeology; and our collections in the fine arts range comprehensively from Old Masters to cutting-edge international contemporary art. This scope places the material heritage of the Jewish world in the wider context of world culture, revealing both distinctions and commonalities that are illuminating.

For this project, we have had to select only 365 images to convey something of the essence of the Jewish world. This has been a twofold challenge—to select a relative handful of objects and images from among collections numbering well over 250,000 items and, even

more difficult, to distill their significance in a way that achieves some sense of "essence." We hope that the result offers a visual overview of the idea of a "Jewish world" which, relating to the 365 days of the year, also provides an opportunity to explore the cycles of Jewish life within the continuum of Jewish history. In this way, this book opens 365 windows onto a varied landscape of communal and private faith, creativity, and engagement with Jewish tradition.

We wish to thank Harry N. Abrams, Inc., and its Editor-in-Chief, Eric Himmel, for inviting us to participate in this publication series. In Jerusalem, Rita Gans, General Manager, Israel Museum Products, took on the challenge of leading the project with Rosemary Eshel, who coordinated the project, and Bella Zaichik, who coordinated the compilation of images. They executed their work with devotion and success. Many members of the Museum staff assisted importantly in the selection and editing of images, preparation of photography, and writing and editing of texts, under the direction of Daisy Raccah-Djivre, Chief Curator of Judaica and Jewish Ethnography; Silvia Rozenberg, Chief Curator of Archaeology; and Yigal Zalmona, Chief Curator-at-Large. They worked smoothly and effectively in this cooperative enterprise.

We acknowledge all of them by name elsewhere in this publication, but we thank them here collectively for their part in the pleasure and success of this undertaking.

JAMES S. SNYDER
ANNE AND JEROME FISHER DIRECTOR

This book is based on the Gregorian calendar year 2005, which corresponds with the Hebrew calendar years 5765/5766. Please refer to pp. 736 for "About the Jewish Calendar."

Corresponding English and Hebrew date lines appear at the bottom of each page throughout the book.

Small Torah scroll
Poland, 18th century

This small Torah scroll, consisting of the first five books of the Bible, may have been used in a private home or while traveling. The ends of the scroll are usually tied to wooden staves called *azei hayyim* (trees of life), which have ornamental handles that serve as a means of rolling the scroll. The handles are engraved with the Hebrew inscription "The teaching of the Lord is perfect renewing life" (Psalms 19:8–9).

TORAH SCROLL:
PEN AND INK ON VELLUM
HANDLES: CAST, ENGRAVED, AND
PARTLY GILT SILVER;
DIAMONDS; EMERALDS
113 CM (HEIGHT)
THE STIEGLITZ COLLECTION WAS
DONATED TO THE ISRAEL MUSEUM,
JERUSALEM WITH THE CONTRIBUTION
OF ERICA AND LUDWIG JESSELSON,
NEW YORK, THROUGH THE AMERICAN
FRIENDS OF THE ISRAEL MUSEUM
PHOTOGRAPH: ISRAEL MUSEUM/
AVI GANOR

January | I 2 3 4 5 6 7 8 9 10 11 12 13 14 15 16 17 18 19 20 21 22 23 24 25 26 27 28 29 30 31

טבת | א ב ג ד ה ו ז ח ט י יא יב יג יד טו טז יז יח יט כ כא כב כג כד כה כו כז כח כט

Marriage contract (*KETUBBAH*)
Padua, Italy, 1732

The marriage contract (*ketubbah*) in which the bridegroom formally accepts responsibility for the bride, was often richly decorated, especially in Italy. This *ketubbah* bears the family coats of arms flanked by a couple dressed in the costume of Italian nobility. In addition, the depiction of Jerusalem is surrounded by the zodiac signs and pictures of the Temple utensils and biblical scenes: Jacob's dream, the Binding of Isaac, Aaron and Moses, Samson and the lion, and Jonah and the whale, as well as scenes relating to the "Woman of Valor" from Proverbs 31:10–31.

GROOM: SAMUEL, SON OF GERSON
HA-COHEN ME-HA-HAZANIM
(CANTARINI)
BRIDE: COLOMBA,
DAUGHTER OF DAVID AZIZ
TEMPERA, GOLD POWDER, AND
PEN AND INK ON PARCHMENT
88.7 X 59 CM

ACQUIRED WITH THE HELP OF
BAMBI AND ROGER FELBERBAUM NEW YORK
IN MEMORY OF MR. AND MRS. WILLIAM OLDEN
PHOTOGRAPH: ISRAEL MUSEUM/NAHUM SLAPAK

January | 1 **2** 3 4 5 6 7 8 9 10 11 12 13 14 15 16 17 18 19 20 21 22 23 24 25 26 27 28 29 30 31

טבת | א ב ג ד ה ו ז ח ט י יא יב יג יד טו טז יז יח יט כ **כא** כב כג כד כה כו כז כח כט

בס״מנא טבא ובמזלא מעל״א

ירושלם   הרים   סביב   לה

BLESSING FOR A WEDDING
TURKEY, 19TH–20TH CENTURY

The themes usually depicted in Jewish papercuts are connected with religion or folk beliefs. In Turkey they most frequently were made to celebrate life-cycle events such as weddings, or for use on synagogue plaques (*shiviti*), based on the verse "I have set the Lord always before me" (Psalms 16:8). This papercut plaque celebrates a wedding and contains a verse from Proverbs (18:22): "He who finds a wife has found happiness and obtains favor of the Lord."

PAPERCUT; PAPER; EMBOSSED GOLD
PAPER; INK; COLORED PENCILS
43 X 30 CM
PHOTOGRAPH: ISRAEL MUSEUM/
DAVID HARRIS

January | 1 2 **3** 4 5 6 7 8 9 10 11 12 13 14 15 16 17 18 19 20 21 22 23 24 25 26 27 28 29 30 31

טבת | א ב ג ד ה ו ז ח ט י יא יב יג יד טו טז יז יח יט כ כא **כב** כג כד כה כו כז כח כט

Prayer book cover
Tripoli, Libya, 1937

The ancient Jewish community in Libya traces its origins back to the third century BCE. The remnants of this once-flourishing community today live mostly in Italy and Israel. Metalworking was a prestigious profession in Libya. Jewish silversmiths and artisans fashioned ritual and ceremonial objects and were much prized for their skills. This silver prayer book cover, which was commissioned on the occasion of a bar mitzvah celebration, is engraved with a seven-branched candelabrum on one side and the Temple Mount on the other, testifying to the community's yearnings for and ties to the Holy Land.

Repoussé and engraved silver
Gift of Nessim (Nuccio) Habib,
Herzliya
Photograph: Israel Museum/
Avshalom Avital

January | 1 2 3 **4** 5 6 7 8 9 10 11 12 13 14 15 16 17 18 19 20 21 22 23 24 25 26 27 28 29 30 31

טבת | א ב ג ד ה ו ז ח ט י י'א י'ב י'ג י'ד ט'ו ט'ז י'ז י'ח י'ט כ כ'א כ'ב **כ'ג** כ'ד כ'ה כ'ו כ'ז כ'ח כ'ט

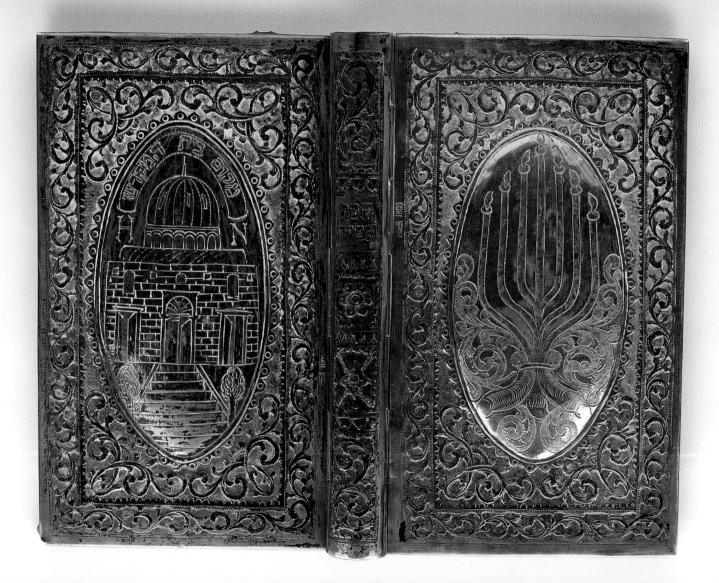

ARTIST: SHMUEL BEN-DAVID (1884–1927)
GROOM: EPHRAIM,
SON OF NAHMAN SONNENSCHEIN
BRIDE: REBEKAH BAT-ZION,
DAUGHTER OF HAIM ARYEH ZUTA
WATERCOLOR AND
PEN AND INK ON PARCHMENT
45 X 35.5 CM
BEQUEST OF ZIONA ZUTA, JERUSALEM
PHOTOGRAPH: ISRAEL MUSEUM/
DAVID HARRIS

MARRIAGE CONTRACT (*KETUBBAH*) JERUSALEM, 1926

This *ketubbah* was drawn for a Jerusalem couple who were married on the twenty-fourth of Tevet, 1926. The artist was Shmuel Ben-David, who taught at Jerusalem's Bezalel School of Arts and Crafts in its early days. It features an interesting representation of Jerusalem combining the new with the old. Against the traditional city background are a couple of pioneers (*halutzim*) entering a white tent arm in arm. Two witnesses who signed the *ketubbah* were notable Zionist leaders Menahem Ussishkin and David Yellin.

January | 1 2 3 4 **5** 6 7 8 9 10 11 12 13 14 15 16 17 18 19 20 21 22 23 24 25 26 27 28 29 30 31

טבת | א ב ג ד ה ו ז ח ט י יא יב יג יד טו טז יז יח יט כ כא כב כג **כד** כה כו כז כח כט

Rings
Yemen, late 19th–early 20th century

All Yemenite women wore rings, but styles varied according to the region.
A bride was given rings as a gift to be worn at her wedding. In rural areas rings would be worn on the toes and the thumbs as well as the fingers.

Gilt silver; silver; carnelian;
pearls; glass; filigree;
granulation
3 cm (max. diameter)
Four rings on permanent loan
Salman Schocken, Tel Aviv;
purchased with the help of
Ellen and Jerome Stern,
New York
Photograph: Israel Museum/
David Harris

January | 1 2 3 4 5 **6** 7 8 9 10 11 12 13 14 15 16 17 18 19 20 21 22 23 24 25 26 27 28 29 30 31

טבת | א ב ג ד ה ו ז ח ט י יא יב יג יד טו טז יז יח יט כ כא כב כג כד **כה** כו כז כח כט

Sabbath candlesticks
Lvov, Poland, 18th century

Women light the candles every Friday evening at dusk, welcoming the Sabbath. The lights have many forms, including hanging lamps, candlesticks for wax candles, and lamps with backplates and oil pans. These candlesticks, engraved with Hebrew letters representing a Kabbalistic formula for God's name, are not identical and show cracks. Their imperfection and the addition of the Hebrew letters contribute to their singular charm.

Repoussé and engraved silver
23 x 20 cm
The Stieglitz Collection was donated to the Israel Museum, Jerusalem with the contribution of Erica and Ludwig Jesselson, New York, through the American Friends of the Israel Museum
Photograph: Israel Museum/ Avi Ganor

January | 1 2 3 4 5 6 **7** 8 9 10 11 12 13 14 15 16 17 18 19 20 21 22 23 24 25 26 27 28 29 30 31

טבת | א ב ג ד ה ו ז ח ט י יא יב יג יד טו טז יז יח יט כ כא כב כג כד כה **כו** כז כח כט

Left to right:
Ciechucinek, Poland, 19th century
Glass; enamel
65 x 42 cm

Poland, 19th century
Repoussé, engraved, and gilt silver
70 x 57 cm

Augsburg (?), Germany, 18th century
Repoussé, engraved, and gilt silver
127 x 68 cm

Bukhara, 1785
Repoussé and engraved silver; niello
64 x 75 cm

The Stieglitz Collection was donated to the Israel Museum, Jerusalem with the contribution of Erica and Ludwig Jesselson, New York, through the American Friends of the Israel Museum
Photograph: Israel Museum/ Avi Ganor

Kiddush cups
Poland, Germany, and Uzbekistan, 18th and 19th centuries

A special prayer, the Kiddush (sanctification blessing) is recited before the Sabbath (and holiday) meal over a glass of wine. It is customary to use goblets and cups specially made for this purpose, and traditional forms such as those depicted here evolved in various countries.

January | 1 2 3 4 5 6 7 **8** 9 10 11 12 13 14 15 16 17 18 19 20 21 22 23 24 25 26 27 28 29 30 31

טבת | א ב ג ד ה ו ז ח ט י יא יב יג יד טו טז יז יח יט כ כא כב כג כד כה כו **כז** כח כט

Torah binder (*WIMPEL*) (detail)
Germany, 1845

The Torah binder was made from the linen spread on which the child was circumcised. It was later cut into pieces and sewn together to form a long strip and embroidered or painted with the names of the boy and his father, the boy's birth date, and part of the blessing from the circumcision ceremony "to the Torah, to the marriage canopy and a life of good deeds." In this painted detail of the bride and groom under the marriage canopy, the Jewish folk artist humorously intermingled the Hebrew scripts with the illustrations.

Watercolor on linen
20 x 305 cm
Gift IRSO
Photograph: Israel Museum/
Nahum Slapak

January | 1 2 3 4 5 6 7 8 **9** 10 11 12 13 14 15 16 17 18 19 20 21 22 23 24 25 26 27 28 29 30 31

טבת | א ב ג ד ה ו ז ח ט י יא יב יג יד טו טז יז יח יט כ כא כב כג כד כה כו כז **כח** כט

GLASS PAINTING
ERETZ ISRAEL, EARLY 20TH CENTURY

The biblical story of the young David triumphing over the Philistine warrior Goliath despite his great size has inspired many Jewish folk artists. This glass painting decorated in a folk style is attributed to Moses Shah, who was born in Tehran and moved to Jerusalem at the end of the nineteenth century.

OILS ON GLASS
49 X 59.5 CM
THE FEUCHTWANGER COLLECTION
PURCHASED AND DONATED TO THE
ISRAEL MUSEUM BY BARUCH AND
RUTH RAPPAPORT OF GENEVA
PHOTOGRAPH: ISRAEL MUSEUM/
YORAM LEHMANN

January | 1 2 3 4 5 6 7 8 9 **IO** 11 12 13 14 15 16 17 18 19 20 21 22 23 24 25 26 27 28 29 30 31

טבת | א ב ג ד ה ו ז ח ט י יא יב יג יד טו טז יז יח יט כ כא כב כג כד כה כו כז כח **כט**

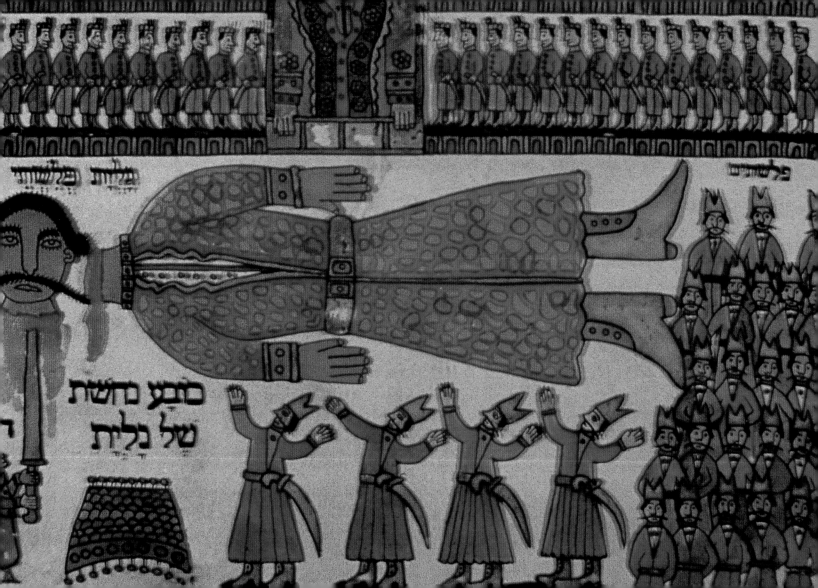

RAISED SILVER THREAD AND WOOL
EMBROIDERY ON SILK DAMASK;
SILVER STRIPS WOVEN INTO RIBBONS;
SILK APPLIQUÉ; TASSELS OF
INTERTWINED METAL AND
LINEN THREAD; LINEN LINING
68.5 x 160 CM
THE STIEGLITZ COLLECTION WAS
DONATED TO THE ISRAEL MUSEUM,
JERUSALEM WITH THE CONTRIBUTION
OF ERICA AND LUDWIG JESSELSON,
NEW YORK, THROUGH THE AMERICAN
FRIENDS OF THE ISRAEL MUSEUM
PHOTOGRAPH: ISRAEL MUSEUM/
AVI GANOR

TORAH ARK VALANCE
GERMANY, 1766

The valance usually forms part of the Torah Ark curtain set and hangs above the curtain in front of or inside the Ark. The three crowns at the top illustrate the Mishnaic verse: "Rabbi Shimon says: There are three crowns: Crown of Torah, Crown of priesthood, Crown of royalty, and the Crown of a good name surpasses them all" (Mishnah Tractate Avot 4:13). Also depicted on the valance are the utensils of the Tabernacle, such as the seven-branched menorah, the Tablets of the Law, and the shewbread (the twelve loaves of bread placed in the Sanctuary every Sabbath).

January | 1 2 3 4 5 6 7 8 9 10 **11** 12 13 14 15 16 17 18 19 20 21 22 23 24 25 26 27 28 29 30 31

שבט א | ב ג ד ה ו ז ח ט י יא יב יג יד טו טז יז יח יט כ כא כב כג כד כה כו כז כח כט ל

כתר ... בהונך

כתר תורה

שלש כתרים הם כתר מלכות ... קרבן ... על המ... בשעה ...

אהל מועד

The Great Isaiah Scroll (columns 26–30) Qumran, Cave 1, Hellenistic-Roman Period, ca. 100 BCE

The Great Isaiah Scroll is one of the original seven Dead Sea Scrolls discovered in Qumran in 1947. It is the longest and best preserved of all the biblical scrolls, and the only one discovered in its entirety (its fifty-four columns contain all sixty-six chapters of the book of Isaiah). The scroll dates from about 100 BCE and is thus some thousand years older than any other Hebrew biblical manuscript known today.

Parchment
23 CM X 734 CM
On permanent exhibition at
the Shrine of the Book,
The Israel Museum, Jerusalem
Photograph: Israel Museum/
David Harris

January | 1 2 3 4 5 6 7 8 9 10 11 **12** 13 14 15 16 17 18 19 20 21 22 23 24 25 26 27 28 29 30 31

שבט | א **ב** ג ד ה ו ז ח ט י יא יב יג יד טו טז יז יח יט כ כא כב כג כד כה כו כז כח כט ל

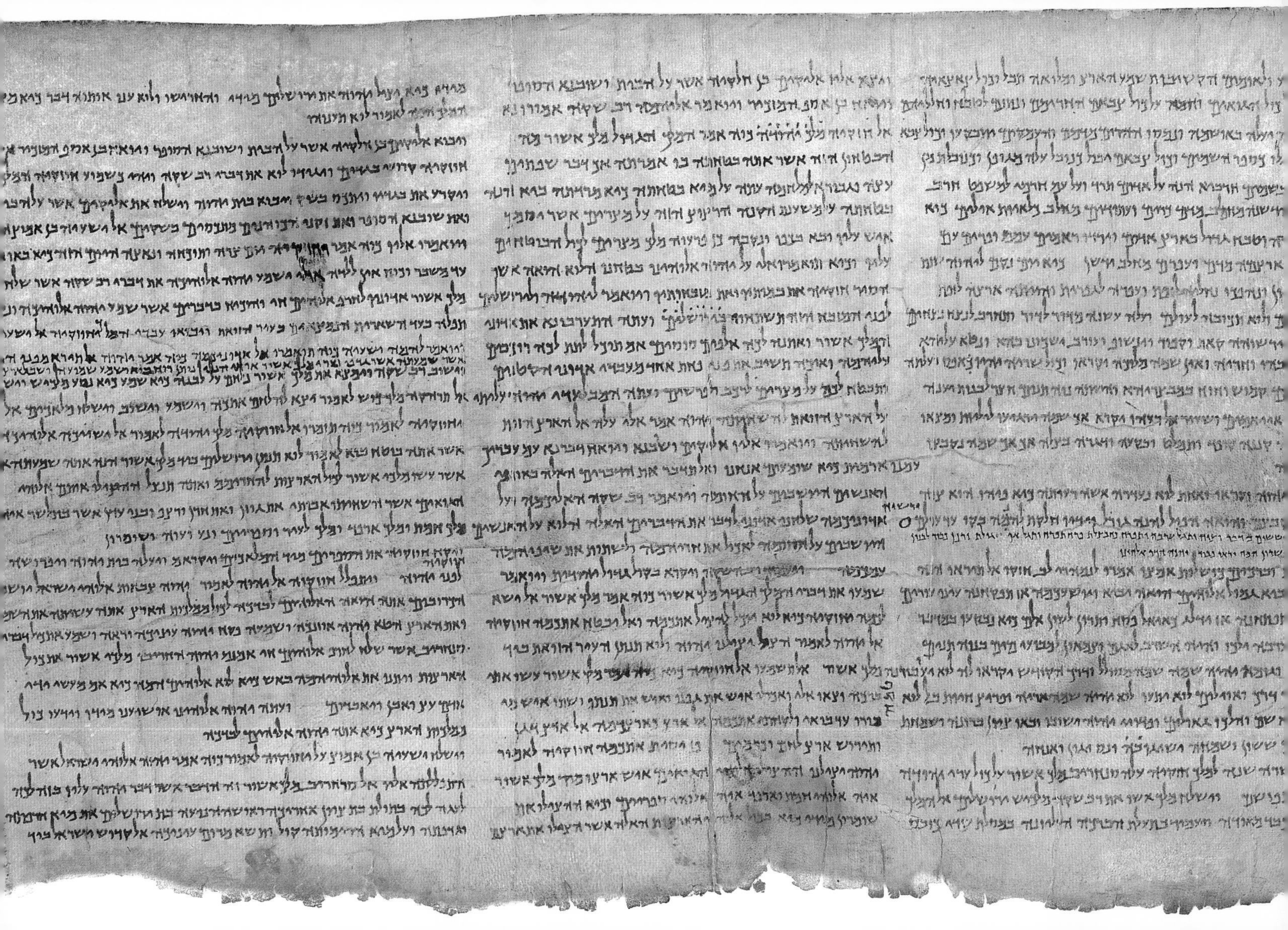

Bodices
Fez, Tetouan, and Rabat, Morocco,
19th–20th century

These bodices, worn under a vest, were an important part of the ceremonial costume and wedding dress of urban Jewish women in Morocco. They were richly embroidered with regional variations. Jewish men and women both made gold-thread embroidery, a tradition believed to have been brought to Morocco by Jews expelled from Spain.

Velvet; gold- and
metal-thread embroidery
upper left, Fez: 40 x 49 cm
upper right, Tetouan: 32 x 41 cm
lower left, Rabat: 46 x 48 cm
lower right, Tetouan: 38 x 43 cm
Photograph: Israel Museum/
Zeev Radovan

January | 1 2 3 4 5 6 7 8 9 10 11 12 **13** 14 15 16 17 18 19 20 21 22 23 24 25 26 27 28 29 30 31

שבט | א ב ג ד ה ו ז ח ט י יא יב יג יד טו טז יז יח יט כ כא כב כג כד כה כו כז כח כט ל

A Passing Cloud, 1975

Late in her life, when Anna Ticho was housebound, she drew the landscapes of the Jerusalem hills from memory. The views that had been so accurately portrayed earlier on became a blend of actual places and a more personal, introspective landscape based on her own interpretation of and emotional response to the scenery that she had loved for so many years. In this wintry drawing Ticho portrays the dark shadow of a cloud on the ground as it passes by. The demarcation of the cloud is clear, creating a swath of dark scrub while the hillside on either side is of a much lighter hue. The charcoal and pastel were applied quickly, creating a turbulence of lines and color, fitting to such a stormy day.

Anna Ticho
(1894, Brno–1980, Israel)
Charcoal and pastel on paper
50.5 x 74.5 cm
Bequest of Anna Ticho, Jerusalem
451.80
Photograph: Israel Museum

January | 1 2 3 4 5 6 7 8 9 10 11 12 13 **14** 15 16 17 18 19 20 21 22 23 24 25 26 27 28 29 30 31

שבט | א ב ג **ד** ה ו ז ח ט י יא יב יג יד טו טז יז יח יט כ כא כב כג כד כה כו כז כח כט ל

TORAH FINIALS (*RIMMONIM*) BURMA AND INDIA, 19TH AND 20TH CENTURY

These rare finials from Burma and Cochin fit over the two upper handles of the staves of a Torah scroll. Attached bells and other suspended ornaments often make a distinctive tinkling sound as the Scroll is removed from the Ark. Apparently the sound was traditionally thought to ward off the forces of evil.

January | 1 2 3 4 5 6 7 8 9 10 11 12 13 14 **15** 16 17 18 19 20 21 22 23 24 25 26 27 28 29 30 31

שבט | א ב ג ד ה ו ו ז ח ט י יא יב יג יד טו טז יז יח יט כ כא כב כג כד כה כו כז כח כט ל

Oil lamps with Jewish symbols
Provenance unknown,
Byzantine Period, 4th–5th century ce

Despite their small size, oil lamps sometimes bear meaningful messages.
These examples, which depict symbols associated with the Temple in Jerusalem—
most prominently the menorah (seven-branched candelabrum)—reflect the Jewish
longing for the rebuilding of the Temple, which was destroyed by the Romans
in 70 ce.

Pottery
8.8, 7.7 cm (length)
left: On loan from the
A. Reifenberg Collection,
Jerusalem
Photograph: Israel Museum/
Avraham Hay

right: Gift of Tamar and
Teddy Kollek, Jerusalem
Photograph: Israel Museum

January | 1 2 3 4 5 6 7 8 9 10 11 12 13 14 15 **16** 17 18 19 20 21 22 23 24 25 26 27 28 29 30 31

שבט | א ב ג ד ה | ז ח ט י יא יב יג יד טו טז יז יח יט כ כא כב כג כד כה כו כז כח כט ל

Astarte figurines
Judah, Iron Age, 8th– early 6th century BCE

Pottery figurines of this type were household objects believed to ensure fertility and abundance. Their use was vehemently condemned by the prophets of ancient Israel.

Pottery
12.5–17 cm (height)
Israel Antiquities Authority
On long term loan from the
Reifenberg Family, Jerusalem
Photograph: Israel Museum/
Nahum Slapak

January | 1 2 3 4 5 6 7 8 9 10 11 12 13 14 15 16 **17** 18 19 20 21 22 23 24 25 26 27 28 29 30 31

שבט | א ב ג ד ה ו **ז** ח ט י יא יב יג יד טו טז יז יח יט כ כא כב כג כד כה כו כז כח כט ל

A JEWISH WEDDING, 1861

The son of a wealthy merchant, M. D. Oppenheim started taking art lessons as a teenager, enrolling in the Munich Art Academy in 1817. After spending four years in Rome during the 1820s he returned to Frankfurt and soon became acquainted with Goethe as well as with the members of the wealthy Rothschild family, whose portraits he painted. By depicting traditional events from the Jewish circle of life, Oppenheim, who was not a religious Jew himself, reacquainted himself and his audience with major events in the life of the Jewish family and community.

MORITZ DANIEL OPPENHEIM,
GERMAN (1800–1882)
OIL ON CANVAS
37.5 X 28.2 CM
ACQUISITION, 1956
1149/3/56
PHOTOGRAPH: ISRAEL MUSEUM

January | 1 2 3 4 5 6 7 8 9 10 11 12 13 14 15 16 17 **18** 19 20 21 22 23 24 25 26 27 28 29 30 31

שבט | א ב ג ד ה ו ז **Π** ט י יא יב יג יד טו טז יז יח יט כ כא כב כג כד כה כו כז כח כט ל

Shrine of the Book, D. Samuel and Jeane H. Gottesman Center for Dead Sea Scrolls and Biblical Manuscripts, 1965

The Shrine of the Book is a building containing the Dead Sea Scrolls and the oldest manuscripts of the Bible found to date. In 1957 the commission to design the shrine was given to two American architects, Frederick Kiesler and Armand Bartos. It was one of the most fascinating architectural challenges in the history of the new State of Israel. The building was intended to demonstrate the range of meanings concealed within the scrolls, which had been buried for two thousand years and then discovered close to the time when the U.N. voted on Israel's independence; it had to do nothing less than create a symbol of identity for Israeli society. The building blends the religious and national aspects of the scrolls with universal concepts of light and dark, good and evil. The interior design suggests a tomb or cave, and its atmosphere is ceremonial and dramatic. The structure's dome is shaped like the lid of the jars in which the scrolls were found in the cave by the Dead Sea. The black wall symbolizes the burden of the past carried by the Jewish people. The contrast between the white and the black symbolizes the struggle of the people of light against the people of darkness, the subject of one of the important scrolls.

ARCHITECTS: FREDERICK KIESLER (1890–1965) AND ARMAND BARTOS (B. 1910)
PHOTOGRAPH: ISRAEL MUSEUM

January | 1 2 3 4 5 6 7 8 9 10 11 12 13 14 15 16 17 18 **19** 20 21 22 23 24 25 26 27 28 29 30 31

שבט | א ב ג ד ה ו ז ח **ט** י יא יב יג יד טו טז יז יח יט כ כא כב כג כד כה כו כז כח כט ל

RECONSTRUCTED BY ESTHER
BEZALEL, JERUSALEM, 1997
DECORATED WITH GILT PAPER,
COTTON THREADS, AND TASSELS
8 KG, 32 CM (DIAMETER)
PHOTOGRAPH: ISRAEL MUSEUM/
NAHUM SLAPAK

BOWL MADE OF HARDENED SUGAR
IN THE TRADITION OF HERAT, AFGHANISTAN

In Herat, Afghanistan, there were two betrothal ceremonies. The first usually took place at the bride's home, and the second was celebrated in the home of the bridegroom. At the end of the first night the groom was presented with a decorated sugar cone; wealthier families would send sugar bowls with tree-like cones in the center (as this picture shows). In Jewish and Muslim betrothals and wedding ceremonies sugar cones are seen as a symbol of blessing (because of their sweetness), purity (because of their white color), fertility (because of their phallic shape), and prosperity (because of their many grains).

January | 1 2 3 4 5 6 7 8 9 10 11 12 13 14 15 16 17 18 19 **20** 21 22 23 24 25 26 27 28 29 30 31

שבט | א ב ג ד ה ו ז ח ט י יא יב יג יד טו טז יז יח יט כ כא כב כג כד כה כו כז כח כט ל

THE HEDER, 1870

In this small painting Brandon tried his brush at "Jewish genre" painting. The children and their teacher (a *melamed*) are in a large, almost empty classroom. A vast map covers one of the bare walls, hinting that the education the children are receiving is more than rabbinical in nature. The rabbi, clad in a dark overcoat, sits behind his desk, while the children, uniformly dressed in white, are busy with their work. By depicting synagogues and classrooms, Brandon tried approaching Jewish themes from a point of view that focused on tradition and education as characteristics of the Jewish community, pointing out the main events in every (male) Jew's life, and relating him to a warm, embracing congregation.

JACQUES EMILE EDOUARD
BRANDON,
FRENCH (1831–1897)
OIL ON PANEL
34 X 44.7 CM
ACQUISITION, 1948
M399/9/48
PHOTOGRAPH: ISRAEL MUSEUM

January | 1 2 3 4 5 6 7 8 9 10 11 12 13 14 15 16 17 18 19 20 **21** 22 23 24 25 26 27 28 29 30 31

שבט | א ב ג ד ה ו ז ח ט י **י"א** י"ב י"ג י"ד ט"ו ט"ז י"ז י"ח י"ט כ כ"א כ"ב כ"ג כ"ד כ"ה כ"ו כ"ז כ"ח כ"ט ל

SHEET SILVER

LEFT TO RIGHT: POLAND
135 X 55 CM

VIENNA, AUSTRIA
100 X 35 CM

POLAND-JERUSALEM
127 X 35 CM

POLAND
110 X 32 CM

THE STIEGLITZ COLLECTION WAS
DONATED TO THE ISRAEL MUSEUM,
JERUSALEM WITH THE CONTRIBUTION
OF ERICA AND LUDWIG JESSELSON,
NEW YORK, THROUGH THE AMERICAN
FRIENDS OF THE ISRAEL MUSEUM
PHOTOGRAPH: ISRAEL MUSEUM/
AVI GANOR

FISH-SHAPE SPICE BOXES
AUSTRIA AND POLAND, 19TH CENTURY

The ceremony of Havdalah marks the end of the Sabbath and the transition to the new week. The ceremony involves blessings on wine, fire, and spices. The use of spices has inspired the creation of different forms such as these specially shaped containers.

January | 1 2 3 4 5 6 7 8 9 10 11 12 13 14 15 16 17 18 19 20 21 **22** 23 24 25 26 27 28 29 30 31

שבט | א ב ג ד ה ו ז ח ט י יא י"ב י"ג יד טו טז יז יח יט כ כא כב כג כד כה כו כז כח כט ל

Necklace (*Gardana*)
Iraqi Kurdistan, early 20th century

This type of necklace, characterized by several rows of chains, was adopted in Kurdistan following the Ottoman conquest. The heart patterns are drawn from the local repertoire, while the bow is evidence of European influence.

Hammered gold; colored stones
43 x 7 cm
Purchased through the generosity
of Bruce Kovner, New York
Photograph: Israel Museum/
Oded Loebl

January | 1 2 3 4 5 6 7 8 9 10 11 12 13 14 15 16 17 18 19 20 21 22 **23** 24 25 26 27 28 29 30 31

ל כט כח כז כו כה כד כג כב כא כ יט יח יז טז טו יד **י'ג** י'ב י'א י ט ח ז ו ה ד ג ב א | שבט

LANDSCAPE, 1928

Israel Paldi's pastoral landscape from 1928 depicts the land of Israel in all its natural wealth. In the foreground of the painting is an olive tree, and behind it a grove of blossoming almond trees. The hills behind are covered with plowed fields still brown with the turned earth. These elements place the time at the change of the seasons from winter to spring. The trees stand erect in straight lines demarcating the fields. These lines, along with those of the furrowed land, indicate that this is the new Israel, strong and robust, a place where European Jewish immigrants were putting down strong roots; it is not the idealized, romantic, and imaginary landscape of earlier depictions. This point is emphasized by the figure wearing modern blue work clothes typical of *kibbutz* and *moshav* workers, rather than Arab dress.

ISRAEL PALDI
(1892, UKRAINE–1979, ISRAEL)
OIL ON CANVAS
63 X 73 CM
ACQUISITION,
BATSHEVA DE ROTHSCHILD FUND
2185/3/63
PHOTOGRAPH: ISRAEL MUSEUM/
YAAKOV HARLAP

January | 1 2 3 4 5 6 7 8 9 10 11 12 13 14 15 16 17 18 19 20 21 22 23 **24** 25 26 27 28 29 30 31

א ב ג ד ה ו ז ח ט י'א י'ב י'ג **י'ד** ט'ו ט'ז י'ז י'ח י'ט כ כ'א כ'ב כ'ג כ'ד כ'ה כ'ו כ'ז כ'ח כ'ט ל | שבט

Tu B'Shevat trays with nuts, dried fruits, and preserved summer fruits In the tradition of Herat, Afghanistan

Tu B'Shevat is known as the New Year for Trees. Many Jewish communities observe the holiday by eating fifteen different kinds of fruit, especially the new fruits of the season. In Herat on Tu B'Shevat the newlywed bride would receive several large copper trays loaded with dried fruits arranged in circles and adorned with gilt paper.

Small tray: 15 cm (diameter)
Medium tray: 38 cm (diameter)
Large tray: 80 cm (diameter)
Reconstructed by Rachel Rabi,
Jerusalem, 1997
Photograph: Israel Museum/
David Harris

January | 1 2 3 4 5 6 7 8 9 10 11 12 13 14 15 16 17 18 19 20 21 22 23 24 **25** 26 27 28 29 30 31

שבט | א ב ג ד ה ו ז ח ט י יא יב יג יד **טו** טז יז יח יט כ כא כב כג כד כה כו כז כח כט ל

Shekel of the Jewish War against Rome
Struck in Jerusalem, Roman Period, 66 CE

The Jewish War against Rome began in the summer of 66 CE. Silver shekels and half-shekels were minted in Jerusalem immediately after the outbreak of hostilities. This particular shekel was struck during the late summer/early fall of 66 CE. It is assumed to be the first coin-type of the Jewish War, a prototype for later issues. Only two specimens of this experimental issue are known.

SILVER
2.2 CM (DIAMETER)
PHOTOGRAPH: ISRAEL MUSEUM/
DAVID HARRIS

January | 1 2 3 4 5 6 7 8 9 10 11 12 13 14 15 16 17 18 19 20 21 22 23 24 25 **26** 27 28 29 30 31

שבט | א ב ג ד ה ו ז ח ט י יא יב יג יד טו **טז** יז יח יט כ כא כב כג כד כה כו כז כח כט ל

Forehead ornament (*parkhona*)
Bukhara, Uzbekistan, early 20th century

This forehead ornament represents the most typical jewelry worn by urban women of Bukhara. Brides usually wore it for the first time at their wedding. The wealthiest would wear a pair of such ornaments fastened to their foreheads with the row of "feet" dangling down over the brow, with a sweet-smelling rose in the middle.

Embossed gold; tourmaline; pearls
9 x 8 cm
Photograph: Israel Museum/
Pierre-Alain Ferrazzini, Geneva

January | 1 2 3 4 5 6 7 8 9 10 11 12 13 14 15 16 17 18 19 20 21 22 23 24 25 26 **27** 28 29 30 31

שבט | א ב ג ד ה ו ז ח ט י י'א י'ב י'ג י'ד ט'ו ט'ז **י'ז** י'ח י'ט כ כא כב כג כד כה כו כז כח כט ל

THE BLESSING OF THE CANDLES, 1920

Jakob Steinhardt was born in the small Polish town of Zercow, but spent most of his childhood in Berlin. During World War I he was posted in Lithuania with the German army, and became reconnected with his shtetl roots. Jewish rituals and shtetl life became central themes in his work in the period following the war and before his immigration to Eretz Israel in 1933. This oil painting depicts a Jewish woman making the traditional blessing over the Sabbath candles. A young boy sits at the table, while the men can be seen through the door.

JAKOB STEINHARDT
(1887, POLAND–1968, ISRAEL)
OIL ON CANVAS
82 X 101 CM
366.3.47
PHOTOGRAPH: ISRAEL MUSEUM/
AVRAHAM HAY

January | 1 2 3 4 5 6 7 8 9 10 11 12 13 14 15 16 17 18 19 20 21 22 23 24 25 26 27 **28** 29 30 31

שבט | א ב ג ד ה ו ז ח ט י יא יב יג יד טו טז יז **יח** יט כ כא כב כג כד כה כו כז כח כט ל

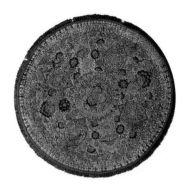

Sabbath cloth
Sakhiz, Iranian Kurdistan,
19th century

This relatively large round cloth is placed on the Sabbath table, which usually is festively decorated. The cloth includes embroidered water lilies, birds, and almond shapes along with Hebrew verses from the Mishnah. Magical mystic texts give this cloth amuletic power and provide protection and blessings.

Silk embroidered on cotton
73 cm (diameter)
Photograph: Israel Museum/
Yoram Lehmann

January | 1 2 3 4 5 6 7 8 9 10 11 12 13 14 15 16 17 18 19 20 21 22 23 24 25 26 27 28 **29** 30 31

שבט | א ב ג ד ה ו ז ח ט י׳א י׳ב י׳ג י׳ד ט׳ו ט׳ז י׳ז י׳ח **י׳ט** כ כ׳א כ׳ב כ׳ג כ׳ד כ׳ה כ׳ו כ׳ז כ׳ח כ׳ט ל

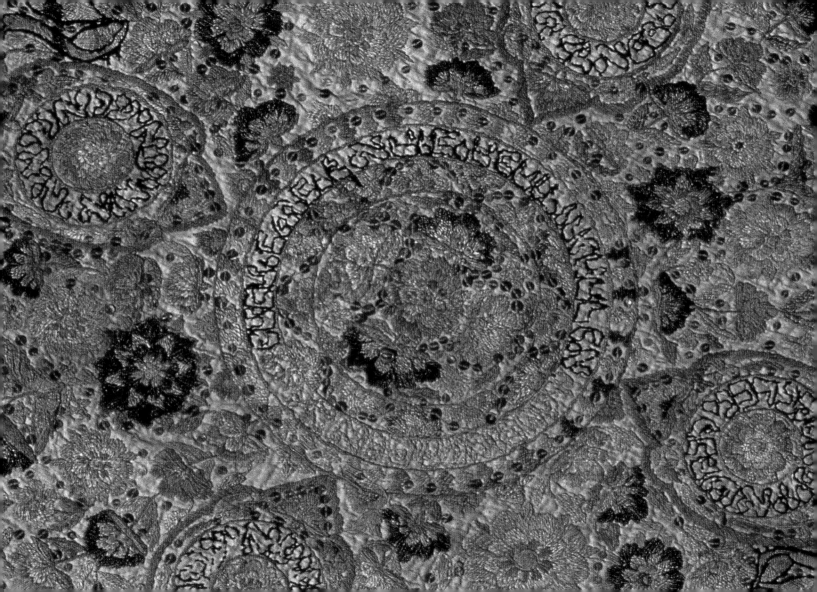

PRAYING MINHAH AT KFAR ETSION, 1947

Before the establishment of the State of Israel in 1948, most of the Jewish settlements were small agriculturally based communities. The photographer's words reveal their dreams and desires for a safe, healthy life and bountiful crops: "It is for such success that this *minyan* [a quorum of ten men] for nine farmers and one watchman, gathered together for the afternoon prayers, beseeches God: Bless this year unto us, together with every kind of the produce thereof, for our welfare; give a blessing upon the face of the earth." —J. Rosner, 1947

DR. JACOB ROSNER
(1902, GERMANY–1950, ISRAEL),
IMMIGRATED TO ERETZ ISRAEL, 1936
GELATIN SILVER PRINT
GIFT OF NAOMI SCHWARTZ

January │ 1 2 3 4 5 6 7 8 9 10 11 12 13 14 15 16 17 18 19 20 21 22 23 24 25 26 27 28 29 **30** 31

ל כט כח כז כו כה כד כג כב כא **כ** יט יח יז טז טו יד יג יב יא י ט ח ז ו ה ד ג ב א │ שבט

Proto-Aeolic capital
Ramat Rachel, Iron Age,
8th–7th century bce

Such capitals, inspired by the shape of the palm tree, mark the height of royal architecture in the kingdoms of Israel and Judah.

Limestone
50 x 108 cm
Israel Antiquities Authority
Photograph: Israel Museum/
David Harris

January | 1 2 3 4 5 6 7 8 9 10 11 12 13 14 15 16 17 18 19 20 21 22 23 24 25 26 27 28 29 30 31

שבט | א ב ג ד ה ו ז ח ט י יא יב יג יד טו טז יז יח יט כ כא כב כג כד כה כו כז כח כט ל

Bell earrings
Herat, Afghanistan,
early 20th century

These typical earrings worn by Jewish women from Herat and Meshed are made in the Qajar tradition, which developed in Iran and India in the eighteenth and nineteenth centuries. The bird design is popular in this region, perhaps a version of the mythological bird that heals, ensures fertility, and grants everlasting life.

Enameled gold; pearls;
lapis lazuli
7 cm (length)
Photograph: Israel Museum/
David Harris

February | I 2 3 4 5 6 7 8 9 10 11 12 13 14 15 16 17 18 19 20 21 22 23 24 25 26 27 28

שבט | א ב ג ד ה ו ז ח ט י יא יב יג יד טו טז יז יח יט כ כא **כב** כג כד כה כו כז כח כט ל

Mosaic floor
Hulda, Byzantine period, 5th century ce

Framed in the center of a plain white mosaic floor, this panel features the most common Jewish symbols of the period: the *lulav, etrog* (citron), incense shovel, menorah, and shofar. The mosaic was found in a secular public building belonging to Jews, which is unusual, for so far, all the other mosaics bearing such motifs have come from synagogues.

Stone
92 cm (width)
Israel Antiquities Authority
Photograph: Israel Museum

February | 1 **2** 3 4 5 6 7 8 9 10 11 12 13 14 15 16 17 18 19 20 21 22 23 24 25 26 27 28

שבט | א ב ג ד ה ו ז ח ט י יא יב יג יד טו טז יז יח יט כ כא כב **כג** כד כה כו כז כח כט ל

MAP OF THE HOLY LAND, 1488

La mer des hystoires conveys the history of the world according to the medieval Christian view, accompanied by copious illustrations, including what are thought to be the two earliest printed maps: *Map of the World* and *Map of the Holy Land*. This one, oriented to the east, centers on Jerusalem, in accordance with the medieval prototype of a city enclosed by a circular wall. Acre (Akko) is the second most important city, in memory of the Crusader period. Damascus and Sidon lie to the north and the Red Sea to the south. The map, which is interwoven with illustrations of scenes from the Bible and the eight personifications of the winds, is based on a misinterpretation of a text by Burchard of Mt. Sion, a thirteenth-century monk who lived for ten years in the Land of Israel. De Schass uses Burchard's text as an introduction to his book.

Pierre le Rouge, French,
15th century
After Lucas Brandis de Schass,
15th century
Woodcut on paper,
on two blocks
38.7 x 55.2 cm
From: La mer des hystoires,
Pierre le Rouge pour
Vincent Commin, Paris, 1488
Norman Bier Section for
Maps of the Holy Land
Gift of Norman and
Frieda Bier, London
B95.0684
Photograph: Israel Museum/
Ilan Stzulman

February | 1 2 **3** 4 5 6 7 8 9 10 11 12 13 14 15 16 17 18 19 20 21 22 23 24 25 26 27 28

שבט | א ב ג ד ה ו ז ח ט י יא יב יג יד טו טז יז יח יט כ כא כב כג **כד** כה כו כז כח כט ל

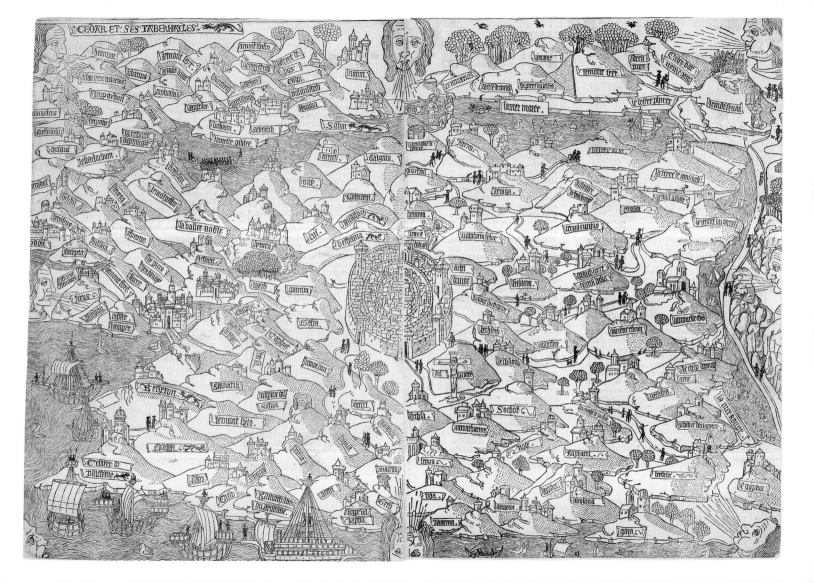

THE REDEMPTION OF THE FIRST BORN, 18TH CENTURY

ANONYMOUS ARTIST,
AFTER BERNARD PICART
(1673, FRANCE–1733),
ACTIVE HOLLAND
ETCHING ON PAPER
17.5 X 30.5 CM
PRINTED AND SOLD BY
H. OVERTON & J. HOOLE, LONDON
766-6-44
PHOTOGRAPH: ISRAEL MUSEUM

"Sanctify unto me all the first-born that opens the womb among the Children of Israel...and all the firstborn of man among your sons shall you redeem" (Exodus 13:2; 13–15). *Pidyon ha-ben*, the redemption of the firstborn son, is carried out after the thirtieth day following the birth of a firstborn son, as a reminder of the miracle that happened when God saved the Israelite firstborn sons and delivered the Children of Israel from Egyptian slavery. The firstborn were to be entrusted with the sacrificial service in the Tabernacle that was to be built. After the Israelites sinned by worshiping the Golden Calf, God commanded Moses to take the Levites instead of all the firstborn Israelites. In the print after Picart, the *cohen* (descendant of the priestly tribe), stands in the center of the composition, holding the child, while his father places silver coins on a special tray, thus ceremonially and symbolically redeeming his son. The mother sits by the cradle.

February | 1 2 3 **4** 5 6 7 8 9 10 11 12 13 14 15 16 17 18 19 20 21 22 23 24 25 26 27 28

א ב ג ד ה ו ז ח ט י י״א י״ב י״ג י״ד ט״ו ט״ז י״ז י״ח י״ט כ כ״א כ״ב כ״ג כ״ד **כה** כו כז כח כט ל | שבט

REPOUSSÉ, CAST, PUNCHED, ENGRAVED,
AND PARTLY GILT SILVER; GEMSTONES
390 X 250 CM
THE STIEGLITZ COLLECTION WAS
DONATED TO THE ISRAEL MUSEUM,
JERUSALEM WITH THE CONTRIBUTION OF
ERICA AND LUDWIG JESSELSON,
NEW YORK, THROUGH THE AMERICAN
FRIENDS OF THE ISRAEL MUSEUM
PHOTOGRAPH: ISRAEL MUSEUM/
AVI GANOR

TORAH CROWN
POLAND, 1729

This Torah crown placed on top of the Torah scroll takes its inspiration from royal crowns in its shape, use of inlaid stones, and richly patterned decoration. It is part of a set of Torah decorations that also includes the shield, finials, and pointer. Inside the base is an inscription bearing the Hebrew date equivalent to 1729 and a verse from the book of Proverbs 4:2: "Do not forsake my teaching."

February | 1 2 3 4 **5** 6 7 8 9 10 11 12 13 14 15 16 17 18 19 20 21 22 23 24 25 26 27 28

שבט | א ב ג ד ה ו ז ח ט י יא יב יג יד טו טז יז יח יט כ כא כב כג כד כה **כו** כז כח כט ל

Lachish Letter no. 3
Lachish, Iron Age, ca. 586 bce

This letter, one of a group of eighteen, is written in biblical Hebrew. It deals with a prophet who ran away to Egypt but was pursued and brought back to the king. The text recalls an episode related by the prophet Jeremiah (26:20–22): "There was also a man prophesying in the name of the Lord.... King Jehoiakim...heard about his address, and...wanted to put him to death."

Ink on pottery
14 cm (height)
Israel Antiquities Authority
Photographs: Israel Museum/
Nahum Slapak

February | 1 2 3 4 5 **6** 7 8 9 10 11 12 13 14 15 16 17 18 19 20 21 22 23 24 25 26 27 28

שבט | א ב ג ד ה ו ז ח ט י י״א י״ב י״ג י״ד טו טז יז יח יט כ כא כב כג כד כה כו **כז** כח כט ל

III 4025 38.127

Marc Chagall
(Russia, 1887–1985, France)
active Russia, France, USA
Oil on canvas
73 x 92 cm
Purchase made possible by Janine
Bernheim and Antoine Wertheimer
in memory of their parents,
Madeleine and Paul Wertheimer,
and by the Crown Family (Chicago),
Edith Haas, Averell Harriman,
Loula Lasker, Edward D. Mitchell,
David Rockefeller,
and Charles Ullman
B91.500

Interior of a Synagogue in Safed, 1931

Marc Chagall painted this canvas on his first visit to Eretz Israel in 1931. During this trip, he was trying to get a feel for the Holy Land before undertaking a commission by the art dealer and publisher Ambroise Vollard to produce a series of illustrations of the Bible. He painted a number of synagogue interiors, including this one of the Sephardic Ha-Ari Synagogue in Safed, which dates back to the sixteenth century. The interior is suffused with a pale-blue luminosity, testimony to Chagall's first encounter with the overwhelming light and intense colors of Eretz Israel. The human figures, one on the staircase of the *bimmah* and one sitting on a bench wrapped in a prayer shawl, seem to hover in true Chagallian manner and add an incorporeal aspect that enhances the serenely spiritual atmosphere of the synagogue.

February | 1 2 3 4 5 6 **7** 8 9 10 11 12 13 14 15 16 17 18 19 20 21 22 23 24 25 26 27 28

שבט | א ב ג ד ה ו ז ח ט י י'א י'ב י'ג י'ד ט'ו ט'ז י'ז י'ח י'ט כ כ'א כ'ב כ'ג כ'ד כ'ה כ'ו כ'ז **כ'ח** כ'ט ל

Child's Drawing of Jerusalem, 1996

On the occasion of Jerusalem 3000, the three-thousandth anniversary of the establishment of the city of Jerusalem, children from Israel and around the world were asked to draw pictures of the city. Some had seen it with their own eyes and others only in their imagination. Thousands of pictures by children of different religions and races were collected from all over the world, and a selection was assembled in an exhibition that took place in the Museum in 1996. The pictures depicted a city of landscapes and symbols and a city of memories and dreams, merged with scenery from the children's native countries. This drawing by a thirteen-year-old Israeli child shows a real Jerusalem, surrounded by hills and fields, but glowing with an eternal spiritual light.

COLORED PENCILS ON PAPER
50 X 35 CM
PHOTOGRAPH: ISRAEL MUSEUM

February | 1 2 3 4 5 6 7 **8** 9 10 11 12 13 14 15 16 17 18 19 20 21 22 23 24 25 26 27 28

שבט | א ב ג ד ה ו ז ח ט י יא יב יג יד טו טז יז יח יט כ כא כב כג כד כה כו כז כח **כט** ל

BRINGING WATER FROM THE WELL
BENE ISRAEL COMMUNITY,
BOMBAY AREA, INDIA, 1984

Water is not piped to individual buildings in rural India, and it must be fetched from a well—traditionally a female task. The Bene Israel women and girls would do the laundry at the well, and then carry two or three copper cans of water on their heads, one on top of the other, back to their houses. The village well served as a meeting place where the women and girls could chat and rest for a while before returning home.

PHOTOGRAPH: ISRAEL MUSEUM/
ORPA SLAPAK

February | 1 2 3 4 5 6 7 8 **9** 10 11 12 13 14 15 16 17 18 19 20 21 22 23 24 25 26 27 28

שבט | א ב ג ד ה ו ז ח ט י יא יב יג יד טו טז יז יח יט כ כא כב כג כד כה כו כז כח כט ל

ADAR PLAQUE
ROMANIA, EARLY 20TH CENTURY

Adar is the month of the Jewish festival of Purim, celebrating the deliverance of the Jews in the Persian Empire. Starting at the beginning of the month, plaques such as this would be hung in synagogues and private homes to announce the festivities of the coming month: "When Adar arrives, festivity thrives" (Talmud, Ta'anit 29a). Two fish are depicted here, probably since the zodiac sign for the month of Adar is Pisces, the fish.

PAINTED GLASS; SILVER FOIL; WOOD
41.43 x 36.3 CM
GIFT OF BEILE FRIEDMAN-ROSENBERG
PHOTOGRAPH: ISRAEL MUSEUM

February | 1 2 3 4 5 6 7 8 9 **IO** 11 12 13 14 15 16 17 18 19 20 21 22 23 24 25 26 27 28

אדר א ‎ ל כט כח כז כו כה כד כג כב כא כ יט יח יז טז טו יד יג יב יא י ט ח ז ו ה ד ג ב

Ossuary of "Simon Builder of the Temple"
Jerusalem, Second Temple Period,
1st century bce–1st century ce

This simple and unadorned ossuary bears two Aramaic inscriptions that read: "Simon Builder of the Temple." Simon must have taken part in the ambitious project of enlarging and renovating the Second Temple carried out in the days of Herod the Great. We do not know if he was an architect or a simple workman. His family, however, clearly wanted him to be remembered for his role in the renovation.

Stone
60 cm (width)
Israel Antiquities Authority
Photograph: Israel Museum/
Avraham Hay

February | 1 2 3 4 5 6 7 8 9 10 **11** 12 13 14 15 16 17 18 19 20 21 22 23 24 25 26 27 28

אדר | א **ב** ג ד ה ו ז ח ט י יא יב יג יד טו טז יז יח יט כ כא כב כג כד כה כו כז כח כט ל

Torah ornaments:
finials, shield, and pointer
Germany, 1904

Silversmith: Jacob Posen
Repoussé, cast, engraved,
and gilt silver; enamel; lapis
17 x 12 cm (finials); 18.5 x 15 x .8 cm
(shield); 24 x 2 cm (pointer)
Courtesy the Ari Ackerman
Foundation; Moshe and
Charlotte Green, New York;
Meir Kaufman Estate, Jerusalem;
Erica and Ludwig Jesselson,
New York; anonymous donors from
Switzerland and South Africa
Photograph: Israel Museum/
Max Richardson

This Torah ornament set was fashioned by the well-known Jewish Posen silver and gold manufacturing firm, famous for its cutlery and Jewish ceremonial art. Two outstanding Jewish women—Brendina Posen, the manufacturer, and Bertha Pappenheim, the feminist and social worker who ordered it on the occasion of her brother's marriage—were involved in its design and commission. Pappenheim was successfully treated by a colleague of Sigmund Freud's. (She was known in psychoanalysis circles as "Anna O.") She was active throughout her life in human and social rights, becoming headmistress of an orphanage. A stamp issued by the German government in 1954 pays tribute to her and is inscribed "Helper of Humanity."

February | 1 2 3 4 5 6 7 8 9 10 11 **12** 13 14 15 16 17 18 19 20 21 22 23 24 25 26 27 28

אדר א ב ג ד ה ו ז ח ט י יא יב יג יד טו טז יז יח יט כ כא כב כג כד כה כו כז כח כט ל

TERRACES, 1930S

Traditional local agriculture found unique solutions to the steep hills common to the Israeli landscape. The terraces that striate the hillsides create small, functional parcels of land that can be efficiently farmed. The stone walls keep the topsoil from running down the hillside. On a compositional level, this photograph reveals the patchwork pattern of the terraces, and their gridlike quality gives the photograph an air of abstraction.

S. J. SCHWEIG
(1905, AUSTRIA–1984, ISRAEL),
IMMIGRATED TO ERETZ ISRAEL, 1923
GELATIN SILVER PRINT
BEQUEST OF THE ARTIST

February | 1 2 3 4 5 6 7 8 9 10 11 12 **13** 14 15 16 17 18 19 20 21 22 23 24 25 26 27 28

אדר | א ב ג ד ה ו ז ח ט י יא יב יג יד טו טז יז יח יט כ כא כב כג כד כה כו כז כח כט ל

The Priestly Benediction on a silver amulet
Jerusalem, Iron Age, late 7th century bce

This silver plaque, inscribed in ancient Hebrew script, represents the oldest copy of biblical verses ever found. The text (Numbers 6:24–26), which forms part of the Jewish liturgy to this day, is known as the "Priestly Benediction."

3.9 CM (HEIGHT)
ISRAEL ANTIQUITIES AUTHORITY
PHOTOGRAPH: ISRAEL MUSEUM

February | 1 2 3 4 5 6 7 8 9 10 11 12 13 **14** 15 16 17 18 19 20 21 22 23 24 25 26 27 28

94

אדר | א ב ג ד ה ו ז ח ט י יא יב יג יד טו טז יז יח יט כ כא כב כג כד כה כו כז כח כט ל

BRACELETS
MOROCCO, EARLY 20TH CENTURY

These bracelets were worn by Jewish women from rural areas of Morocco, often several pairs at the same time. Because of their heavy weight they might also have been used in self defense. The variety of techniques show the long and rich tradition of silversmith work by Jewish craftsmen in this area.

SILVER; SEMIPRECIOUS STONES
6–7 CM (DIAMETER)
PHOTOGRAPH: ISRAEL MUSEUM/
CHANAN SADEH

February | 1 2 3 4 5 6 7 8 9 10 11 12 13 14 **15** 16 17 18 19 20 21 22 23 24 25 26 27 28

אדר | א ב ג ד ה ו ז ח ט י יא יב יג יד טו טז יז יח יט כ כא כב כג כד כה כו כז כח כט ל

Bezalel carpet depicting David's Tower and the Site of the Temple
Eretz Israel, ca. 1909

This carpet was woven in the workshop of the Zionist Bezalel School of Arts and Crafts, which was founded in Jerusalem in 1906. The combination of a depiction of the Mosque of Omar (located on Jerusalem's Temple Mount) and the seven-armed menorah—a vessel from the Temple and a common Zionist symbol—directs the carpet user's awareness toward the concept of the Temple, its destruction, and its symbolic rebuilding. The basic tenet underlying these kinds of combined images was the idea that the Zionist return to the Land of Israel in the twentieth century was in fact the redemption of the Jewish people and the renewal of ancient independence. The carpet-weaving department at Bezalel was one of the first to open at the institution, answering the founders' desires to create work for Jerusalem's Jewish residents and to design a Hebrew living environment based on the new Eretz Israel–Zionist style, using images that create a sense of national collective identity.

Wool
72 x 136 cm
Gift of Mrs. Rosa Kipnis,
Tel Aviv, in memory of Rabbi
Dr. Yeshayahu Rafaelowitz
420.78
Photograph: Israel Museum

February | 1 2 3 4 5 6 7 8 9 10 11 12 13 14 15 **16** 17 18 19 20 21 22 23 24 25 26 27 28

אדר | א ב ג ד ה ו **ז** ח ט י יא יב יג יד טו טז יז יח יט כ כא כב כג כד כה כו כז כח כט ל

Study for *Bar Mitzvah Boy Reading from the Torah*, 19th Century

J. E. E. Brandon was born into a wealthy family of Spanish-Portuguese descent. He studied at the Ecole des Beaux-Arts in Paris and under Camille Corot, and during the 1850s became a close friend of Edgar Degas. He began to depict Jewish subjects in the 1860s; some of these paintings were exhibited in the Salon and even won him a medal. Though he exhibited with the Impressionists in 1874, his work remained academic in nature. In this study, Brandon depicted a Saturday morning at the synagogue, with a boy who has reached the age of thirteen (bar mitzvah) standing on the *bimmah* in the center of the congregation, flanked by guiding and observing adults. The boy reaches for the Scroll and reads, pointing at the passage in front of him. An imposing Gothic-style wooden Ark (*Aron ha'Kodesh*) completes the composition of both private and public ceremony.

Jacques Emile Edouard Brandon,
French (1831–1897)
Oil on canvas
38 x 61.5 cm
Acquisition, 1966
519.66
Photograph: Israel Museum

February | 1 2 3 4 5 6 7 8 9 10 11 12 13 14 15 16 **17** 18 19 20 21 22 23 24 25 26 27 28

אדר ‏ א ב ג ד ה ו ז ח ט י יא יב יג יד טו טז יז יח יט כ כא כב כג כד כה כו כז כח כט ל

Names of Jerusalem on coins Persian to Crusader Period, 4th century BCE–12th century CE

Minting in Jerusalem continued intermittently for some 1,600 years, from ca. 380 BCE to ca. 1200 CE. During this long period, the name of the city changed several times. Top row from left: *YHD* (Aramaic), ca. 380 BCE; *Yerushalayim* (ancient Hebrew), 68 CE; *COL(ONIA) AEL(IA) KAPIT(OLINA)* (Latin), 130 CE. Bottom row from left: *Iliya* (Arabic), 660–680 CE; *IERVSALEM* (Latin), 1163–1174 CE; *CIV(ITAS) CR(UX)* ("City of the Cross," Latin), 1187 CE.

SILVER AND BRONZE
0.6–2.3 CM (DIAMETER)
PHOTOGRAPHS: ISRAEL MUSEUM/
DAVID HARRIS

February | 1 2 3 4 5 6 7 8 9 10 11 12 13 14 15 16 17 **18** 19 20 21 22 23 24 25 26 27 28

אדר | א ב ג ד ה ו ז ח **ט** י יא יב יג יד טו טז יז יח יט כ כא כב כג כד כה כו כז כח כט ל

CASE: WOOD; VELVET;
REPOUSSÉ SILVER; GLASS BEADS
107 X 30 CM

MANTLE: VELVET; SILK; METALLIC
THREAD EMBROIDERY
67 X 29 CM
GIFT OF SHLOMO ZINI, MOSHAV YAD
RAMBAM, ISRAEL
PHOTOGRAPH: ISRAEL MUSEUM/
DAVID HARRIS

TORAH SCROLL CASE
IRAN, 1973
TORAH MANTLE
MOGADOR (?), MOROCCO, 1926

Torah scrolls are always protected by textile mantles or cases. In most Middle Eastern communities the scroll is traditionally kept in a wooden or metal case, which is usually decorated, as is this example from Iran. However in Morocco, especially in places where Jewish Spanish exiles settled, an embroidered mantle with a hard top was used to cover the Torah scroll. In the early mantles leather was used as a stiffener; it was later replaced by cardboard.

February | 1 2 3 4 5 6 7 8 9 10 11 12 13 14 15 16 17 18 **19** 20 21 22 23 24 25 26 27 28

אדר | א ב ג ד ה ו ז ח ט י יא יב יג יד טו טז יז יח יט כ כא כב כג כד כה כו כז כח כט ל

VIEW OF JERUSALEM, 1930S

This photograph of the Temple Mount with the empty, bare hills surrounding it was taken from a site east of the Augusta Victoria Hospital on the Mount of Olives. This vantage point was often used by nineteenth-century photographers, and Ben-Dov follows this tradition. His sky, however, is his own. In the nineteenth century it was usual to see the sky as a single color with no details, typical of the summer in this region, yet Ben-Dov made his photograph on a cloudy day, creating a unique dramatic atmosphere.

YAACOV BEN-DOV
(1882, RUSSIA–1968, ISRAEL),
IMMIGRATED TO ERETZ ISRAEL, 1908
GELATIN SILVER PRINT
GIFT OF RENA (FISCH) AND
ROBERT LEWIN, LONDON

February | 1 2 3 4 5 6 7 8 9 10 11 12 13 14 15 16 17 18 19 **20** 21 22 23 24 25 26 27 28

אדר ‏| א ב ג ד ה ו ו ח ט י **י'א** ‏ י'ב י'ג י'ד ט'ו ט'ז י'ז י'ח י'ט כ כ'א כ'ב כ'ג כ'ד כ'ה כ'ו כ'ז כ'ח כ'ט ל

Cult stand with musicians
Ashdod, Iron Age,
late 11th–early 10th century bce

Each of the five musicians shown emerging from the windows of this cult stand plays an instrument: one plays the cymbals, two a double-pipe, another a stringed instrument, and the last a timbrel. The stand recalls the passage from I Samuel (10:5): "You will encounter a band of prophets coming down from the shrine, preceded by lyres, timbrels, flutes, and harps."

Pottery
34.7 cm (height)
Israel Antiquities Authority
Photograph: Israel Museum/
Pierre Alan Ferrazzini

February | 1 2 3 4 5 6 7 8 9 10 11 12 13 14 15 16 17 18 19 20 **21** 22 23 24 25 26 27 28

אדר | א ב ג ד ה ו ז ח ט י **י'א** **י'ב** י'ג יד טו טז יז יח יט כ כא כב כג כד כה כו כז כח כט ל

Gold glass bases with Jewish symbols
Catacombs of Rome(?), Roman-Byzantine period, 4th century CE

Hundreds of plaques like these, probably the bases of vessels whose walls were broken off, were found embedded in the walls of the catacombs of Rome. Made from two layers of glass encasing designs in gold leaf, they presumably served as grave markers. Most of the plaques bear Christian motifs but a few have Jewish symbols related to the Temple and its rituals.

Glass and gold leaf
100, 117 cm (diameter)
Gift of Jakob Michael,
New York, in memory of his wife,
Erna Sondheimer-Michael
Photograph: Israel Museum/
David Harris

February | 1 2 3 4 5 6 7 8 9 10 11 12 13 14 15 16 17 18 19 20 21 **22** 23 24 25 26 27 28

אדר | א ב ג ד ה ו ז ח ט י יא יב **יג** יד טו טז יז יח יט כ כא כב כג כד כה כו כז כח כט ל

Living room of the Ortenau family Reconstruction, Munich, Germany, 19th century

This reconstructed room in the Israel Museum belonged to the Ortenau family, descendants of the Wertheimers, who were court bankers for more than two hundred years. It reflects a typical bourgeois nineteenth-century living room with objects of the Biedermeier and Art Nouveau styles. This reconstruction demonstrates how Jews were assimilated into the German way of life in that period. Only some objects such as a Hanukkah lamp, a Kiddush cup, and a spice box hint at the Jewish identity of the room's inhabitants. The desk was given to Mr. Ortenau's great uncle by the German-Jewish poet Heinrich Heine, who was Dr. Ortenau's patient towards the end of his life.

Gift of Erich and
Cornelie Ortenau, Munich
Photograph: Israel Museum/
David Harris

February | 1 2 3 4 5 6 7 8 9 10 11 12 13 14 15 16 17 18 19 20 21 22 **23** 24 25 26 27 28

אדר | א ב ג ד ה ו ז ח ט י א י ב י ג **י׳ד** ט ו ט ז י ז י ח י ט כ כ א כ ב כ ג כ ד כ ה כ ו כ ז כ ח כ ט ל

"House of David"
INSCRIBED ON A VICTORY STELE
Tel Dan, Iron Age, 9th century bce

This unique inscription, written in Aramaic, is from the First Temple period. It contains the first extra-biblical reference to the Davidic dynasty.

Basalt
32 cm (height)
Israel Antiquities Authority
Photograph: Israel Museum/
Peter Lanyi

February | 1 2 3 4 5 6 7 8 9 10 11 12 13 14 15 16 17 18 19 20 21 22 23 **24** 25 26 27 28

אדר | א ב ג ד ה ו ז ח ט י יא יב יג יד **טו** טז יז יח יט כ כא כב כג כד כה כו כז כח כט ל

CARVED IVORIES
SAMARIA, IRON AGE, 9TH–8TH CENTURY BCE

It is likely that these carved ivory plaques were once inlaid in wall panels or luxurious wooden furniture in the royal palace at Samaria, capital of the northern kingdom of Israel. This palace is referred to in I Kings 22:39 as "the ivory palace" built by King Ahab. Reference to the ivory furnishings of the northern kingdom's aristocracy is found in the words of the prophet Amos (6:4): "They lie on ivory beds, lolling on their couches, feasting on lambs from the flock and on calves from the stalls."

SACRED TREE: 17.6 CM (HEIGHT)
STRIDING SPHINX: 7.5 CM (HEIGHT)
LION AND BULL: 4.2 CM (HEIGHT)
ISRAEL ANTIQUITIES AUTHORITY
PHOTOGRAPH: ISRAEL MUSEUM/
DAVID HARRIS

February | 1 2 3 4 5 6 7 8 9 10 11 12 13 14 15 16 17 18 19 20 21 22 23 24 **25** 26 27 28

אדר | א ב ג ד ה ו ז ח ט י י״א י״ב י״ג י״ד ט״ו **ט״ז** י״ז י״ח י״ט כ כ״א כ״ב כ״ג כ״ד כ״ה כ״ו כ״ז כ״ח כ״ט ל

SHIVITI TORAH ARK CURTAIN ISTANBUL, TURKEY, EARLY 20TH CENTURY

This Torah Ark curtain with the *shiviti* inscription "I have set the Lord always before me" (Psalms 16:8) is profusely embroidered with biblical quotations and prayers. The shape of the seven-branched menorah is created with written words from Psalm 67. On either side of the Tablets of the Law is the *magen david* (star, literally the Shield of David) with the word *Shaddai* (the name of God) in the center. The open hands represent the priestly blessing.

WOOL; WOOL-THREAD EMBROIDERY;
CHAIN STITCH
208 X 162 CM
PHOTOGRAPH: ISRAEL MUSEUM/
DAVID HARRIS

February | 1 2 3 4 5 6 7 8 9 10 11 12 13 14 15 16 17 18 19 20 21 22 23 24 25 **26** 27 28

אדר | א ב ג ד ה ו ז ח ט י יא יב יג יד טו טז **י'** יח יט כ כא כב כג כד כה כו כז כח כט ל

Women's earrings in basket form
Iranian and Iraqi Kurdistan,
early 20th century

Metalwork in Kurdistan was mainly a Jewish profession, and goldsmiths and silversmiths enjoyed great prestige. Usually each artisan had his own specialty, such as filigree, casting, or stamping. Basket earrings are made in a variety of patterns such as lotus flowers, double-headed birds, and floral designs, all expressing the wish for a long and fertile life.

Cast, beaten, and stamped gold;
filigree
3 cm (diameter)
Photograph: Israel Museum/
Nahum Slapak

February | 1 2 3 4 5 6 7 8 9 10 11 12 13 14 15 16 17 18 19 20 21 22 23 24 25 26 **27** 28

ל כט כח כז כו כה כד כג כב כא כ יט **ח'** יז טז טו יד יג י'ב י'א י ט ח ז ו ה ד ג ב א | אדר

Pomegranate-shaped vessel
Provenance unknown, Iron Age,
10th–8th century bce

The pomegranate, a symbol of fertility and abundance, is frequently mentioned in the Bible and is counted among the seven kinds of fruit with which the land of Israel is blessed (Deuteronomy 8:7–8).

Pottery
7 cm (height)
Photograph: Israel
Museum/Avraham Hay

February | 1 2 3 4 5 6 7 8 9 10 11 12 13 14 15 16 17 18 19 20 21 22 23 24 25 26 27 **28**

אדר | א ב ג ד ה ו ז ח ט י יא יב יג יד טו טז יז יח **יט** כ כא כב כג כד כה כו כז כח כט ל

TITLE PAGE FOR A SERIES OF POSTCARDS, EARLY 20TH CENTURY

This title page from an album of photographic postcards, taken by the most important Jewish Eretz-Israeli photographers from the early twentieth century, was created by one of the most prominent teachers at the Bezalel School of Arts and Crafts in Jerusalem. The school, which opened its doors on March 1, 1906, was named after Bezalel ben Uri, the biblical builder of the Ark of the Covenant. Boris Schatz, the school's founder, envisioned it as a temple to new art representing the spiritual values of the Jewish people. Schatz saw himself and his artist-colleagues as priests serving the temple. In this illustration, the figure depicting the biblical Bezalel designing the temple menorah resembles one of the craftsmen who worked in the school workshop, and the menorah is in the style of pieces created there. In the background photograph Boris Schatz can be seen against the Bezalel buildings; on one roof is a menorah produced by the institution. Thus reality rests on a biblical dimension and the title page's design symbolically expresses the ideological connection between the biblical past and Zionist present.

PUBLISHED BY Y. BEN-DOV
(1882–1968)
SHMUEL BEN-DAVID
(1884, BULGARIA–1927, ERETZ ISRAEL)
PHOTOGRAPH,
INDIA INK AND
BROWN WASH ON PAPER
18 X 26 CM
O.S. 3003.66
PHOTOGRAPH: ISRAEL MUSEUM

March | 1 2 3 4 5 6 7 8 9 10 11 12 13 14 15 16 17 18 19 20 21 22 23 24 25 26 27 28 29 30 31

אדר | א ב ג ד ה ו ז ח ט י י״א י״ב י״ג י״ד ט״ו ט״ז י״ז י״ח י״ט כ כ״א כ״ב כ״ג כ״ד כ״ה כ״ו כ״ז כ״ח כ״ט ל

ואקרא אתכם בשם
בצלאל
ואמלא אתו רוח
אלהים בחכמה
ובתבונה ובדעת
ובכל מלאכה

SERIE „II" VERLAG BEN-DOV JERUSALEM BEZALEL

סריה ב.: הוצאת יבן דוב ירושלם

UPPER LEFT:
PROVENANCE UNKNOWN, IRON AGE,
8TH CENTURY BCE
AMAZONITE MOUNTED IN GOLD
SEAL: 1.5 CM (HEIGHT)
SETTING: 2.5 CM (HEIGHT)

UPPER RIGHT:
PROVENANCE UNKNOWN, IRON AGE,
9TH–8TH CENTURY BCE
OPAL
3.1 CM (HEIGHT)
ISRAEL ANTIQUITIES AUTHORITY

LOWER LEFT:
MIZPAH (TELL EN NASBEH), IRON
AGE, LATE 8TH–7TH CENTURY BCE
AGATE
1.9 CM (HEIGHT)
ISRAEL ANTIQUITIES AUTHORITY

LOWER RIGHT:
PROVENANCE UNKNOWN, IRON AGE,
8TH CENTURY BCE
CARNELIAN
0.7 CM (HEIGHT)
GIFT OF TAMAR AND TEDDY
KOLLEK, JERUSALEM

SEALS, IRON AGE, 9TH–7TH CENTURY BCE

The Seal of Shaphat (upper left) is mounted in a gold ring and bears the inscription "(belonging) to Shaphat" in ancient Hebrew script. Shaphat is a common biblical name, meaning "God has judged." The richly ornamented Seal of Jezebel (upper right) bears the name "Jezebel" in Phoenician script. Jezebel is mentioned in the Bible (I Kings 16:31) as the wife of King Ahab, ruler of the northern kingdom of Israel. The two upper registers of the Seal of Yaazanyahu (lower left) are engraved with the name and title of the seal's owner "(belonging) to Yaazanyahu, servant of the king." This title, known from the Bible, was borne by high-ranking officials in the royal administration (II Kings 22:12). The excellent workmanship of the Seal of Jeremiah (lower right) indicates that it was carved by a master engraver. It bears the inscription "(belonging) to Jeremiah" incised in ancient Hebrew script.

PHOTOGRAPH: ISRAEL MUSEUM/DAVID HARRIS

March | 1 **2** 3 4 5 6 7 8 9 10 11 12 13 14 15 16 17 18 19 20 21 22 23 24 25 26 27 28 29 30 31

אדר ‏| א ב ג ד ה ו ז ח ט י יא יב יג יד טו טז יז יח יט כ **כא** כב כג כד כה כו כז כח כט ל

Leggings
San'a, Yemen, early 20th century

Most women in Yemen wore leggings attached to their undergarments (loose trousers worn underneath the dress) covering the lower part of the leg. The leggings worn by unmarried girls had many special decorations, such as mother-of-pearl triangles, coral, and cowrie shells, which were believed to have amuletic properties especially protective of young girls.

Embroidered velvet;
mother-of-pearl; coral;
shells; silverwork
22 x 15 cm
Lent by WIZO (Women's International Zionist Organization) in memory of Martha Bamberger, a longtime member of the World WIZO Executive
Photograph: Israel Museum/ David Harris

March | 1 2 **3** 4 5 6 7 8 9 10 11 12 13 14 15 16 17 18 19 20 21 22 23 24 25 26 27 28 29 30 31

אדר | א ב ג ד ה ו ו ז ח ט י יא יב יג יד טו טז יז יח יט כ כא **כב** כג כד כה כו כז כח כט ל

Snow in Jerusalem, 1927

A thick blanket of white snow covering the domed rooftops of Jerusalem's Old City is a rare sight. This view of the Old City from the east could only have been taken pre-1948, after which Schweig would not have been able to gain access to Jordanian-controlled East Jerusalem. The white snow gives a new view of the city, pure and quiet.

S. J. Schweig
(1905, Austria–1984, Israel)
immigrated to Eretz Israel, 1923
Gelatin silver print
Bequest of the artist
Photograph: Israel Museum

March │ 1 2 3 **4** 5 6 7 8 9 10 11 12 13 14 15 16 17 18 19 20 21 22 23 24 25 26 27 28 29 30 31

ל כט כח כז כו כה כד **כג** כב כא כ יט יח יז טז טו יד יג יב יא י ט ח ז ו ה ד ג ב א │ אדר

Balustrade
Ramat Rachel, Iron Age,
late 8th–early 7th century bce

This window balustrade from a royal fortress south of Jerusalem reflects a Phoenician influence, introduced in the time of King Solomon, who brought Phoenician artisans to Jerusalem for the construction of the Temple and the royal palace.

Limestone
37 x 125 cm
Israel Antiquities Authority
Photograph: Israel Museum/
David Harris

March | 1 2 3 4 **5** 6 7 8 9 10 11 12 13 14 15 16 17 18 19 20 21 22 23 24 25 26 27 28 29 30 31

אדר | א ב ג ד ה ו ז ח ט י יא יב יג יד טו טז יז יח יט כ כא כב כג **כד** כה כו כז כח כט ל

PROBABLY BY JOSEPH ZVI GEIGER
OIL PAINT ON GLASS
52.5 X 32 CM
THE FEUCHTWANGER COLLECTION,
PURCHASED AND DONATED BY
BARUCH AND RUTH RAPPAPORT,
GENEVA
PHOTOGRAPH: ISRAEL MUSEUM

PURIM PAINTING
SAFED, ERETZ ISRAEL, 1893

This glass painting depicts scenes from the Purim story along with the Hebrew inscription from the narrative. The various characters shown are dressed in contemporary Ottoman clothes and the scenes feature Esther meeting the Persian King Ahasuerus, Mordechai being crowned, and the overthrow and hanging of the King's officer, Haman.

March | 1 2 3 4 5 **6** 7 8 9 10 11 12 13 14 15 16 17 18 19 20 21 22 23 24 25 26 27 28 29 30 31

אדר | א ב ג ד ה ו ז ח ט י יא יב יג יד טו טז יז יח יט כ כא כב כג כד **כה** כו כז כח כט ל

BOWL AND THREE OSTRACA
ARAD, IRON AGE, LATE 8TH CENTURY BCE

These objects were found in the temple that stood in Arad during the time of the Judean monarchy. The bowl, found near the sacrificial altar, is inscribed with the word "sacred" in ancient Hebrew script. Each of the ostraca (inscribed pottery shards) bears a single name, two of which (Pashhur and Meremot) appear in the Bible as the names of priests (Jeremiah 21:1, Nehemiah 3:4).

INK ON POTTERY
BOWL: 13.5 CM (DIAMETER)
ISRAEL ANTIQUITIES AUTHORITY
PHOTOGRAPH: ISRAEL MUSEUM/
AVRAHAM HAY

March │ 1 2 3 4 5 6 **7** 8 9 10 11 12 13 14 15 16 17 18 19 20 21 22 23 24 25 26 27 28 29 30 31

א ב ג ד ה ו ז ח ט י יא יב יג יד טו טז יז יח יט כ כא כב כג כד כה **כו** כז כח כט ל │ אדר

THE ROTHSCHILD MISCELLANY MANUSCRIPT
NORTHERN ITALY, CA. 1450–80

The Rothschild Miscellany is one of the most magnificent Hebrew illuminated manuscripts in existence. Almost every one of its very thin refined vellum leaves is richly decorated with colorful miniatures and marginal paintings in tempera colors and gold leaf. The book assembles thirty-seven religious and secular units, meticulously copied, giving it an encyclopedic flavor. Profusely illuminated, it was decorated, apparently in the workshops of the painters Bonifacio Bembo and Cristoforo de Predis. The figures and border decorations of the miniatures such as this page illustration of *Eshet Hayil*, "Woman of Valor" (Proverbs 31:10–31), describes her industrious works in the typically rich Italian Renaissance style. The manuscript, which belonged to the Rothschild family library in Paris, disappeared during World War II, later reappearing when it was offered for sale in New York and eventually given to the Israel Museum.

March | 1 2 3 4 5 6 7 **8** 9 10 11 12 13 14 15 16 17 18 19 20 21 22 23 24 25 26 27 28 29 30 31

אדר | א ב ג ד ה ו ז ח ט י יא יב יג יד טו טז יז יח יט כ כא כב כג כד כה כו **כז** כח כט ל

Thomas Fuller, English
(1608–1661)
Hand-colored engraving on
paper, by Robert Vaughan
28.3 x 36 cm
From: Thomas Fuller, *A Pisgah
Sight of Palestine*, London,
John Williams, 1650
Norman Bier Section for
Maps of the Holy Land
Gift of Norman and
Frieda Bier, London
B95.0660
Photograph: Israel Museum/
Ilan Stzulman

From Zebulon to the Sea..., 1650

The map shows the lower Galilee, which was allotted to the tribe of Zebulon (Joshua 19:10–18). At the upper right is a ship with a mast, the emblem of the tribe. The map includes depictions of many events in the Old and New Testaments, such as in the Carmel area near the Kishon River, where we see Elijah slaying the false prophets; or the shores of the Sea of Galilee, where Jesus preaches to the masses. Special emphasis is placed on geographical detail such as mountains, rivers, and vegetation, and on defining settled areas, royal cities (which are noted with a crown), and Levite cities (surrounded by circled dots). Fuller was an English clergyman who wrote historical and theological works. This map is from a book of biblical historical research, and it includes a full map of the Holy Land, as well as detailed double-page maps of the tribes' patrimonies.

March │ 1 2 3 4 5 6 7 8 **9** 10 11 12 13 14 15 16 17 18 19 20 21 22 23 24 25 26 27 28 29 30 31

אדר │ א ב ג ד ה ו ז ח ט י יא יב יג יד טו טז יז יח יט כ כא כב כג כד כה כו כז **כח** כט ל

MEDITER
Ptolomais
RANEVM

TRIBUS

VALLIS IEPHTAEL

TRIBUS

Naasson

Hanathon

Misheal

Canah

ASHER

Hukkok

Bethsaida

Gunereth

Capernaum

Iephtahel torrens sive Shihor Libnah

Beth-lehem

Iordanus Parvus

Aznoth Tabor

Leah

VALLIS

Iepha torrens

Neah Remmon Methoara

CARMEL

Ittah-kazin

LEVI

Iokneam

Zebulon

Ajalon

Sephoris Dionesarea

Gath Hepher

Kattah Kartah

LEVI

Sepulchrum Elonis

Dothaim

Magdala

SALTVS

Nazareth

Dalman Atha

CARMELI

MONS

Iotopata

Naphieh

Bethuli

MEL

Naim

Tiberias

CAP MEL

Cain

Shimron-meron

Kishon fluv.

LEVI

Idalah

LEVI

Ingel Tiger

GA IN FERIOR GALILEA

LEVI

Nahalal Tabor

TABOR MONS

MARE Galilææ Tiberiadis

Rimmon Dimnah

LEVI

Tarichea

YELLOW SYNAGOGUE, 1950S

Nahum Gutman is considered one of Israel's most important modernist artists. He is especially renowned for his use of vibrant colors to depict the strong Israeli light. During the late 1940s and 1950s he painted many watercolors of synagogue interiors in Tel Aviv, Tiberias, and Safed. The translucent colors glow with a warmth that expresses the sanctity of the site. The tall pillars that dominate the foreground of this work and the high, arched ceiling are echoed in the Holy Ark that sweeps upward in a gentle curve.

NAHUM GUTMAN
(1898, ROMANIA–1980, ISRAEL)
WATERCOLOR ON PAPER
49.2 X 61 CM
GIFT VIA THE AMERICA-ISRAEL
CULTURAL FOUNDATION
360.70
PHOTOGRAPH: ISRAEL MUSEUM/
MEIDAD SUCHOWOLSKI

March | 1 2 3 4 5 6 7 8 9 **10** 11 12 13 14 15 16 17 18 19 20 21 22 23 24 25 26 27 28 29 30 31

אדר | א ב ג ד ה ו ז ח ט י יא יב יג יד טו טז יז יח יט כ כא כב כג כד כה כו כז כח **כט** ל

CHILDBIRTH BAG
MARRAKESH, MOROCCO,
EARLY 20TH CENTURY

The bag was used to hold aromatic herbs, presents, and babies' clothes. It was hung above the mother's bed, and given to her by her husband when their first child was born. The most common motifs decorating such bags are the mother's initials, the tree of life, and birds.

VELVET; GOLD-THREAD EMBROIDERY
41 X 29.5 CM
DONATED BY RAPHAEL BENAZERAF,
PARIS
PHOTOGRAPH: ISRAEL MUSEUM/
CHANAN SADEH

March | 1 2 3 4 5 6 7 8 9 10 **11** 12 13 14 15 16 17 18 19 20 21 22 23 24 25 26 27 28 29 30 31

ל   א ב ג ד ה ו ז ח ט י יא יב יג יד טו טז יז יח יט כ כא כב כג כד כה כו כז כח כט | אדר

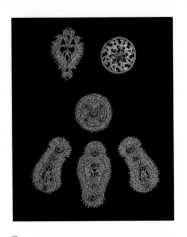

HOOD PLAQUES
SAN'A, YEMEN,
LATE 19TH–EARLY 20TH CENTURY

Plaques of different sizes and shapes were sewn onto the luxurious brocade headgear that the married Jewish women of San'a wore to weddings and other festivities. The characteristic dainty filigree work and small-shot granulation of the plaques recall ancient Etruscan jewelry, while their shapes are reminiscent of Indian filigree jewelry.

March | 1 2 3 4 5 6 7 8 9 10 11 **12** 13 14 15 16 17 18 19 20 21 22 23 24 25 26 27 28 29 30 31

אדר ב | א ב ג ד ה ו ז ח ט י יא יב יג יד טו טז יז יח יט כ כא כב כג כד כה כו כז כח כט

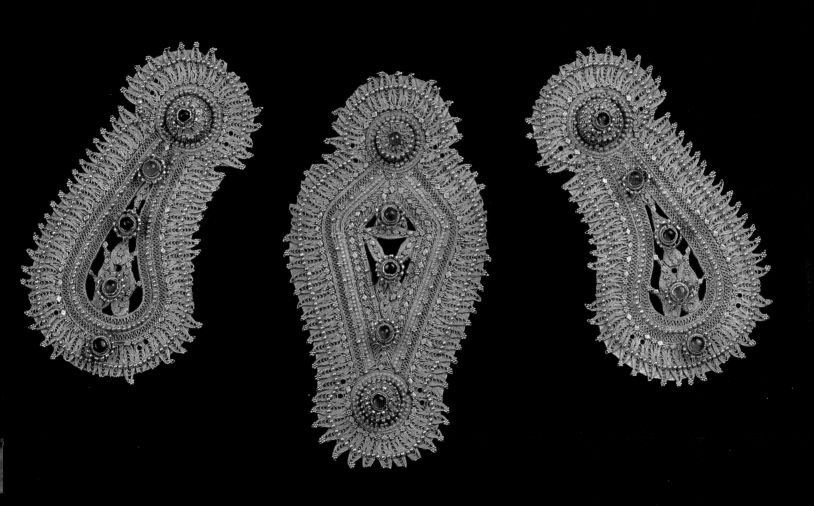

Bread stamps with Jewish symbols
Provenance unknown, Byzantine Period

The practice of stamping bread dough before baking was customary in different cultures. These stamps bear a menorah flanked by a shofar and the Four Species. The motif symbolizes the Temple in Jerusalem and the hope for redemption.

BRONZE
4.5, 5.5 CM (WIDTH)
GIFT OF LEO MILDENBERG,
REIFENBERG COLLECTION
PHOTOGRAPH: ISRAEL MUSEUM/
DAVID HARRIS

March | 1 2 3 4 5 6 7 8 9 10 11 12 **13** 14 15 16 17 18 19 20 21 22 23 24 25 26 27 28 29 30 31

אדר ב | א **ב** ג ד ה ו ז ח ט י יא יב יג יד טו טז יז יח יט כ כא כב כג כד כה כו כז כח כט

Necklace
San'a, Yemen,
Late 19th–Early 20th Century

This type of richly worked necklace was made by Jewish silversmiths exclusively for the Jewish women of San'a. It was given to the bride by her father or future husband and worn at the wedding, framing the bride's chin. Later on it was worn to after-birth celebrations and other important events. The painstaking work that went into the fashioning of the small but double-sided filigree pendants made it a particularly costly piece of jewelry.

Gilt silver; glass;
silk tassel; filigree
30 x 15 cm
Lent by WIZO
(Women's International
Zionist Organization)
in memory of Martha Bamberger,
a longtime member of the
World WIZO Executive
Photograph: Israel Museum/
David Harris

March | 1 2 3 4 5 6 7 8 9 10 11 12 13 **14** 15 16 17 18 19 20 21 22 23 24 25 26 27 28 29 30 31

אדר ב | א ב **ג** ד ה ו ז ח ט י יא יב יג יד טו טז יז יח יט כ כא כב כג כד כה כו כז כח כט

Purim Performance in the Museum's Galleries, 1995

Ten-to-fifteen-year-old art students created this installation, which is based on a David Hockney opera set. The children studied the artist, created their own masks, built the set, and on the day of Purim performed in the Museum's art galleries for the pleasure of the visitors.

March | 1 2 3 4 5 6 7 8 9 10 11 12 13 14 **15** 16 17 18 19 20 21 22 23 24 25 26 27 28 29 30 31

אדר ב | א ב ג ד ה ו ז ח ט י יא יב יג יד טו טז יז יח יט כ כא כב כג כד כה כו כז כח כט

ESTHER SCROLL
ITALY, 18TH CENTURY

The reading of the story of Esther, which commemorates the deliverance of the Jews of Persia from the tyranny of the King's officer Haman, is the central event of the Purim holiday. This scroll is illustrated with depictions of the heroes of the story dressed in eighteenth-century European-style garments and inscribed with their names. The unknown illustrator of this scroll imitated the copper etchings widely circulated in Europe.

PEN AND INK AND SEPIA ON PARCHMENT;
INCISED WOODEN ROD
210 X 1822 CM
THE STIEGLITZ COLLECTION WAS
DONATED TO THE ISRAEL MUSEUM,
JERUSALEM WITH THE CONTRIBUTION OF
ERICA AND LUDWIG JESSELSON,
NEW YORK, THROUGH THE AMERICAN
FRIENDS OF THE ISRAEL MUSEUM
PHOTOGRAPH: ISRAEL MUSEUM/
AVI GANOR

March | 1 2 3 4 5 6 7 8 9 10 11 12 13 14 15 **16** 17 18 19 20 21 22 23 24 25 26 27 28 29 30 31

אדר ב | א ב ג ד ה ו ז ח ט י י'א י'ב י'ג י'ד ט'ו ט'ז י'ז י'ח י'ט כ כ'א כ'ב כ'ג כ'ד כ'ה כ'ו כ'ז כ'ח כ'ט

המלך להשמיד להרג ולאבד את כל היהודים מנער ועד זקן
טף ונשים ביום אחד בשלושה עשר לחדש שנים עשר הוא חדש
אדר ושללם לבוז פתשגן הכתב להנתן דת בכל מדינה ומדינה
גלוי לכל העמים להיות עתדים ליום הזה הרצים יצאו דחופים בדבר
המלך והדת נתנה בשושן הבירה והמלך והמן ישבו לשתות
והעיר שושן נבוכה
ומרדכי ידע את כל אשר נעשה ויקרע
מרדכי את בגדיו וילבש שק ואפר ויצא בתוך העיר ויזעק זעקה
גדולה ומרה ויבוא עד לפני שער המלך כי אין לבוא אל שער המלך
בלבוש שק ובכל מדינה ומדינה מקום אשר דבר המלך
ודתו מגיע אבל גדול ליהודים וצום ובכי ומספד שק ואפר יצע
לרבים ותבואינה נערות אסתר וסריסיה ויגידו לה ותתחלחל המלכה
מאד ותשלח בגדים להלביש את מרדכי ולהסיר שקו מעליו ולא
קבל ותקרא אסתר להתך מסריסי המלך אשר העמיד לפניה
ותצוהו על מרדכי לדעת מה זה ועל מה זה ויצא התך אל מרדכי
אל רחוב העיר אשר לפני שער המלך ויגד לו מרדכי את כל אשר
קרהו ואת פרשת הכסף אשר אמר המן לשקול על גנזי המלך
ביהודים לאבדם ואת פתשגן כתב הדת אשר נתן בשושן להשמידם
נתן לו להראות את אסתר ולהגיד לה ולצוות עליה לבוא אל המלך
להתחנן לו ולבקש מלפניו על עמה ויבא התך ויגד לאסתר את דברי
מרדכי ותאמר אסתר להתך ותצוהו אל מרדכי
ועם מדינות המלך יודעים אשר כל איש ואשה אשר יבא אל המלך
אל החצר הפנימית אשר לא יקרא אחת דתו להמית לבד מאשר
יושיט לו המלך את שרביט הזהב וחיה ואני לא נקראתי לבוא אל
המלך זה שלושים יום ויגידו למרדכי את דברי אסתר ויאמר
מרדכי להשיב אל אסתר אל תדמי בנפשך להמלט בית המלך
מכל היהודים כי אם החרש תחרישי בעת הזאת רוח והצלה
יעמוד ליהודים ממקום אחר ואת ובית אביך תאבדו ומי יודע
אם לעת כזאת הגעת למלכות ותאמר אסתר להשיב אל מרדכי לך כנוס את
כל היהודים הנמצאים בשושן וצומו עלי ואל תאכלו ואל תשתו שלשת
ימים לילה ויום גם אני ונערתי אצום כן ובכן אבוא אל

המלך אשר לא כדת וכאשר אבדתי אבדתי ויעבר מרדכי ויעש ככל
אשר צותה עליו אסתר ויהי ביום השלישי ותלבש אסתר מלכות
ותעמד בחצר בית המלך הפנימית נכח בית המלך והמלך יושב על
כסא מלכותו בבית המלכות נכח פתח הבית ויהי כראות המלך את
אסתר המלכה עמדת בחצר נשאה חן בעיניו ויושט המלך לאסתר
את שרביט הזהב אשר בידו ותקרב אסתר ותגע בראש השרביט
ויאמר לה המלך מה לך אסתר המלכה ומה בקשתך עד חצי המלכות
וינתן לך ותאמר אסתר אם על המלך טוב יבא המלך והמן היום אל
המשתה אשר עשיתי לו ויאמר המלך מהרו את המן לעשות את
דבר אסתר ויבא המלך והמן אל המשתה אשר עשתה אסתר
ויאמר המלך לאסתר במשתה היין מה שאלתך וינתן לך ומה
בקשתך עד חצי המלכות ותעש ותען אסתר ותאמר שאלתי
ובקשתי אם מצאתי חן בעיני המלך ואם על המלך טוב לתת את
שאלתי ולעשות את בקשתי יבא המלך והמן אל המשתה אשר
אעשה להם ומחר אעשה כדבר המלך ויצא המן ביום ההוא שמח
וטוב לב וכראות המן את מרדכי בשער המלך ולא קם ולא זע ממנו
וימלא המן על מרדכי חמה ויתאפק המן ויבא אל ביתו וישלח ויבא
את אהביו ואת זרש אשתו ויספר להם המן את כבוד עשרו ורב
בניו ואת כל אשר גדלו המלך ואת אשר נשאו על השרים ועבדי
המלך ויאמר המן אף לא הביאה אסתר המלכה עם המלך אל
המשתה אשר עשתה כי אם אותי וגם למחר אני קרוא לה עם
המלך וכל זה איננו שוה לי בכל עת אשר אני ראה את מרדכי
היהודי יושב בשער המלך ותאמר לו זרש אשתו וכל אהביו
יעשו עץ גבה חמשים אמה ובבקר אמר למלך ויתלו את מרדכי
עליו ובא עם המלך אל המשתה שמח וייטב הדבר לפני המן
ויעש העץ
בלילה ההוא נדדה שנת המלך ויאמר להביא
את ספר הזכרנות דברי הימים ויהיו נקראים לפני המלך וימצא
כתוב אשר הגיד מרדכי על בגתנא ותרש שני סריסי המלך
משמרי הסף אשר בקשו לשלח יד במלך אחשורוש ויאמר
המלך מה נעשה יקר וגדלה למרדכי על זה ויאמרו נערי

READING THE MEGILLAT ESTHER, SHTIBELECH SYNAGOGUE, MEA SHEARIM, JERUSALEM, 1983

This photograph was taken at a small synagogue in the ultra-orthodox Jerusalem neighborhood of Mea Shearim. It is traditional to come to the reading of Megillat Esther at Purim in costume, and here the figure of an Arab sitting apart in his kaffiyah and grotesque mask in the foreground is very striking. Although at the time the photograph was taken, it was quite common to see people dressed in this costume, in light of political developments of the last twenty years, it has become rare, and even shocking. The contrast of the Arab and the orthodox Jews in traditional dress touches political issues, as well as compositional ones such as light and dark areas of the image.

JOEL KANTOR (B. CANADA, 1948),
IMMIGRATED TO ISRAEL, 1976
GELATIN SILVER PRINT
GIFT OF THE ARTIST, JERUSALEM

March | 1 2 3 4 5 6 7 8 9 10 11 12 13 14 15 16 **17** 18 19 20 21 22 23 24 25 26 27 28 29 30 31

אדר ב | א ב ג ד ה | ו ז ח ט י יא יב יג יד טו טז יז יח יט כ כא כב כג כד כה כו כז כח כט

Burial Society glass
Prague, Bohemia, 1713

This burial glass, one of the few surviving Bohemian glasses, was used by the Burial Society (*Hevra Kadisha*) at their annual banquets, held on the traditional anniversary of the death of Moses. Such benevolent societies took care of all the ceremonies surrounding death and burial. The painting on this glass, a depiction of a funeral procession, reflects the tradition of painting on glass, whose standards were high in Bohemia. The inscription on the upper section consists of biblical and talmudic phrases relating to death and mourning, as well as to drinking wine and preaching.

Glass; enamel; paint
24.5 x 15.7 cm
Photograph: Israel Museum/
Yoram Lehmann

March   1 2 3 4 5 6 7 8 9 10 11 12 13 14 15 16 17 **18** 19 20 21 22 23 24 25 26 27 28 29 30 31

אדר ב | א ב ג ד ה ו ז ח ט י יא יב יג יד טו טז יז יח יט כ כא כב כג כד כה כו כז כח כט

Spice box
Israel, 1986

The Havdalah ceremony takes place on Saturday evening, marking the end of the Sabbath and the beginning of the new week. The ceremony includes blessings recited over wine, spices, and a lit candle. The aromatic spices were often kept in decorated containers. Zelig Segal, who was born in Jerusalem, studied at the Bezalel School of Arts and Crafts. He created this unusual spice box by fusing tradition with new innovative ideas in design. The perforated, detachable ball was designed to hold the spices to be smelled by each member of the family.

Designer: Zelig Segal
Spun and fabricated silver
9.5 x 6.3 x 9.5 cm
Purchased by Eric Estorick Fund
Photograph: Israel Museum

March | 1 2 3 4 5 6 7 8 9 10 11 12 13 14 15 16 17 18 **19** 20 21 22 23 24 25 26 27 28 29 30 31

אדר ב | א ב ג ד ה ו ז **ח** ט י יא יב יג יד טו טז יז יח יט כ כא כב כג כד כה כו כז כח כט

Purim bread
In the Moroccan tradition,
Jerusalem, Israel, 2002

On Purim Jews send each other gifts of food. In Morocco these foods included a special bread, *khebza di Purim* or *boyoza*. This bread was baked in various shapes and forms, but always contained eggs in their shell. Usually the number of eggs referred to the number of the children in the family but they also symbolized the eyes of Haman who had plotted to destroy the Jews.

Photograph: Israel Museum/
Orpa Slapak

March | 1 2 3 4 5 6 7 8 9 10 11 12 13 14 15 16 17 18 19 **20** 21 22 23 24 25 26 27 28 29 30 31

אדר ב | א ב ג ד ה ו ז ח **ט** י יא יב יג יד טו טז יז יח יט כ כא כב כג כד כה כו כז כח כט

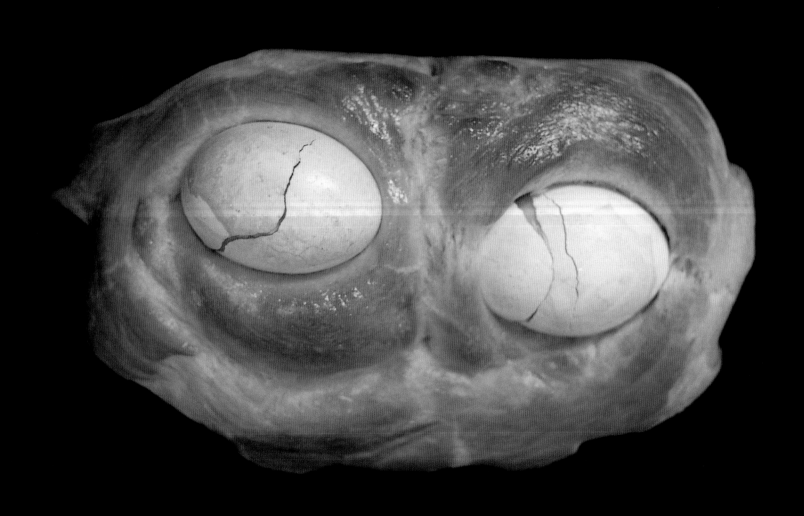

PURIM DOLLS
SAN'A AND ENVIRONS, YEMEN, 1930S

These Yemenite Purim dolls made of wood and rags represent Haman and Zeresh, the villains in the biblical book of Esther. On Purim young boys would pull them through the streets on a wooden cart to the sounds of laughter and toy guns shooting explosive noisemakers. Eventually the dolls were kicked off or burned, symbolically "smiting Haman." This custom was also known in other Jewish communities.

WOOD; RAGS; PLASTIC; METAL
LEFT TO RIGHT: 37 X 24.5, 39 X 29.5 CM
PERMANENT LOAN
BY SALMAN SCHOCKEN, TEL AVIV
PHOTOGRAPH: ISRAEL MUSEUM/
DAVID HARRIS

March | 1 2 3 4 5 6 7 8 9 10 11 12 13 14 15 16 17 18 19 20 **21** 22 23 24 25 26 27 28 29 30 31

אדר ב | א ב ג ד ה ו ז ח ט 'י א' י ב' י ג' י ד' ט ו' ט ז' י ז' י ח' י ט' כ כא כב כג כד כה כו כז כח כט

Purim plate for *Mishloah manot* (sending gifts of food)
Les Islettes, France, 18th century

Festive meals on Purim inspired a large range of Purim plates, mostly of pewter or faience. This faience plate was used for the Purim custom of exchanging gifts of food with friends and neighbors. It shows a scene in the Esther narrative in which Mordechai, Queen Esther's uncle, wearing royal clothes and a plumed hat, is being led on horseback by the King's officer Haman.

March | 1 2 3 4 5 6 7 8 9 10 11 12 13 14 15 16 17 18 19 20 21 **22** 23 24 25 26 27 28 29 30 31

אדר ב | א ב ג ד ה ו ז ח ט **י'** י"א יב יג יד טו טז יז יח **י"ט** כ כא כב כג כד כה כו כז כח כט

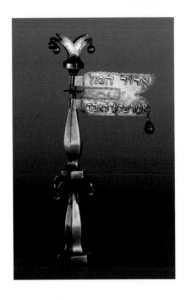

NOISEMAKER
VIENNA, AUSTRIA, 1826

During the reading of the Esther Scroll at Purim, the congregants make noise to drown out the name of Haman whenever it is mentioned. Special clappers and rattles were made for the purpose. This silver noisemaker is surmounted by a clown's hat and makes noise when shaken.

REPOUSSÉ SILVER
22 X 9.5 CM
GIFT OF ELIEZER BURSTEIN
COLLECTION, LUGANO
PHOTOGRAPH: ISRAEL MUSEUM/
DAVID HARRIS

March | 1 2 3 4 5 6 7 8 9 10 11 12 13 14 15 16 17 18 19 20 21 22 **23** 24 25 26 27 28 29 30 31

אדר ב | א ב ג ד ה ו ז ח ט י' י"א י"ב י"ג י"ד ט"ו ט"ז י"ז י"ח י"ט כ כ"א כ"ב כ"ג כ"ד כ"ה כ"ו כ"ז כ"ח כ"ט

PLATE OF PAINTED AND DECORATED EGGS
IN THE TRADITION OF HERAT, AFGHANISTAN

In Herat it was customary for the women of the family to get together in the courtyard on the Fast of Esther (eve of Purim festival) to dye the eggs for the *mishloah manot*, the traditional custom of exchanging platters of sweetmeats and cakes with friends and family during Purim. The dyed eggs were ornamented with gilt-paper cutouts and embroidery threads.

RECONSTRUCTED BY ESTHER BEZALEL, LEAH GOL, RACHEL NA'AMAD, JERUSALEM; AND MALKA AND LEA YAZDI, TEL AVIV PHOTOGRAPH: ISRAEL MUSEUM/ DAVID HARRIS

March | 1 2 3 4 5 6 7 8 9 10 11 12 13 14 15 16 17 18 19 20 21 22 23 **24** 25 26 27 28 29 30 31

אדר ב | א ב ג ד ה ו ז ח ט י יא יב **ג'** יד טו טז יז יח יט כ כא כב כג כד כה כו כז כח כט

Esther scroll
Iran, 1848

The Scroll of Esther recounts the story of Purim, which commemorates the deliverance of the Jews of Persia from the tyranny of Haman, the King's officer. The biblical text of the Scroll of Esther is usually handwritten on parchment. Neither it nor the Torah scroll read in synagogue are ever decorated. However, private scrolls are often illustrated. Geometric designs are typical of manuscripts from Middle Eastern Jewish communities because they generally avoided depicting human figures. The inscriptions in the first four columns in this scroll include part of the traditional blessing before the reading of the scroll, the genealogy of Mordechai and Haman, a dedication in honor of the person who commissioned it (David Yeshua Menahem Avraham), and the date.

March | 1 2 3 4 5 6 7 8 9 10 11 12 13 14 15 16 17 18 19 20 21 22 23 24 **25** 26 27 28 29 30 31

אדר ב | א ב ג ד ה ו ז ח ט י יא יב יג י' טו טז יז יח יט כ כא כב כג כד כה כו כז כח כט

Purim in Jerusalem
Mea Shearim,
Jerusalem, Israel, 1983

In Jerusalem, the festival of Purim is celebrated on a special day called Shushan Purim, on the fifteenth of Adar. The photograph shows a typical Hasidic family in Jerusalem, the children dressed up and holding *mishloah manot*, traditional gifts of food, while the father wears a fur *streimel* hat, worn on the Sabbath and festivals.

9 X 14 CM
PHOTOGRAPH: ISRAEL MUSEUM/
AVI NILSSON BEN-ZVI

March | 1 2 3 4 5 6 7 8 9 10 11 12 13 14 15 16 17 18 19 20 21 22 23 24 25 **26** 27 28 29 30 31

אדר ב | א ב ג ד ה ו ז ח ט י יא יב יג יד טו טז יז יח יט כ כא כב כג כד כה כו כז כח כט

Decorated hen
In the tradition of Herat, Afghanistan

One of the humorous betrothal gifts given to the bride by her future mother-in-law
on Purim was a painted and dressed live white hen. As it was meant to represent
the bride, its beak was painted red and its eyes made up with kohl; the "eyebrows"
were drawn with green paint, and gilt paper and sequins were added. The hen wore
a cape and tiny trousers with silver bells. When it wandered around the courtyard,
the sound of the tinkling bells delighted the child-bride and her family.

Reconstructed by Esther Bezalel,
Jerusalem, 1980
Photograph: Israel Museum/
Nahum Slapak

March | 1 2 3 4 5 6 7 8 9 10 11 12 13 14 15 16 17 18 19 20 21 22 23 24 25 26 **27** 28 29 30 31

אדר ב | א ב ג ד ה ו ז ח ט .י.א .י'ב .י'ג יד טו **טז** יז יח יט כ כא כב כג כד כה כו כז כח כט

LEGGINGS
CENTRAL PLATEAU, YEMEN,
EARLY 20TH CENTURY

Most women in Yemen wore leggings attached to their undergarments, which covered the lower part of the leg. The embroidery designs existed in great variety, depending on the origin and status of the wearer as well as the occasion on which the leggings were worn. The most festive examples, such as these, were part of a ceremonial outfit worn by Jewish brides and made by Jewish embroiderers in San'a. The bridegrooms presented them to their brides as a wedding gift.

GOLD BROCADE; SILVER-AND
SILK-THREAD EMBROIDERY
36 X 20 CM
PHOTOGRAPH: ISRAEL MUSEUM/
AVRAHAM HAY

March | 1 2 3 4 5 6 7 8 9 10 11 12 13 14 15 16 17 18 19 20 21 22 23 24 25 26 27 **28** 29 30 31

אדר ב | א ב ג ד ה ו ז ח ט י יא יב יג יד טו טז **יז** יח יט כ כא כב כג כד כה כו כז כח כט

Chancel screen engraved and decorated in relief
Synagogue at Susiya, southern Hebron hill region, Byzantine Period, 5th–7th century ce

The marble screens that separated the *bimmah* (pulpit) from the rest of the main hall in synagogues of the Byzantine period were decorated in relief. This panel was part of the screen surrounding the *bimmah* of the synagogue at Susiya, a flourishing Jewish village south of Hebron. It is decorated with a geometric menorah in high relief, from which two engraved censers hang. Below the menorah, the tops of a *lulav* (palm branch) and an incense shovel are visible. The reconstruction of the *bimmah* of the Susiya synagogue is at The Israel Museum, Jerusalem.

Marble
71.5 cm (width)
Staff Archaeological Officer
in the Civil Administration of
Judea and Samaria
Photograph: Israel Museum

March | 1 2 3 4 5 6 7 8 9 10 11 12 13 14 15 16 17 18 19 20 21 22 23 24 25 26 27 28 **29** 30 31

אדר ב | א ב ג ד ה ו ז ח ט י יא יב יג יד טו טז יז **יח** יט כ כא כב כג כד כה כו כז כח כט

Esther scroll
Holland, early 18th century

The Book of Esther is read during the festival of Purim. According to the biblical story, lots were cast to determine the month of execution for the Jews in Persia, and the fatal lot fell on the month of Adar. This is shown in the depiction featuring the wheel of the zodiac where a man is pointing at the sign of Pisces, equivalent to the month of Adar. Eventually, the plot to annihilate the Jews failed, and they were delivered from danger.

Pen and ink and gouache
on parchment; handwritten
25.5 x 297 cm
Photograph: Israel Museum/
Yoram Lehmann

March | 1 2 3 4 5 6 7 8 9 10 11 12 13 14 15 16 17 18 19 20 21 22 23 24 25 26 27 28 29 **30** 31

אדר ב | א ב ג ד ה ו ז ח ט י יא יב יג יד טו טז יז יח **יט** כ כא כב כג כד כה כו כז כח כט

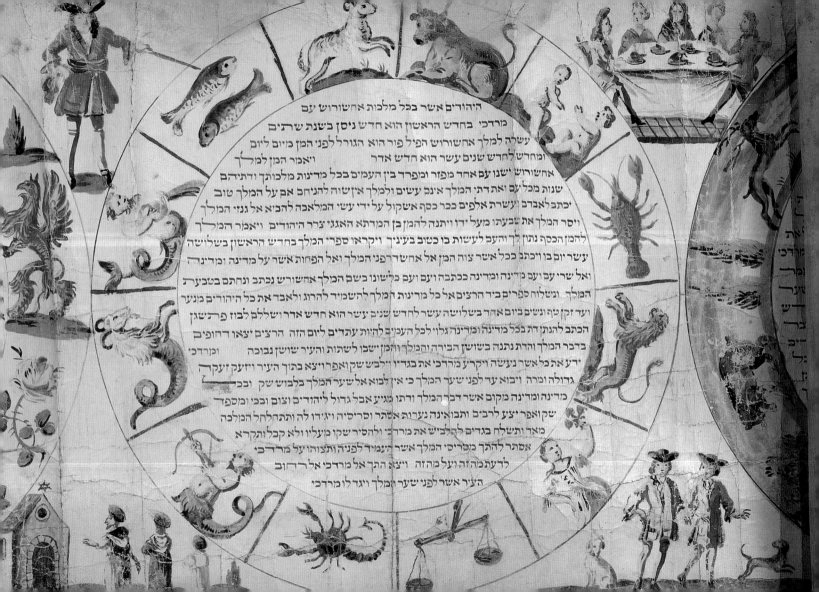

היהודים אשר בכל מלכות אחשורוש עם

מרדכי בחדש הראשון הוא חדש ניסן בשנת שתים

עשרה למלך אחשורוש הפיל פור הוא הגורל לפני המן מיום ליום

ומחדש לחדש שנים עשר הוא חדש אדר ויאמר המן למלך

אחשורוש ישנו עם אחד מפזר ומפרד בין העמים בכל מדינות מלכותך ודתיהם

שנות מכל עם ואת דתי המלך אינם עשים ולמלך אין שוה להניחם אם על המלך טוב

יכתב לאבדם ועשרת אלפים ככר כסף אשקול על ידי עשי המלאכה להביא אל גנזי המלך

ויסר המלך את טבעתו מעל ידו ויתנה להמן בן המדתא האגגי צרר היהודים ויאמר המלך

להמן הכסף נתון לך והעם לעשות בו כטוב בעיניך ויקראו ספרי המלך בחדש הראשון בשלושה

עשר יום בו ויכתב ככל אשר צוה המן אל אחשדרפני המלך ואל הפחות אשר על מדינה ומדינה

ואל שרי עם ועם מדינה ומדינה ככתבה ועם ועם כלשונו בשם המלך אחשורוש נכתב ונחתם בטבעת

המלך ונשלוח ספרים ביד הרצים אל כל מדינות המלך להשמיד להרג ולאבד את כל היהודים מנער

ועד זקן טף ונשים ביום אחד בשלושה עשר לחדש שנים עשר הוא חדש אדר ושללם לבוז פתשגן

הכתב להנתן דת בכל מדינה ומדינה גלוי לכל העמים להיות עתדים ליום הזה הרצים יצאו דחופים

בדבר המלך והדת נתנה בשושן הבירה והמלך והמן ישבו לשתות והעיר שושן נבוכה ומרדכי

ידע את כל אשר נעשה ויקרע מרדכי את בגדיו וילבש שק ואפר ויצא בתוך העיר ויזעק זעקה

גדולה ומרה ויבוא עד לפני שער המלך כי אין לבוא אל שער המלך בלבוש שק ובכל

מדינה ומדינה מקום אשר דבר המלך ודתו מגיע אבל גדול ליהודים וצום ובכי ומספד

שק ואפר יצע לרבים ותבואינה נערות אסתר וסריסיה ויגידו לה ותתחלחל המלכה

מאד ותשלח בגדים להלביש את מרדכי ולהסיר שקו מעליו ולא קבל ותקרא

אסתר להתך מסריסי המלך אשר העמיד לפניה ותצוהו על מרדכי

לדעת מה זה ועל מה זה ויצא התך אל מרדכי אל רחוב

העיר אשר לפני שער המלך ויגד לו מרדכי

Mortar
Verona, Italy, late 16th century

The mortar is decorated with a seven-branched candelabrum and Hebrew letters crowned with dots, suggesting that a Jewish physician commissioned the making of the object. Medicine was widely practiced by Italian Jews, particularly during the Renaissance. The most renowned physicians served the Papal court as well as royalty and aristocracy and were also known for their medical textbooks.

Artist: Servius de Levis
Cast bronze
14 x 15.5 cm
The Stieglitz Collection was donated to the Israel Museum, Jerusalem with the contribution of Erica and Ludwig Jesselson, New York, through the American Friends of the Israel Museum
Photograph: Israel Museum/ Avi Ganor

March | 1 2 3 4 5 6 7 8 9 10 11 12 13 14 15 16 17 18 19 20 21 22 23 24 25 26 27 28 29 30 **31**

אדר ב | א ב ג ד ה ו ז ח ט י יא יב יג יד טו טז יז יח יט כ כא כב כג כד כה כו כז כח כט

Three-dimensional menorah
Synagogue at Ma'on, southern Hebron hill region, Byzantine Period, 6th–7th century ce

Talmudic sources do not mention the use of three-dimensional menorahs in synagogues. We do, however, know of the prohibition against imitating the menorah that stood in the Temple in Jerusalem, destroyed in 70 ce. This large menorah, from the synagogue at Ma'on, is one of a kind. The top of its stems are in the shape of oil lamps that could actually be lit. We do not know if it had a ceremonial function or if it was merely decorative.

Marble
88 cm (height)
Staff Archaeological Officer
in the Civil Administration of
Judea and Samaria
Reconstructed in the Israel
Museum Laboratories through
a donation by Janis and
Harold Cooper, Florida
Photograph: Israel Museum

April | **1** 2 3 4 5 6 7 8 9 10 11 12 13 14 15 16 17 18 19 20 21 22 23 24 25 26 27 28 29 30

אדר ב | א ב ג ד ה ו ז ח ט י יא יב יג יד טו טז יז יח יט כ **כא** כב כג כד כה כו כז כח כט

READINGS AND SONGS (*PIYUTIM*) MANUSCRIPT
IRANIAN KURDISTAN, 1864

This handwritten and decorated prayer book comprises the Song of Songs and other liturgical texts read at various festivals. The decoration of this manuscript includes cypress trees, a symbol of the tree of life, flower cartouches, and other motifs used in local embroidery.

SCRIBE: HAYYIM BEN MOSHE
PEN AND INK AND
WATERCOLOR ON PAPER
18 X 11.5 CM
GIFT OF ELIEZER BEN DOV, TEHRAN
PHOTOGRAPH: ISRAEL MUSEUM/
DAVID HARRIS

April | 1 **2** 3 4 5 6 7 8 9 10 11 12 13 14 15 16 17 18 19 20 21 22 23 24 25 26 27 28 29 30

כט כח כז כו כה כד כג **כב** כא כ יט יח יז טז טו יד יג יב יא י ט ח ז ו ה ד ג ב א | ב אדר

אני

ישנה ולבי ער קול
דודי דופק פתחי לי
אחותי רעיתי יונתי
תמתי שראשי נמלא
טל שראשי קוצתי
רסיסי לילה
כתר   כל פתגמייא האלין
חבו עמא בית דישראל
ומסר יוי יתהון ביד נבודנצאר

Depiction of the Temple menorah
Jerusalem, Second Temple Period,
1st century bce

Found in the excavations of the Old City of Jerusalem, this fragment of plaster bears the earliest known representation of the Temple menorah. It was incised on the wall of a house by an artist who, in all likelihood, had actually seen the Temple menorah himself. The objects on the right are probably the shewbread table and the altar.

Plaster
20 cm (height)
Israel Antiquities Authority
Photograph: Israel Museum

April ┃ 1 2 **3** 4 5 6 7 8 9 10 11 12 13 14 15 16 17 18 19 20 21 22 23 24 25 26 27 28 29 30

אדר ב ┃ א ב ג ד ה ו ז ח ט י יא יב יג יד טו טז יז יח יט כ כא כב **גכ** כד כה כו כז כח כט

On the Jordan River, 1920s

This pastoral image shows a rowboat full of people on one of the tributaries of the Jordan River. They are dressed in formal European attire and seem to be a group of tourists enjoying their vacation. In the nineteenth century, taking a boat down the Jordan and its tributaries became a common leisure-time activity, a transplant of European habits to the local environment.

Yaacov Ben-Dov
(1882, Russia–1968, Israel),
immigrated to Eretz Israel, 1908
Gelatin silver print
gift of Rena (Fisch)
and Robert Lewin, London

April | 1 2 3 **4** 5 6 7 8 9 10 11 12 13 14 15 16 17 18 19 20 21 22 23 24 25 26 27 28 29 30

אדר ב | א ב ג ד ה ו ז ח ט י יא יב יג יד טו טז יז יח יט כ כא כב כג **כד** כה כו כז כח כט

Two crouching lions
Samaria, Iron Age, 9th–8th century bce

This pair of crouching lions from the royal palace at Samaria brings to mind the description of Solomon's ivory throne: "Two lions stood beside the arms, and twelve lions on the six steps, six on either side" (I Kings 10:19–20).

Ivory
4 cm (height)
Israel Antiquities Authority
Photograph: Israel Museum/
David Harris

April | 1 2 3 4 **5** 6 7 8 9 10 11 12 13 14 15 16 17 18 19 20 21 22 23 24 25 26 27 28 29 30

אדר ב | א ב ג ד ה ו ז ח ט י יא יב יג יד טו טז יז יח יט כ כא כב כג כד **כה** כו כז כח כט

Frans Hogenberg
Flemish (1535–1590)
Hand-colored etching on paper
33 x 41.8 cm (plate)
From: Braun & Hogenberg,
Civitates Orbis Terrarum,
Köln
Norman Bier Section for
Maps of the Holy Land
Gift of Karl and Li Handler,
Vienna
P 1157-5-61
Photograph: Israel Museum/
Ilan Stzulman

Jerusalem, the Holy City, by far the most famous city of Judea and the East, 1575

This bird's-eye view of "modern" Jerusalem, oriented to the east, is titled "This is Jerusalem: I have set it in the midst of the nations and countries that are around her" (Ezekiel 5:5). The bottom left, inside the frame, is inscribed: "Jerusalem, the Holy City, since time immemorial the most famous city of Judea and the East, in size and greatness." The legend at the lower right identifies this work as a map. In the lower center stand "Oriental" figures dressed in robes and turbans. Hogenberg was a Flemish etcher, cartographer, and publisher. He etched most of the maps in Ortelius's atlases. Although this map is considered relatively reliable, the facade of the Church of the Holy Sepulchre is tilted ninety degrees eastward, for emphasis. Notably, place names cited in the map's legend are those that were given by the Crusaders, such as "Pisans' Tower" on the fortress, "Templum Salomonis" for the Dome of the Rock, and "Sepulchrum Domini" for the Al-Aqsa Mosque.

April | 1 2 3 4 5 **6** 7 8 9 10 11 12 13 14 15 16 17 18 19 20 21 22 23 24 25 26 27 28 29 30

אדר ב | א ב ג ד ה ו ז ח ט י יא יב יג יד טו טז יז יח יט כ כא כב כג כד כה כו כז כח כט

EZECHIELIS V.
Hæc est Ierusalem, Ego eam in medio Gentium
posui, et in eius circuitu terras.

HIEROSOLYMA VRBS SANC
TA, IVDEAE, TOTIVSQVE
ORIENTIS LONGE CLARIS-
SIMA, QVA AMPLITVDINE AC
MAGNIFICENTIA HOC NOS-
TRO ÆVO CONSPICVA EST.

JEWELRY FROM THE JEWISH WORLD ISLAMIC COUNTRIES, LATE 19TH– EARLY 20TH CENTURY

The Israel Museum's jewelry collection represents an important chapter in the material culture of the Jewish communities in Islamic countries, testifying to a longstanding tradition of craftsmanship usually confined to Jews. Their skilled hands created jewelry in a variety of techniques and styles, the knowledge of which was passed from father to son.

VARIOUS MEDIA
PHOTOGRAPH: ISRAEL MUSEUM/
NAHUM SLAPAK

April | 1 2 3 4 5 6 **7** 8 9 10 11 12 13 14 15 16 17 18 19 20 21 22 23 24 25 26 27 28 29 30

אדר ב | א ב ג ד ה ו ז ח ט י יא יב יג יד טו טז יז יח יט כ כא כב כג כד כה **כו** כז כח כט

THE JEWISH QUARTER, OLD CITY OF JERUSALEM, 1920S

Standing prominently above the roofs of the Jewish Quarter is the Tiferet Israel Synagogue, named after the Admor Rabbi Israel Friedman from Ruzhin who financially supported its construction, which was completed in 1872. The synagogue was positioned so that its windows overlooked the Western Wall and Temple Mount. Most of the synagogues in the Jewish Quarter were destroyed when the Jordanians conquered the Old City during the 1948 War of Independence. Many photographers made images of Jerusalem since the invention of the camera, but the Jewish Quarter has mainly interested only Jewish photographers. The Dome of the Rock and the Temple Mount can be seen in the background of the photograph.

YAACOV BEN-DOV
(1882, RUSSIA–1968, ISRAEL),
IMMIGRATED TO ERETZ ISRAEL, 1908
GELATIN SILVER PRINT
GIFT OF RENA (FISCH) AND
ROBERT LEWIN, LONDON

April | 1 2 3 4 5 6 7 **8** 9 10 11 12 13 14 15 16 17 18 19 20 21 22 23 24 25 26 27 28 29 30

אדר ב | א ב ג ד ה ו ז ח ט י יא יב יג יד טו טז יז יח יט כ כא כב כג כד כה כו כז **כח** כט

THE ROTHSCHILD MISCELLANY MANUSCRIPT
NORTHERN ITALY, CA. 1450–80

The Rothschild Miscellany is one of the most magnificent Hebrew illuminated manuscripts in existence. It is unrivaled in the richness and quality of its illuminations and marginal texts. It assembles thirty-seven religious and secular units encompassing in minute detail almost every custom of religious and secular Jewish life. Of the 948 pages, 816 are decorated in minute detail in vibrant colors, including word panels decorated with gold and silver, as seen in these profusely illustrated pages. On one of the pages can be seen a picture of Haman and his ten sons hung from a tree.

VELLUM; PEN AND INK;
TEMPERA; GOLD LEAF
21 X 15.9 CM
GIFT OF JAMES A. DE ROTHSCHILD,
LONDON
PHOTOGRAPH: ISRAEL MUSEUM/
DAVID HARRIS

April | 1 2 3 4 5 6 7 8 **9** 10 11 12 13 14 15 16 17 18 19 20 21 22 23 24 25 26 27 28 29 30

אדר ב | א ב ג ד ה ו ז ח ט י יא יב יג יד טו טז יז יח יט כ כא כב כג כד כה כו כז **כח כט**

RECONSTRUCTION OF A ROOM IN AN URBAN JEWISH HOME
FEZ, MOROCCO, EARLY 20TH CENTURY

This room was used to receive guests and celebrate family events. It was usually situated on the lower floor of the house. Guests would sit on the cushion-strewn bench while tea and refreshments were served from silver and copper vessels and dishes. The room was furnished with Persian-style patterned carpets, curtains, and embroidered fabrics. Lattice windows (*mushrabiyya*), made of painted wood and metal, enabled women of the household to look out without being seen.

GIFTS OF MR. RAPHAEL BENAZERAF, PARIS; MR. AND MRS. EDWARD TOLEDANO, LONDON; MR. RAFI MOSCUNA, TEL AVIV; BARONESS ALIX DE ROTHSCHILD, PARIS; SOCIÉTÉ DES AMIS DU MUSÉE DE L'HOMME, PARIS; THE JERUSALEM FOUNDATION LOAN BY CARMIT AND ALEX GUTMAN, TEL AVIV
PHOTOGRAPH: ISRAEL MUSEUM/ DAVID HARRIS

April | 1 2 3 4 5 6 7 8 9 **IO** 11 12 13 14 15 16 17 18 19 20 21 22 23 24 25 26 27 28 29 30

נ'ס | א ב ג ד ה ו ז ח ט י י'א י'ב י'ג י'ד ט'ו ט'ז י'ז י'ח י'ט כ כ'א כ'ב כ'ג כ'ד כ'ה כ'ו כ'ז כ'ח כ'ט ל

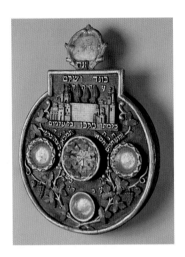

SEDER PLATE
ERETZ ISRAEL, 1889

This three-tiered Seder plate, from the late nineteenth century, was designed for the symbolic foods of Passover. Four small gilded dishes are inscribed with their Hebrew names. Above them is a decorative plaque with a view of the Western Wall in Jerusalem, maybe alluding to the hope traditionally expressed at the end of the ceremony: "Next year in Jerusalem."

April | 1 2 3 4 5 6 7 8 9 10 **11** 12 13 14 15 16 17 18 19 20 21 22 23 24 25 26 27 28 29 30

נ יסן | א **ב** ג ד ה ו ז ח ט י י"א י"ב י"ג י"ד ט ו ט ז י"ז י"ח י"ט כ כ"א כ"ב כ"ג כ"ד כ"ה כ ו כ ז כ ח כ ט ל

NECKLACE
MESHED, IRAN,
EARLY 20TH CENTURY

The fish—a repeated motif on this necklace—is an ancient symbol of fertility and a means of warding off the evil eye. It figures in various Eastern cultures, as do the crescent and the star, which, considered cosmic symbols, are also seen on protective amulets.

HAMMERED GOLD,
15 CM (DIAMETER)
PHOTOGRAPH: ISRAEL MUSEUM/
ODED LOEBL

April | 1 2 3 4 5 6 7 8 9 10 11 **12** 13 14 15 16 17 18 19 20 21 22 23 24 25 26 27 28 29 30

ל כט כח כז כו כה כד כג כב כא כ יט יח יז טז טו יד יג יב יא י ט ח ז ו ה ד ג ב א | ניסן

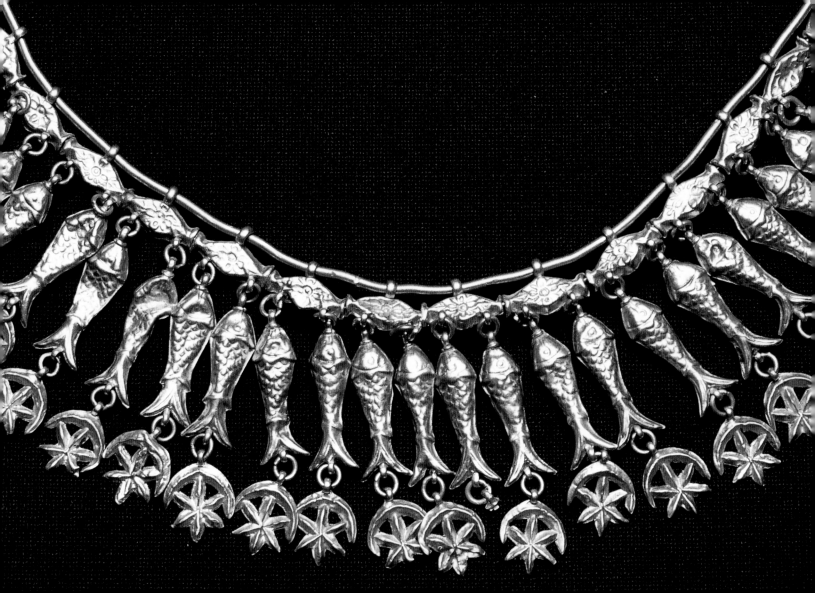

"Jerusalem" inscription
Amaziah, near Lachish, Iron Age, early 6th century BCE

Incised on the wall of a rock-cut burial cave in ancient Hebrew script, this is the earliest-known mention of Jerusalem in a Hebrew inscription.

STONE
62.5 x 123.2 CM
ISRAEL ANTIQUITIES AUTHORITY
PHOTOGRAPH: ISRAEL MUSEUM

April │ 1 2 3 4 5 6 7 8 9 10 11 12 **13** 14 15 16 17 18 19 20 21 22 23 24 25 26 27 28 29 30

נ׳ס│ן א ב ג **ד** ה ו ז ח ט י׳א י׳ב י׳ג י׳ד ט׳ו ט׳ז י׳ז י׳ח י׳ט כ כ׳א כ׳ב כ׳ג כ׳ד כ׳ה כ׳ו כ׳ז כ׳ח כ׳ט ל

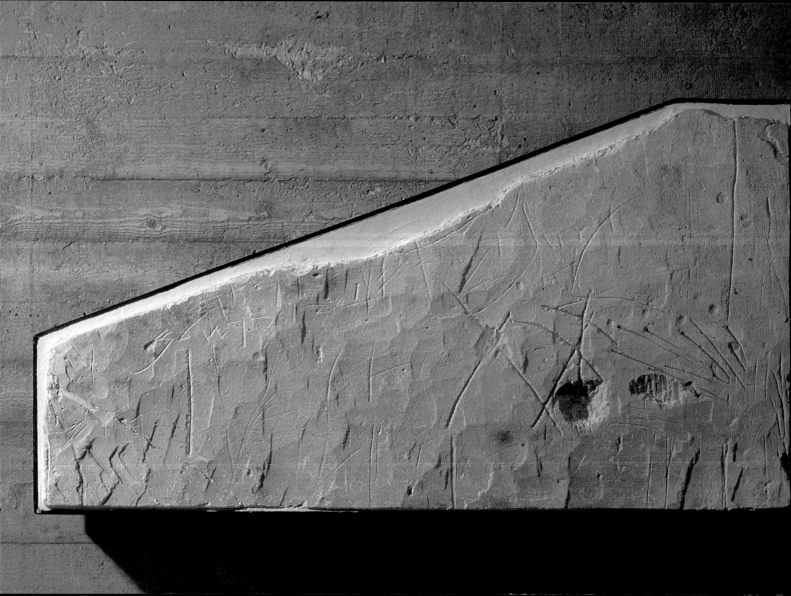

"House of God" ostracon
Arad, Iron Age, early 7th century BCE

The letter inscribed on this pottery shard was written in biblical Hebrew, using ancient Hebrew script. Addressed to the commander of the Judean fortress at Arad, it informs him that the individual in the Temple (probably Solomon's Temple in Jerusalem), about whom he had inquired, is well.

INK ON POTTERY
6.2 CM (HEIGHT)
ISRAEL ANTIQUITIES AUTHORITY
PHOTOGRAPH: ISRAEL MUSEUM

April | 1 2 3 4 5 6 7 8 9 10 11 12 13 **14** 15 16 17 18 19 20 21 22 23 24 25 26 27 28 29 30

ניסן | א ב ג ד ה ו ז ח ט י יא יב יג יד טו טז יז יח יט כ כא כב כג כד כה כו כז כח כט ל

VIEW OF JERUSALEM FROM THE MOUNT OF OLIVES, 1858

Lear made two trips to Jerusalem, once in 1858 and again in 1867. This watercolor dates from his first visit. The artist arrived on March 27, and began exploring the area immediately outside the walls the very next day. He spent the week of April 20 encamped on the Mount of Olives making drawings for a painting of Jerusalem at sunset that had been commissioned by Lady Waldegrave. Lear's ambitious paintings aimed for exact naturalistic representation. What he usually achieved, however, was a dramatic, brilliantly colored, and idealized view of a very picturesque setting at a time of day when the light effects are most memorable. Lear's watercolors are remarkable as jewels of observation and nostalgia, capturing the pleasure and poetry of distant lands.

EDWARD LEAR,
ENGLISH (1812–1888)
INK AND WATERCOLOR ON
THICK BROWN PAPER
29.5 X 46.2 CM
GIFT OF RUDOLF G. SONNEBORN,
NEW YORK, TO AMERICA-ISRAEL
CULTURAL FOUNDATION, 1964
M 3535-4-64
PHOTOGRAPH: ISRAEL MUSEUM

April | 1 2 3 4 5 6 7 8 9 10 11 12 13 14 **15** 16 17 18 19 20 21 22 23 24 25 26 27 28 29 30

ניסן | א ב ג ד ה | ז ח ט י יא יב יג יד טו טז יז יח יט כ כא כב כג כד כה כו כז כח כט ל

TORAH CROWN AND FINIALS
ADEN, SOUTHERN YEMEN,
SECOND HALF OF THE 19TH CENTURY

This exceptional Torah crown with finials is placed on the top of the Torah scroll. Its design, unique to Aden, reflects a combination of local styles and foreign motifs; the inspiration may have come from neighboring countries such as India, Ethiopia, or Somalia. Along the crown are engraved various biblical quotations. Since Jewish ceremonial objects were produced only by Jewish silversmiths in Aden, these engravings attest to their wide knowledge of Hebrew and the Bible.

REPOUSSÉ AND STAMPED
SHEET SILVER
41 X 35 CM
PURCHASED THROUGH A DONATION
OF THE WEISZ CHILDREN IN MEMORY
OF THEIR FATHER, DAVID WEISZ
PHOTOGRAPH: ISRAEL MUSEUM/
YORAM LEHMANN

April | 1 2 3 4 5 6 7 8 9 10 11 12 13 14 15 **16** 17 18 19 20 21 22 23 24 25 26 27 28 29 30

ניסן | א ב ג ד ה ו ז ח ט י יא יב יג יד טו טז יז יח יט כ כא כב כג כד כה כו כז כח כט ל

L'EXAMEN DU LEVAIN (THE SEARCH FOR LEAVENED BREAD), 18TH CENTURY

BERNARD PICART
(1673, FRANCE–1733),
ACTIVE HOLLAND
HAND-COLORED ENGRAVING AND
ETCHING ON PAPER
16.5 X 21.5 CM
FROM: *CÉRÉMONIES DES JUIFS IN
CÉRÉMONIES ET COSTUMES
RELIGIEUSES DE TOUS LES PEUPLES
DU MONDE*, PUBLISHED IN
AMSTERDAM 1723–1738
GIFT OF MRS. ERIKA ELIZABETH
MAUER, NEW YORK,
IN MEMORY OF HER PARENTS
GEORG AND RENEE HOLÄNDER
B95.0871
PHOTOGRAPH: ISRAEL MUSEUM

"And there shall be no leavened bread seen with you, nor shall there be leaven seen with you in all your borders. And you shall tell your son in that day, saying: It is because of that which the Lord did for me when I came out of Egypt" (Exodus 13:7–8).

The search for leaven (*bedikat hametz*) is an integral part of the preparations for Passover. As shown here by Picart, after the house has been cleaned, a number (ten is customary) of bread crumbs are placed in key places around the home so that when the blessing for the search of *hametz* is recited, God's name should not be taken in vain. On the night of the fourteenth of Nisan, a candle is used to make it possible to see into deep cracks and corners. A feather is used to brush the crumbs onto a tray. The morning after, the *hametz* is burnt outside. This ritual may also symbolize, according to the Kabbalah, the desire to search ourselves and destroy the spiritual imperfections within us.

April | 1 2 3 4 5 6 7 8 9 10 11 12 13 14 15 16 **17** 18 19 20 21 22 23 24 25 26 27 28 29 30

ניסן | א ב ג ד ה ו ז **ח** ט י יא יב יג יד טו טז יז יח יט כ כא כב כג כד כה כו כז כח כט ל

L' EXAMEN du LEVAIN &c.

ERNA MICHAEL HAGGADAH
MIDDLE RHINE, GERMANY, CA. 1340

The Erna Michael Haggadah has richly colored illustrations according to the German and Italian tradition. The gold and painted initial word panels are highly ornamented, as in this page, which shows the decorated letter *aleph*, the first letter in the Hebrew alphabet. This manuscript was known in Germany during the sixteenth and seventeenth centuries, reappearing in France in 1950. It was presented to the Israel Museum in 1966 by Mr. Jakob Michael of New York in memory of his wife, Erna, thereby giving the Haggadah its name.

PEN AND INK, TEMPERA, AND
GOLD LEAF ON PARCHMENT,
HANDWRITTEN
35 X 25.5 CM
GIFT OF JAKOB MICHAEL,
NEW YORK, IN MEMORY OF HIS WIFE,
ERNA SONDHEIMER-MICHAEL, 1966
PHOTOGRAPH: ISRAEL MUSEUM/
MOSHE CAINE

April | 1 2 3 4 5 6 7 8 9 10 11 12 13 14 15 16 17 **18** 19 20 21 22 23 24 25 26 27 28 29 30

נ יס ן | א ב ג ד ה ו ז ח **ט** י יא יב יג יד טו טז יז יח יט כ כא כב כג כד כה כו כז כח כט ל

BIRDS' HEAD HAGGADAH
SOUTHERN GERMANY, CA. 1300

The Haggadah is read during the festive seder on the first night of Passover and recounts the story of the Exodus from Egypt. The Birds' Head Haggadah is the earliest known illustrated Ashkenazi Haggadah to have survived as a separate book. It is richly illustrated in the margins with mostly biblical and ritual scenes. The page reproduced here depicts the preparation, pricking, and baking of *matzah*, the unleavened bread eaten on Pesach. The most striking feature of this Haggadah are the human figures with pronounced birds' heads. Although there are various explanations for this intriguing phenomenon, it may well have arisen in order to avoid the depiction of human figures according to the second commandment: "Thou shall not make unto thee any graven image, or any likeness" (Exodus 20:4). Men are depicted here wearing conical hats, which was a distinctive mark in the dress of Jews at that time.

PEN AND INK AND TEMPERA ON
PARCHMENT; HANDWRITTEN
27 X 19 CM
PHOTOGRAPH: ISRAEL MUSEUM/
MOSHE CAINE

April | 1 2 3 4 5 6 7 8 9 10 11 12 13 14 15 16 17 18 **19** 20 21 22 23 24 25 26 27 28 29 30

ניסן | א ב ג ד ה ו ז ח ט י יא יב יג יד טו טז יז יח יט כ כא כב כג כד כה כו כז כח כט ל

להתחכמה וגם צדה לא
עשו להם
מרור זה שאנו אוכ
לים על
שום מה על שום שמררו
המצריים את חיי אבותינו
במצרים שנ׳ וימררו את
חייהם בעבודה קשה בחומר
ובלבנים ובכל עבודה בשדה
את כל עבדתם אשר עב
דו בהם בפרך
בכל דור ודור חיב

אדם לראות את עצמו . כ
אלו הוא יצא ממצרים
שנ׳ והגדת לבנך ביום ההו
ההוא לאמר בעבור זה
עשה יי׳ לי בצאתי ממצרי
לא את אבותינו גאל
הקבה בלבד אלא
אף אותנו גאל עמהם שנ
שנ׳ ואותנו הוציא משם
למען הביא אותנו לתת
לנו את הארץ אשר נשבע
לאבותינו

Utensils for making *Matzah*
Sweden, late 19th century

During the festival of Passover, Jews eat *matzah*, which symbolizes the unleavened bread eaten by their ancestors as they fled from Egypt. The process of making *matzah* requires no more than eighteen minutes from the time the flour is mixed with water and kneaded until it goes into the oven to be baked. It is perforated with little holes to prevent it from rising. The table on the left has a special shaft in the center for kneading the dough for *matzah*. The same type of device is still in use today in bakeries where *matzah* is made by hand.

ABOVE: TABLE FOR KNEADING
MATZAH DOUGH
SWEDEN, LATE 19TH CENTURY
PINEWOOD
11.5 X 50 CM
PHOTOGRAPH: ISRAEL MUSEUM

IRON
LEFT: 20 CM (LENGTH)
RIGHT: 6 CM (DIAMETER)
GIFT OF THE MOSAISKA FOERSAMLINGEN, GOETEBORG,
AND THE CAMILLA AND FRITZ HOLLAENDER FOUNDATION
PHOTOGRAPH: ISRAEL MUSEUM/DAVID HARRIS

April | 1 2 3 4 5 6 7 8 9 10 11 12 13 14 15 16 17 18 19 **20** 21 22 23 24 25 26 27 28 29 30

ניסן | א ב ג ד ה ו ז ח ט י **י"א** י"ב י"ג י"ד ט"ו ט"ז י"ז י"ח י"ט כ כ"א כ"ב כ"ג כ"ד כ"ה כ"ו כ"ז כ"ח כ"ט ל

MAKER: SOLOMON BEN MOSES
PEN AND INK, WATERCOLOR ON
PAPER; CARVED AND PAINTED WOOD;
CLOTH FLOWERS AND GLASS
77 X 64 CM
PHOTOGRAPH: ISRAEL MUSEUM/
DAVID HARRIS

PLAQUE FOR *ERUV TAVSHILIN*
GERMANY, 1806

The biblical prohibition against work on the festivals specifically excluded the preparation of food (Exodus 12:16). When a festival falls on Friday, however, it is permitted to prepare food needed for the Sabbath on condition that the preparations begin before the festival. A special ceremony called *eruv tavshilin*—in which two kinds of foods are set aside to enable cooking to be done—takes place in the home. This decorative wall plaque from Germany is inscribed with the blessing for the ceremony, and is decorated with birds and flowers, together with a carved lion and deer and the verse "Be bold as a leopard, light as an eagle, swift as a deer, and strong as a lion to do the will of God" (Pirkei Avot 5:23).

April | 1 2 3 4 5 6 7 8 9 10 11 12 13 14 15 16 17 18 19 20 **21** 22 23 24 25 26 27 28 29 30

ניסן | א ב ג ד ה ו ז ח ט י י'א **י'ב** י'ג י'ד ט'ו ט'ז י'ז י'ח י'ט כ כ'א כ'ב כ'ג כ'ד כ'ה כ'ו כ'ז כ'ח כ'ט ל

CANDLEHOLDER FOR *BEDIKAT HAMETZ* (SEARCH FOR LEAVEN)
ISRAEL, 1986

On the evening before Passover a symbolic ceremony takes place called *bedikat hametz*, performed by the head of the family. The last crumbs of bread are gathered together to be burned the following morning. In some communities a candle and a feather are used for this ceremony. Moshe Zabari fashioned this silver holder for the candle and the feather, inscribed with the Hebrew blessing recited before the ceremony.

DESIGNER: MOSHE ZABARI
REPOUSSÉ, CUT, PIERCED, AND
WELDED SILVER; FEATHER
19.7 X 7.3 CM
PHOTOGRAPH: ISRAEL MUSEUM/
DAVID HARRIS

April | 1 2 3 4 5 6 7 8 9 10 11 12 13 14 15 16 17 18 19 20 21 **22** 23 24 25 26 27 28 29 30

ניסן | א ב ג ד ה ו ז ח ט י י"א י"ב **י"ג** יד טו טז יז יח יט כ כא כב כג כד כה כו כז כח כט ל

Passover plate
Spain, ca. 1480

This plate is one of the few surviving objects of Jewish ceremonial art from Spain prior to the expulsion of the Jews in 1492. The Hebrew inscription on the center of the plate refers to the three main components of the ritual Passover meal: *pesach* (lamb), *matzah* (unleavened bread), and *maror* (bitter herbs). A naive mistake in the Hebrew spelling of the word *matzah* may indicate that a Jew commissioned the plate from a non-Jewish craftsman who was unfamiliar with the Hebrew characters. Most Seder plates known to us date from the eighteenth century on.

EARTHENWARE
57 CM (DIAMETER)
GIFT OF JAKOB MICHAEL,
NEW YORK, IN MEMORY OF HIS WIFE
ERNA SONDHEIMER-MICHAEL
PHOTOGRAPH: ISRAEL MUSEUM/
NAHUM SLAPAK

April | 1 2 3 4 5 6 7 8 9 10 11 12 13 14 15 16 17 18 19 20 21 22 **23** 24 25 26 27 28 29 30

נ׳סן | א ב ג ד ה ו ז ח ט י י׳א י׳ב י׳ג **י׳ד** ט׳ו ט׳ז י׳ז י׳ח י׳ט כ כ׳א כ׳ב כ׳ג כ׳ד כ׳ה כ׳ו כ׳ז כ׳ח כ׳ט ל

ERNA MICHAEL HAGGADAH
MIDDLE RHINE, GERMANY, CA. 1400

This Haggadah, bearing German and Italian influence in its decoration, illustrates the different stages of the Passover evening service. The page shown here depicts the Seder table with seated men reading the Haggadah. A gold star-shaped hanging lamp used for kindling the Sabbath lights hangs in the middle of the room. This type of domestic oil lamp was used in medieval Europe by Jews and non-Jews alike. Known by its German name *Judenstern* (Star of the Jews), it survived among Jews for festive occasions. This manuscript was known in Germany during the sixteenth and seventeenth centuries, reappearing in France in 1950. It was presented to the Israel Museum in 1966 by Mr. Jakob Michael of New York in memory of his wife, Erna, thereby giving the Haggadah its name.

April | 1 2 3 4 5 6 7 8 9 10 11 12 13 14 15 16 17 18 19 20 21 22 23 **24** 25 26 27 28 29 30

ניסן | א ב ג ד ה ו ז ח ט י יא יב יג יד **טו** טז יז יח יט כ כא כב כג כד כה כו כז כח כט ל

Passover Haggadah
Hamburg, Germany, 1762

The main focus of the Passover celebration is the festive Seder (order) meal, during which the family reads the Haggadah, a compilation with a set text and specific sequence that tells the story of the Exodus from Egypt. This Haggadah was written and illustrated by Nathanel ben Aaron ha-Levi Segal, the scribe in Hamburg, Altona, and Wandsbeck, an important center of Jewish culture. It is in a style characteristic of eighteenth-century Moravia. Among the artists who worked in this area were newcomers from Moravia, where illuminated manuscript art underwent a revival at the beginning of the eighteenth century. These artists were influenced by the copperplate etchings and woodcuts in printed books from Venice and Amsterdam and especially printed Haggadot from Amsterdam from the seventeenth and eighteenth centuries.

Scribe and illustrator:
Nathanel ben Aaron
ha-Levi Segal
Pen and ink on parchment,
handwritten
30.3 x 19.6 cm
The Stieglitz Collection was
donated to the Israel Museum,
Jerusalem with the contribution
of Erica and Ludwig Jesselson,
New York, through the American
Friends of the Israel Museum
Photograph: Israel Museum/
Avi Ganor

April | 1 2 3 4 5 6 7 8 9 10 11 12 13 14 15 16 17 18 19 20 21 22 23 24 **25** 26 27 28 29 30

נ׳ס | א ב ג ד ה ו ז ח ט י י׳א י׳ב י׳ג י׳ד ט׳ו **ט׳ז** י׳ז י׳ח י׳ט כ כ׳א כ׳ב כ׳ג כ׳ד כ׳ה כ׳ו כ׳ז כ׳ח כ׳ט ל

Right page

וְלֹא נָתַן לָנוּ אֶת הַשַּׁבָּת

דַּיֵּנוּ : קֵרְבָנוּ לִפְנֵי הַר סִינַי

וְלֹא קֵרְבָנוּ לִפְנֵי הַר סִינַי

דַּיֵּנוּ : נָתַן לָנוּ אֶת הַתּוֹרָה

וְלֹא נָתַן לָנוּ אֶת הַתּוֹרָה

דַּיֵּנוּ : הִכְנִיסָנוּ לְאֶרֶץ יִשְׂרָאֵל

וְלֹא הִכְנִיסָנוּ לְאֶרֶץ יִשְׂרָאֵל

דַּיֵּנוּ : בָּנָה לָנוּ אֶת בֵּית הַבְּחִירָה

וְלֹא

משֶׁה יְדַבֵּר וְהָאֱלֹהִים יַעֲנֶנּוּ בְקוֹל ✿ וַיְיָחֵילוּ כָּל אֲשֶׁר דִבֶּר ה' נַעֲשֶׂה וְנִשְׁמָע אוֹכִי ה' אֱלֹהֶיךָ

עַל אַחַת כַּמָּה וְכַמָּה טוֹבָה כְפוּלָה וּמְכֻפֶּלֶת לַ
לַמָּקוֹם עָלֵינוּ ׃ שֶׁהוֹצִיאָנוּ מִמִּצְרַיִם ׃ וְעָשָׂה
בָהֶם שְׁפָטִים ׃ וְעָשָׂה בֵאלֹהֵיהֶם ׃ וְהָרַג בְּכוֹרֵיהֶם
וְנָתַן לָנוּ אֶת מָמוֹנָם ׃ וְקָרַע לָנוּ אֶת הַיָּם ׃ וְהֶעֱבִירָנוּ בְּתוֹכוֹ
בֶּחָרָבָה ׃ וְשִׁקַּע צָרֵינוּ בְּתוֹכוֹ ׃ וְסִפֵּק צָרְכֵּנוּ בַּמִּדְבָּר
אַרְבָּעִים שָׁנָה ׃ וְהֶאֱכִילָנוּ אֶת הַמָּן ׃ וְנָתַן לָנוּ אֶת הַשַּׁבָּת
וְקֵרְבָנוּ לִפְנֵי הַר סִינַי ׃ וְנָתַן לָנוּ אֶת הַתּוֹרָה ׃ וְהִכְנִיסָנוּ לְאֶרֶץ

Left page

יִשְׂרָאֵל ׃ וּבָנָה לָנוּ אֶת בֵּית הַבְּחִירָה ׃ לְכַפֵּר עַל
כָּל עֲוֹנוֹתֵינוּ ׃

רַבָּן גַּמְלִיאֵל אוֹמֵר כָּל שֶׁלֹּא אָמַר שְׁלשָׁה
דְּבָרִים אֵלּוּ בְּפֶסַח לֹא יָצָא יְדֵי חוֹבָתוֹ וְאֵלּוּ הֵן
פֶּסַח ׃ מַצָּה ׃ וּמָרוֹר ׃

פֶּסַח שֶׁהָיוּ אֲבוֹתֵינוּ אוֹכְלִים בִּזְמַן שֶׁבֵּית הַמִּקְדָּשׁ
קַיָּים עַל שׁוּם מָה עַל שׁוּם שֶׁפָּסַח הַקָּדוֹשׁ
בָּרוּךְ הוּא עַל בָּתֵּי אֲבוֹתֵינוּ בְּמִצְרַיִם שֶׁנֶּאֱמַר
וַאֲמַרְתֶּם זֶבַח פֶּסַח הוּא לַה' אֲשֶׁר פָּסַח עַל בָּתֵּי בְנֵי יִשְׂרָאֵל
בְּמִצְרַיִם בְּנָגְפּוֹ אֶת מִצְרַיִם וְאֶת בָּתֵּינוּ הִצִּיל וַיִּקּוֹד הָעָם
וַיִּשְׁתַּחֲווּ ׃

וּכְכָה תּאֹכְלוּ אֹתוֹ מָתְנֵיכֶם חֲגֻרִים עַל בְּנֵי בֵּיתוֹ וַיֹּאכְלוּ וַיֹּאכְלוּ בִּידְכֶם פֶּסַח הוּא לַה'

מַצָּה זוֹ שֶׁאָנוּ אוֹכְלִים עַל שׁוּם מָה עַל שׁוּם
שֶׁלֹּא הִסְפִּיק בְּצֵקָם שֶׁל אֲבוֹתֵינוּ לְהַחֲמִיץ
עַד שֶׁנִּגְלָה עֲלֵיהֶם מֶלֶךְ מַלְכֵי הַמְּלָכִים
הַקָּדוֹשׁ בָּרוּךְ הוּא וּגְאָלָם שֶׁנֶּאֱמַר וַיֹּאפוּ אֶת הַבָּצֵק אֲשֶׁר
הוֹצִיאוּ מִמִּצְרַיִם עֻגֹת מַצּוֹת כִּי לֹא חָמֵץ כִּי גֹרְשׁוּ מִמִּצְרַיִם
וְלֹא יָכְלוּ לְהִתְמַהְמֵהַּ וְגַם צֵדָה לֹא עָשׂוּ לָהֶם

SEDER PLATE
GERMANY, 1769

This plate was used to display the ritual foods of the Seder, the festive meal celebrating the first night of Passover. The plate is decorated with a depiction of the Egyptian cities Pithom and Rameses, named in the Bible as places where the Jews are believed to have been enslaved, as well as a Hebrew quotation from Exodus exhorting the celebration of Passover.

ARTIST: JACOB SCHOTT
ENGRAVED PEWTER
35.6 CM (DIAMETER)
THE STIEGLITZ COLLECTION WAS
DONATED TO THE ISRAEL MUSEUM,
JERUSALEM WITH THE CONTRIBUTION
OF ERICA AND LUDWIG JESSELSON,
NEW YORK, THROUGH THE AMERICAN
FRIENDS OF THE ISRAEL MUSEUM
PHOTOGRAPH: ISRAEL MUSEUM/
AVI GANOR

April | 1 2 3 4 5 6 7 8 9 10 11 12 13 14 15 16 17 18 19 20 21 22 23 24 25 **26** 27 28 29 30

ניסן | א ב ג ד ה ו ז ח ט י יא יב יג יד טו טז **יז** יח יט כ כא כב כג כד כה כו כז כח כט ל

Passover set
Israel, 1989

Since graduating from the Bezalel School of Arts and Crafts, the Israeli artist Amit Shor has been dedicated to the field of Jewish ritual objects, producing many bold and innovative pieces. In this Passover set she has experimented by casting blank images of the traditional Passover foods into the aluminum blocks, making reference to traditional Jewish sources while also creating new forms and ideas.

Designer: Amit Shor
Spun aluminum; gilt brass
36 x 24 cm (tray);
16 cm (height of Elijah cup)
Acquired with the help of the Katherine Sonneborn Falk Fund
Photograph: Israel Museum/ David Harris

April | 1 2 3 4 5 6 7 8 9 10 11 12 13 14 15 16 17 18 19 20 21 22 23 24 25 26 **27** 28 29 30

א ב ג ד ה ו ז ח ט י׳א י׳ב י׳ג י׳ד ט׳ו ט׳ז י׳ז **י׳ח** י׳ט כ כ׳א כ׳ב כ׳ג כ׳ד כ׳ה כ׳ו כ׳ז כ׳ח כ׳ט ל | ניסן

Sassoon Haggadah
Catalonia, Spain, ca. 1320

The Sassoon Spanish Haggadah is a rare example in the Israel Museum Collections of the pre-Expulsion manuscript from Spain. It is written in square Sephardi script. Text illustrations blend local and foreign stylistic influences, depicting grotesque images and floral scrolls. These two illustrated pages show two people in prayer within the ornamented word panel on the first page. On the second page a man leaving prison holding his chains is depicted, illustrating the text, "Out of my distress: The Lord answered me" (Psalms 118:5). Richly illuminated Haggadot belonged to wealthy members of the Jewish community prior to their expulsion in 1492, and this manuscript gives testimony to the once-flourishing Spanish Jewish community.

PEN AND INK, TEMPERA,
AND GOLD LEAF ON PARCHMENT
21 X 16.5 CM
PERMANENT LOAN FROM
THE STATE OF ISRAEL
PHOTOGRAPH: ISRAEL MUSEUM/
NAHUM SLAPAK

April | 1 2 3 4 5 6 7 8 9 10 11 12 13 14 15 16 17 18 19 20 21 22 23 24 25 26 27 **28** 29 30

נ׳ס׳ן | א ב ג ד ה ו ז ח ט י׳א י׳ב י׳ג י׳ד ט׳ו ט׳ז י׳ז י׳ח **י׳ט** כ כ׳א כ׳ב כ׳ג כ׳ד כ׳ה כ׳ו כ׳ז כ׳ח כ׳ט ל

מן המצר

קראתי יה ענני במ
רחב יה ולי לא
אירא מה יעשה לי
אדם יי לי בעזרי

שמרו

נא בית אהרן יי לעו

תסמ

שמח

לעולם

חסדו

First Nuremberg Haggadah
Germany, ca. 1449

The First Nuremberg Haggadah, written in Ashkenazi square script, is richly decorated by hand with biblical scenes and text illustrations. On the last page are six medallions bearing signs of the zodiac. Initial word panels are usually adorned with floral motifs, hunting scenes, various animals, and grotesque creatures. This page illustrates the initial word *Lefichach*, showing the ritual of the Seder. On the right a man lifts a glass of wine; on the left men and women sit at the Seder table with *matzot* and the special Seder dishes. The Haggadah was written, illustrated, and signed by Joel ben Simeon, a noted and prolific scribe-illuminator who was active in Germany and Italy in the second half of the fifteenth century, to whose hand is attributed at least a dozen other manuscripts.

SCRIBE AND ILLUSTRATOR:
JOEL BEN SIMEON
INK ON PARCHMENT, HANDWRITTEN
AV. 28.3 X 18 CM
GIFT OF ERICA JESSELSON AND
THE JESSELSON FAMILY NEW YORK,
IN HONOR OF
TEDDY KOLLEK'S 90TH BIRTHDAY
PHOTOGRAPH: ISRAEL MUSEUM:/
GENNADIY LITIOVGA

April | 1 2 3 4 5 6 7 8 9 10 11 12 13 14 15 16 17 18 19 20 21 22 23 24 25 26 27 28 **29** 30

נ׳ס|ן | א ב ג ד ה ו ז ח ט י יא יב יג יד טו טז יז יח יט כ כא כב כג כד כה כו כז כח כט ל

ויאמרו סגניאף את הבבק אשר חדשאו
מצריים עות מיזת כל וחמיזכב
גרשה ממצריים ולא יכרו להתמהמה
וגם צידה לא עשה להם
מ**צור** זה שיצו אוכלים על
שום מה על שהם ית
שמהרו המצריים את
כיי אבותינו ממצריים שנגבי מפורק את ה
חייתם מעבירה קשה בחמיר ובלבנם ה
ובכל עברה בשדה עברדם אשר עברו
בהם מפרך
ב**כל** דור ודור חייב אדם לראות
עצמו כאלו הוא יצא ממצרים
שנ וחגרת לבנך ביום ההוא
לאמר בעבור זה עשה יי ל בצאתי ת
ממצרים
לא את אבותינו גאל הקבה כלבד
גלא את

אתה גאל עמחב שנ ואתנו הוציא משם
לבש הביא אתנו אל הארץ אשר נשבע
לאבותנו
כל אוחד ואחד דירם
וחם שלו ראמרי
לפיך הקרוב

א**שר** חביבן להורות להלל לשבח
לפאר לרומם להדר לברך לעלה
לקלס למי שעשה נסים לאבותינו
את כל הנסים האלד ורצאור מן מעבד
לחרות מיגון לשמחה ומאבל ליום
טוב

MATZAH COVER
GERMANY, 19TH CENTURY

Matzah is eaten throughout Passover, recalling the unleavened bread eaten by Jews as they fled from Egypt. During Shabbat and festive meals it is covered with a special cloth with separate compartments to hold the *matzah*. On the Seder night a whole *matzah* is inserted into each of the compartments. Around the cloth are embroidered the names of the traditional foods for the Seder ceremony and the blessing said on eating the *matzah*.

COTTON WITH MULTICOLORED WOOL
EMBROIDERY; GOLD THREADS
36 X 34.5 CM
PHOTOGRAPH: ISRAEL MUSEUM

April | 1 2 3 4 5 6 7 8 9 10 11 12 13 14 15 16 17 18 19 20 21 22 23 24 25 26 27 28 29 **30**

ניסן | א ב ג ד ה ו ז ח ט י יא יב יג יד טו טז יז יח יט כ **כא** כב כג כד כה כו כז כח כט ל

"THE PIANO SELLER'S" HAGGADAH
CAIRO, EGYPT, 1908

This colorfully illustrated handwritten Haggadah from early-twentieth-century Cairo is an example of blending the ancient tradition of illustrating the Haggadah with modern elements. The numerous folk-style illustrations include scenes of Passover preparations and celebrations, sometimes with such details as electric lamps and modern architecture. The Haggadah received its name from the text accompanying a full-page illustration of a woman playing the piano, inscribed in Hebrew: "The piano seller, Mordecai Hami." Hami was probably the father of Bekhor Hami, who wrote and illustrated the Haggadah.

PEN AND INK, WATERCOLORS,
SEQUINS, AND METAL FOIL ON PAPER
21 X 16.9 CM
PHOTOGRAPH: ISRAEL MUSEUM/
RONNY TERRY

May | **I** 2 3 4 5 6 7 8 9 10 11 12 13 14 15 16 17 18 19 20 21 22 23 24 25 26 27 28 29 30 31

ניסן | א ב ג ד ה ו ז ח ט י יא יב יג יד טו טז יז יח יט כ כא **כב** כג כד כה כו כז כח כט ל

MAIMOUNA CELEBRATION IN JERUSALEM, 1970S

Moroccan Jews celebrate Maimouna, marking the return to eating bread at the conclusion of Passover. At home the table is set with a white tablecloth and decorated with greens and sheaves of wheat. White flour, symbolizing purity and abundance, is mixed with water and other ingredients to create the first leavened bread eaten after the festival. The table is also set with food and drink and several good luck symbols. The celebration continues throughout the night and the following day, with eating, dancing, and visiting friends. In Israel today, Moroccan Jews still celebrate Maimouna in the traditional way and also mark it with open-air festivities and picnics.

May | 1 **2** 3 4 5 6 7 8 9 10 11 12 13 14 15 16 17 18 19 20 21 22 23 24 25 26 27 28 29 30 31

ניסן | א ב ג ד ה ו ז ח ט י יא יב יג יד טו טז יז יח יט כ כא כב **כג** כד כה כו כז כח כט ל

Ceremonial stand
Megiddo, Iron Age, 12th century bce

This is probably a scaled-down version of full-sized stands that supported the pottery or metal vessels used in cultic ceremonies. It brings to mind the *mehonot*—bases of brass mentioned in the Bible in the description of Solomon's Temple (I Kings 7:27–28).

Bronze
9.8 cm (height)
Israel Antiquities Authority
Photograph: Israel Museum/
David Harris

May 1 2 **3** 4 5 6 7 8 9 10 11 12 13 14 15 16 17 18 19 20 21 22 23 24 25 26 27 28 29 30 31

נ׳סן א ב ג ד ה ו ז ח ט י י׳א י׳ב י׳ג י׳ד ט׳ו ט׳ז י׳ז י׳ח י׳ט כ כ׳א כ׳ב כ׳ג **כד** כ׳ה כ׳ו כ׳ז כ׳ח כ׳ט ל

Kibbutz Merhavia, 1920s

Kibbutz Merhavia, founded in 1911, was the first *kibbutz* in the Jezreel valley. The new communal buildings can be seen in the background, while in the foreground we see the end of the wheat harvest, when the hay is being collected for fodder. A man stands on the horse-drawn cart holding a pitchfork while a woman in a long white robe on the left rests a pitchfork on her shoulder. Ben-Dov wrote the name of the settlement on the bottom right of the negative, and, on the left he marked his name and "Bezalel Jerusalem," linking his work at this time to his position as teacher at the Bezalel School of Arts and Crafts in Jerusalem.

YAACOV BEN-DOV
(1882, RUSSIA–1968, ISRAEL),
IMMIGRATED TO ERETZ ISRAEL, 1908
GELATIN SILVER PRINT
GIFT OF RENA (FISCH) AND
ROBERT LEWIN, LONDON

May | 1 2 3 **4** 5 6 7 8 9 10 11 12 13 14 15 16 17 18 19 20 21 22 23 24 25 26 27 28 29 30 31

נִיסָן | א ב ג ד ה ו ז ח ט י יא יב יג יד טו טז יז יח יט כ כא כב כג כד **כה** כו כז כח כט ל

מרחביה

REFUGEES, 1906

Abel Pann painted this depiction of the wandering of Jewish refugees expelled from their homes when he was a young artist in Paris in his early twenties. He arrived there after his own years of wandering in Eastern Europe, and a few years of study at the Academy of Art in Odessa. As a student he had decided to dedicate his life to the artistic documentation of the Jewish fate and, for example, recorded the aftermath of the infamous Kishinev pogrom (1903). In this painting the displaced wander under a gloomy sky; indeed all the colors are dark and dismal. This is a portrait of a whole community—the rabbi; men, women, and children; the poor and the rich; the intellectual and the artisan—and the meaning of collective identity is reduced to wandering and immigration. Pann was already a Zionist when he painted this scene, and it is clear that his motivation in depicting this destitution included the desire to allude to the alternative of negating the Diaspora and turning toward redemption.

ABEL PANN
(1883, LITHUANIA–1963, ISRAEL)
OIL ON CANVAS
97 X 160 CM
4082
PHOTOGRAPH: ISRAEL MUSEUM/
AVSHALOM AVITAL

May | 1 2 3 4 **5** 6 7 8 9 10 11 12 13 14 15 16 17 18 19 20 21 22 23 24 25 26 27 28 29 30 31

ניסן | א ב ג ד ה ו ז ח ט י יא יב יג יד טו טז יז יח יט כ כא כב כג כד כה **כו** כז כח כט ל

Atlit Detention Camp, 1945

Behind the coiled barbed-wire fence stand rows upon rows of men and women, illegal immigrants interned by the British Mandate forces during and after World War II. After the Declaration of Independence, the detention camp was turned into a transit camp to house the thousands of new immigrants from north Africa and central Europe making *aliyah* to Israel. This photograph, shown here to commemorate Holocaust Memorial Day, depicts survivors from the concentration camps of Europe, those who will become important members of the nascent State of Israel.

Dr. Nahum Tim Gidal
(1909, Germany–1996, Israel),
immigrated to Eretz Israel, 1936
Gelatin silver print

May | 1 2 3 4 5 **6** 7 8 9 10 11 12 13 14 15 16 17 18 19 20 21 22 23 24 25 26 27 28 29 30 31

ניסן | א ב ג ד ה ו ז ח ט י יא יב יג יד טו טז יז יח יט כ כא כב כג כד כה כו **כז** כח כט ל

Interior of the Vittorio Veneto Synagogue
Italy, 1700

The outer facade of this synagogue from the northern Italian town of Vittorio Veneto—it occupied the second and third stories of a plain stone building—gave little hint of its rich, late-Baroque interior decoration. Completed in December 1700, according to the Hebrew inscription on the Torah Ark, it was used by the local Jewish community for more than two hundred years. But during the nineteenth century, the community dwindled, owing to emigration to the large cities, and by the end of World War I the synagogue was no longer in use. In 1965 it was transferred intact to the Israel Museum and the interior was fully reconstructed according to the original plan.

Wood; gilt; brass
10.50 x 5.80 m
Gift of Jakob Michael, New York
In memory of his wife,
Erna Sondheimer-Michael
Photograph: Israel Museum/
David Harris

May | 1 2 3 4 5 6 **7** 8 9 10 11 12 13 14 15 16 17 18 19 20 21 22 23 24 25 26 27 28 29 30 31

ניסן | א ב ג ד ה ו ז ח ט י יא יב יג יד טו טז יז יח יט כ כא כב כג כד כה כו כז **כח** כט ל

CALENDAR FOR THE OMER
PARAMARIBO, SURINAME, 19TH CENTURY

The Jewish Portuguese community of Suriname (formerly Dutch Guiana) dates back to the seventeenth century, when they arrived from Holland via Brazil. Two synagogues were built in the capital city, Paramaribo, during the first half of the eighteenth century, one for Sephardim and one for Ashkenazim. This calendar for counting the Omer, the period from Passover to Shavuot, comes from the Sephardi Zedeq Ve-shalom Synagogue in Paramaribo. Zedeq Ve-shalom, now unused, is one of the oldest synagogues in the Americas. Its interior and ceremonial objects were transferred to The Israel Museum, where the synagogue will be reconstructed.

CARVED AND PAINTED WOOD
70.5 X 33.4 CM
PERMANENT LOAN OF THE
SURINAME COMMUNITY
PHOTOGRAPH: ISRAEL MUSEUM/
PETER LANYI

May | 1 2 3 4 5 6 7 **8** 9 10 11 12 13 14 15 16 17 18 19 20 21 22 23 24 25 26 27 28 29 30 31

ניסן | א ב ג ד ה ו ז ח ט י יא יב יג יד טו טז יז יח יט כ כא כב כג כד כה כו כז כח **כט** ל

FESTIVE BONNET WITH *STERNTICHEL*
EASTERN EUROPE, 18TH–19TH CENTURY

According to Jewish law a basic requirement of modesty is that a married woman's hair be covered. This luxurious bonnet would have been worn on the Sabbath and other festive occasions. It was tight fitting, covering the hair completely, and the woman's forehead was framed by its diadem-like band (*sterntichel*), which was richly embroidered with pearls.

SILK; VELVET; PEARLS
20 X 15 CM
PHOTOGRAPH: ISRAEL MUSEUM/
DAVID HARRIS

May | 1 2 3 4 5 6 7 8 **9** 10 11 12 13 14 15 16 17 18 19 20 21 22 23 24 25 26 27 28 29 30 31

ניסן | א ב ג ד ה ו ז ח ט י יא יב יג יד טו טז יז יח יט כ כא כב כג כד כה כו כז כח כט ל

SEFER BE'ER SHE-HAFAR YITZHAK
(THE WELL DUG BY YITZHAK)
KASSEL, GERMANY, 1715

This manuscript contains commentaries on biblical verses for festivals and includes an index. It is written in elaborate Ashkenazi Hebrew script and illustrated with opening words and three colorful title pages. This picture shows a detail of a title page, with a play on the verse from *Eshet Hayil*, "Woman of Valor" (Proverbs 31). The author and artist, Yitzhak son of Moshe Baruch Halevi of Kassel, also illustrated Esther scrolls.

SCRIBE: YITZHAK, SON OF
MOSHE BARUCH HALEVI
PEN AND INK, WATERCOLOR ON PAPER
HANDWRITTEN
28.5 X 21 CM
PHOTOGRAPH: ISRAEL MUSEUM/
PETER LANYI

May | 1 2 3 4 5 6 7 8 9 **IO** 11 12 13 14 15 16 17 18 19 20 21 22 23 24 25 26 27 28 29 30 31

אייר | **א** ב ג ד ה ו ז ח ט י יא יב יג יד טו טז יז יח יט כ כא כב כג כד כה כו כז כח כט ל

שֶׁקֶר הַחֵן וְהֶבֶל הַיּוֹפִי

מִלְאוּ צְמִיבֶם מִפְּרִידִי

וִיהוֹלֵל בִּשְׁעָרִים מַעֲשֵׂי

בְּעֶזְרַת אֱלֹהֵי עוֹשִׂי

Plaque with engraving of *Hatikvah*, the Zionist anthem
Odessa, Russia, ca. 1900

This silver plaque bears the early version of the music and lyrics to the Israeli national anthem, *Hatikvah*. The plaque was produced by the silversmith Israel Rouchomovsky in honor of the founding of the B'nai Zion movement in Odessa and for the promotion of the Zionist idea. Throughout his life Rouchomovsky was connected with Zionist activity, moving to Paris from Odessa and maintaining contact with the Zionist movement.

Artist: Israel Rouchomovsky
(1860–1934)
Engraved and partly gilt silver
10.5 x 5.5 cm
Photograph: Israel Museum

May │ 1 2 3 4 5 6 7 8 9 10 **11** 12 13 14 15 16 17 18 19 20 21 22 23 24 25 26 27 28 29 30 31

אייר │ א **ב** ג ד ה ו ז ח ט י יא יב יג יד טו טז יז יח יט כ כא כב כג כד כה כו כז כח כט ל

Independence Day Parade, Jerusalem, ca. 1950

This photograph appeared in an album the Jewish National Fund published and distributed to donors in thanks for their support. As can be seen in this photograph, the images in the album give a complete and idealized picture of the enthusiasm and excitement connected to those early days of the State of Israel.

S. J. Schweig
(1905, Austria–1984, Israel),
immigrated to Eretz Israel, 1923
Gelatin silver print
Bequest of the artist

May | 1 2 3 4 5 6 7 8 9 10 11 **12** 13 14 15 16 17 18 19 20 21 22 23 24 25 26 27 28 29 30 31

אייר | א ב **ג** ד ה ו ז ח ט י יא יב יג יד טו טז יז יח יט כ כא כב כג כד כה כו כז כח כט ל

SKETCH FOR A CARPET DEDICATED TO MR. AND MRS. DAVID WOLFSOHN, 1906

This sketch was the basis for a carpet design celebrating the twenty-fifth wedding anniversary of David Wolfsohn, the second president of the World Zionist Congress (after Theodor Herzl). E. M. Lilien created some of Zionism's founding visual images. He came to Jerusalem in 1906 to help establish the Bezalel School of Arts and Crafts and to prepare patterns for the carpet department. In the right-hand panel of the carpet, designed as a triptych after Renaissance religious paintings, the Diaspora (*Galluth*) is depicted by Jews trapped by thorns; in the left-hand panel the end of *Galluth* is symbolized by a man bearing the rose of Jericho, which can bloom after thousands of years of dormancy (a symbol of Zionist redemption) and an angel blowing the *shofar* (ram's horn). The central panel shows an allegorical wedding. The groom resembles both an Assyrian prince and Wolfsohn (and Herzl), and the lily (*Lilien* in German) signifies that the artist himself was present. This typical Lilien melding of Western aesthetics, "Oriental" motifs signifying the biblical period, and symbolic figures of Diaspora became a set visual system for the Zionist movement in its early days.

May | 1 2 3 4 5 6 7 8 9 10 11 12 **13** 14 15 16 17 18 19 20 21 22 23 24 25 26 27 28 29 30 31

אייר | א ב ג **ד** ה ו ז ח ט י יא יב יג יד טו טז יז יח יט כ כא כב כג כד כה כו כז כח כט ל

TORAH ARK CURTAIN
TURKEY, EARLY 20TH CENTURY

In Turkey it was common to dedicate to the synagogue rich embroideries originally made for a dowry. Usually the donated objects were adapted from household objects; this Ark curtain, for example, was made from a bedspread and cushion covers. The dedicatory inscription was made on a separate piece of fabric and sewn onto the Ark curtain, as is often the case.

SATIN; VELVET; MULTICOLORED
CHENILLE AND METAL-THREAD
EMBROIDERY
203 X 147 CM
PHOTOGRAPH: ISRAEL MUSEUM/
DAVID HARRIS

May | 1 2 3 4 5 6 7 8 9 10 11 12 13 **14** 15 16 17 18 19 20 21 22 23 24 25 26 27 28 29 30 31

אייר | א ב ג ד **ה** ו ז ח ט י יא יב יג יד טו טז יז יח יט כ כא כב כג כד כה כו כז כח כט ל

בן פרת יוסף   בן פרת עלי עין

הקדש לק"ק בקור חולים יב"ש ממני הצעיר שמואל קאסטוריאנו ס"ט

בכ"ר אברהם נ"ע:

Woven wool carpet
Iraqi Kurdistan, 20th century

Weaving was mainly a Jewish occupation in Kurdistan and this carpet from Iraqi Kurdistan incorporates various images including a stork, airplane, lighthouse and flag, probably in expectation of immigration to Israel. Woven hangings were used for a variety of purposes: as a room divider to give privacy to the newlywed couple for the first week after their marriage, as sukkah decorations, as table coverings, and to wrap the newly deceased.

200 X 240 CM
PHOTOGRAPH: ISRAEL MUSEUM/
NAHUM SLAPAK

May | 1 2 3 4 5 6 7 8 9 10 11 12 13 14 **15** 16 17 18 19 20 21 22 23 24 25 26 27 28 29 30 31

אייר | א ב ג ד ה | ז ח ט י יא יב יג יד טו טז יז יח יט כ כא כב כג כד כה כו כז כח כט ל

Decorative hatpins (*Rozéta*)
Ottoman Empire, early 20th century

The *rozéta* (rose) pin decorated the velvet *tokádo* cap worn by married Jewish women of Izmir and Rhodes. It was first known as a turban pin worn by the Sultan's wives during the eighteenth century. When people stopped wearing the *tokádo*, the *rozéta* started to be worn as lapel pins.

Gilt silver; diamonds;
diamond chips
Left to right: 4, 4.7, 3.1 cm
(diameter)
Photograph: Israel Museum/
David Harris

May | 1 2 3 4 5 6 7 8 9 10 11 12 13 14 15 **16** 17 18 19 20 21 22 23 24 25 26 27 28 29 30 31

אייר | א ב ג ד ה ו **ז** ח ט י יא יב יג יד טו טז יז יח יט כ כא כב כג כד כה כו כז כח כט ל

Chalice
Provenance unknown, Iron Age,
8th century BCE

Chalices like this one, probably made of metal, are shown being carried off as booty by Assyrian soldiers in a wall relief from Sennacherib's palace in Nineveh, which depicts the sack of the city of Lachish.

Pottery
32 cm (height)
Photograph: Israel Museum/
Avraham Hay

May | 1 2 3 4 5 6 7 8 9 10 11 12 13 14 15 16 **17** 18 19 20 21 22 23 24 25 26 27 28 29 30 31

אייר | א ב ג ד ה ו ז **ח** ט י יא יב יג יד טו טז יז יח יט כ כא כב כג כד כה כו כז כח כט ל

GERARD DE JODE,
FLEMISH (1509–1591)
AFTER TILEMANNUS STELLA,
GERMAN (1525–1589)
HAND-COLORED ETCHING ON PAPER,
BY JOHANNES AND
LUCAS DOETECHUM
30.7 X 51.3 CM
FROM: GERARD DE JODE,
SPECULUM ORBIS TERRAE, ANTWERP,
EDITED BY THE AUTHOR'S SON,
CORNELIS DE JODE, 1593
NORMAN BIER SECTION FOR
MAPS OF THE HOLY LAND
GIFT OF NORMAN AND FRIEDA BIER,
LONDON
B 95.0681
PHOTOGRAPH: ISRAEL MUSEUM/
ILAN STZULMAN

DESCRIPTION OF THE HOLY LAND, LAND OF PROMISE OR PALESTINE..., 1578

In this west-oriented map the coastline is deeply and inaccurately indented, extending from Tyre to Beersheba (!), and the Dead Sea is crescent shaped. At the lower right stands the "new" Jerusalem. The Church of the Nativity in Bethlehem and the Church of the Holy Sepulchre are also indicated. De Jode, apparently of Jewish descent, was a surveyor, copper engraver, and publisher in Antwerp. He published single-sheet maps, among them, two plans of Jerusalem after Peter Lacstain. This map belongs to a familiar genre in which a plan or picture of Jerusalem is combined with a map of the Holy Land. The Jerusalem map belongs to a series of five that were copied from each other in Italy in the sixteenth century. De Jode copied the map from Stella, a German contemporary.

May | 1 2 3 4 5 6 7 8 9 10 11 12 13 14 15 16 17 **18** 19 20 21 22 23 24 25 26 27 28 29 30 31

אייר | א ב ג ד ה ו ז ח **ט** י יא יב יג יד טו טז יז יח יט כ כא כב כג כד כה כו כז כח כט ל

CIVITAS HIERVSALEM

Lebonna. · Sichem · Thabor · Endor · Mero lacus · Sion · Rebasumach · Reuna · interior · Hanaton · NAP. · Necheb.

Iamua · Samaria · Sichem · Nasareth · or. · Lachem · Ribba · BASAN · Saesanu philippi

hmethath · Eduma · Bethulia · Dabraeth · Gitta chepher · Nea · REGNVM

Asedoth · anoach · Asser · Tiberias · Brisemes · Thalla · Samachonites lacus · Seleucia · Gaulon

lexandrium · Salem · Ennon · Tarichee · Magdolum · Rimmon · Sueta · Gessuri · Gaulonites regio.

gia · Enabris · Mare Galilee · Betsaides · Capernam · Iordanis fluuius · Argob Regio. · HERMON MONS.

Vallis · uel Ganesaret mare. · Chorazaim · Argob.

IORDANIS · Ennon · Ephron · Iulias · conitis · GALAAD MONS.

Praud · Gadara · Gala · Gamala · Tra· · MONS.

Nobeth · lacus · tenuis · Ascarot.

Bethnim rach · Machanaim · Astaroth · SAE

Saphon · Edrei · Iabis. · hus.

Bethharan · Iaazer · Ramath · Terra

Chesbon · Hseben · Machane · Charchar · Seb. · Arta ·

Amon flu. · Msimith · Ammonitis regio nunc · Iabor · fluuius · Philadelphia. · THR. ·

Ab· · HABARIM. M. · PHILADELPHIA. · Pella. · ACONI · MONTES.

Per · sian

DISPOSITIO SEPVTVRE DOMINICE

Ioannes à Dentecum Lucas à Dentecum Freecum.

CONTAINERS FOR WATER
PUNE AND BOMBAY, INDIA,
EARLY 20TH CENTURY

These containers were sometimes part of a Jewish bride's dowry and later stood, brightly polished, in the corner of her kitchen. The cans and the buckets were used to bring the water and the clean laundry from the village well. Water was stored in covered containers with a tap, in brass casks, and sometimes earthenware vessels. People used a wide bowl and a pitcher to wash their hands and rinse their mouths after a festive meal. These vessels were brought to elderly people in their honor or to those who were leading the blessings.

BRASS; COPPER; CLAY
10–75 CM (HEIGHT)
SMALL JAR: GIFT OF SARAH AND
SHELIM ABRAHAM, BOMBAY
PHOTOGRAPH: ISRAEL MUSEUM/
AVRAHAM HAY

May | 1 2 3 4 5 6 7 8 9 10 11 12 13 14 15 16 17 18 **19** 20 21 22 23 24 25 26 27 28 29 30 31

אייר | א ב ג ד ה ו ז ח ט ' י א י ב י ג י ד ט ו ט ז י ז י ח י ט כ כא כב כג כד כה כו כז כח כט ל

Menorah in low relief
Synagogue of Hammat Tiberias, Galilee,
Byzantine period, 4th–5th century ce

This menorah has, at the tip of each branch, a depression designed to hold an oil lamp, which would probably have been in the form of a small glass beaker. The alternating pomegranate and flower design is inspired by the biblical description of the Tabernacle menorah: "On one branch there shall be three cups shaped like almond-blossoms, each with calyx and petals" (Exodus 25:33).

Limestone
46 cm (height)
Photograph: Israel Museum/
Yoram Lehmann

May | 1 2 3 4 5 6 7 8 9 10 11 12 13 14 15 16 17 18 19 **20** 21 22 23 24 25 26 27 28 29 30 31

אייר | א ב ג ד ה ו ז ח ט י **י'א** י'ב י'ג י'ד ט'ו ט'ז י'ז י'ח י'ט כ כ'א כ'ב כ'ג כ'ד כ'ה כ'ו כ'ז כ'ח כ'ט ל

GRACE AFTER MEALS MANUSCRIPT
MORAVIA, 1727

This tiny eighteenth-century manuscript of blessings for private use was written and painted by hand. Such books were often presented as personal gifts, given perhaps by a groom to his bride. The naive and colorful illustrations show men and women undertaking various religious duties. The figures wear fashionable clothes against richly decorated surroundings, portraying the lives of upper-class Ashkenazi Jews. Illustrated here are details from the blessings said over spices at the Havdalah ceremony on the conclusion of the Sabbath and on eating fruit and vegetables grown from the ground.

SCRIBE: NATHAN BEN SHIMSHON
OF MEZERITZ
PEN AND INK AND GOUACHE
ON PARCHMENT
7.4 X 5.7 CM
GIFT OF JAKOB MICHAEL,
NEW YORK,
IN MEMORY OF HIS WIFE,
ERNA SONDHEIMER-MICHAEL
PHOTOGRAPH: ISRAEL MUSEUM/
YORAM LEHMANN

May | 1 2 3 4 5 6 7 8 9 10 11 12 13 14 15 16 17 18 19 20 **21** 22 23 24 25 26 27 28 29 30 31

אייר | א ב ג ד ה ו ז ח ט י יא **י'ב** י'ג יד טו טז יז יח יט כ כא כב כג כד כה כו כז כח כט ל

ווען מיינר פאר מיין אפיטיק פֿמר בּיים גיט זמנטדן ∶

בָּא אָ"מֶ"ה בּוֹרֵא מִינֵי בְשָׂמִים

TOMB OF RABBI MEIR BA'AL HANESS, 1948

Rabbi Meir Ba'al Haness (Master of the Miracle) was a Talmudic sage who was able to ward off serious danger to himself and others by declaring, "God of Meir, answer me!" It is traditionally believed that anyone who gives charity in memory of Rabbi Meir will have his prayers answered. The *tzaddik's* tomb in Tiberias is a popular pilgrimage site for those looking to have their prayers answered and miracles performed. Streichman's depiction of the tomb shows the influence of European modernism, both in the bold patches of solid color and the breakdown and abstraction of the landscape and buildings into geometric shapes.

YEHEZKIEL STREICHMAN
(1906, LITHUANIA–1993, ISRAEL)
OIL ON CANVAS
70 X 90 CM
PURCHASE, RECANATI FUND FOR
THE ACQUISITION OF ISRAELI ART
894.78
PHOTOGRAPH: ISRAEL MUSEUM/
NOA STREICHMAN

May | 1 2 3 4 5 6 7 8 9 10 11 12 13 14 15 16 17 18 19 20 21 **22** 23 24 25 26 27 28 29 30 31

אייר | ג'יב יא'י ט ח ז ו ה ד ג ב א יד טו טז יז יח יט כ כא כב כג כד כה כו כז כח כט ל

PHYLACTERY (*TEFILLIN*) CASES
POLAND AND CENTRAL EUROPE,
18TH–19TH CENTURY

These decorated silver cases are containers for storing the *tefillin*, which are made of two leather boxes, each containing a parchment scroll inscribed with the *Shema* prayer, comprising verses from Exodus and Deuteronomy. *Tefillin* are worn strapped to the forehead and left arm by Jewish men during weekday morning prayers.

CAST, ENGRAVED,
AND PARTLY GILT SILVER
LEFT: 5.5 X 6.2 X 8 CM
CENTER AND RIGHT: 5.4 X 8.2 X 6.2 CM
THE STIEGLITZ COLLECTION WAS
DONATED TO THE ISRAEL MUSEUM,
JERUSALEM WITH THE CONTRIBUTION
OF ERICA AND LUDWIG JESSELSON,
NEW YORK,
THROUGH THE AMERICAN
FRIENDS OF THE ISRAEL MUSEUM
PHOTOGRAPH: ISRAEL MUSEUM/
AVI GANOR

May │ 1 2 3 4 5 6 7 8 9 10 11 12 13 14 15 16 17 18 19 20 21 22 **23** 24 25 26 27 28 29 30 31

אייר │ א ב ג ד ה ו ז ח ט י יא יב יג **י'ד** טו טז יז יח יט כ כא כב כג כד כה כו כז כח כט ל

A Family Meal, 1991

The morning after the successful completion of Operation Solomon, in which 14,600 Ethiopian Jews were brought safely to Israel overnight, Youth Wing art teachers brought art materials to the Jerusalem hotels where the immigrants were housed. The children re-created the world they had just left, the language of art offering a medium of expression beyond verbal language. In this scene one can see the family inside the dwelling—parents, children, dog—as well as the food served, including *injera*, the typical Ethiopian bread made from teff, an indigenous grain.

May | 1 2 3 4 5 6 7 8 9 10 11 12 13 14 15 16 17 18 19 20 21 22 23 **24** 25 26 27 28 29 30 31

אייר | א ב ג ד ה ו ז ח ט י יא יב יג יד **טו** טז יז יח יט כ כא כב כג כד כה כו כז כח כט ל

PLANE, BUS, AND SYNAGOGUE, 1991

In 1991, 14,600 Ethiopian Jews were safely brought to Israel overnight. In this drawing one can see the experience, as expressed by one of the children who lived through it. In this drawing, made the morning after the immigrants arrived in Jerusalem, we see them leaving their villages and synagogues in Ethiopia, being driven by buses to the airport, and being brought over by planes. The colors in the drawing are very similar to native Ethiopian embroidery. The Youth Wing art teachers who supplied art materials to the children noted that they were able to depict the world they had just left through the universal language of art.

ARTWORK BY AN ETHIOPIAN
IMMIGRANT CHILD
FELT-TIP PEN ON PAPER
25 X 15 CM
ISRAEL MUSEUM YOUTH WING
COLLECTION
PHOTOGRAPH: ISRAEL MUSEUM

May │ 1 2 3 4 5 6 7 8 9 10 11 12 13 14 15 16 17 18 19 20 21 22 23 24 **25** 26 27 28 29 30 31

אייר │ א ב ג ד ה ו ז ח ט י יא יב יג יד טו **טז** יז יח יט כ כא כב כג כד כה כו כז כח כט ל

HASSIDS RECLINING AGAINST DOME IN MOONLIGHT, MERON, 1935

The tomb of the *tzaddik* Shimon Bar Yochai (the Kabbalist who wrote the *Zohar*) on Mt. Meron is the site of pilgrimage for thousands of Jews at Lag B'Omer. Shimon Bar Yochai was the last of Rabbi Akiva's students. According to tradition, the students of Rabbi Akiva died over a period of thirty-three days beginning on the second day of Pesach and ending on Lag B'Omer. Thus this holiday is celebrated as marking the end of the mourning period. The pilgrimage to Mt. Meron on this evening includes singing, dancing, and bonfires, and it is customary to bring three-year-old boys to the site for their first haircut.

DR. NAHUM TIM GIDAL
(1909, GERMANY–1996, ISRAEL),
IMMIGRATED TO ERETZ ISRAEL, 1936
GELATIN SILVER PRINT

May | 1 2 3 4 5 6 7 8 9 10 11 12 13 14 15 16 17 18 19 20 21 22 23 24 25 **26** 27 28 29 30 31

אייר | א ב ג ד ה ו ז ח ט י יא יב יג יד טו טז **ז׳** יח יט כ כא כב כג כד כה כו כז כח כט ל

Book of customs (*Sefer ha-Minhagim*) Amsterdam, Holland, 1713

Books of customs were written as illustrated guides to Jewish practice in different places in Europe from the end of the Middle Ages to the early nineteenth century. Customs of mourning, such as not cutting the hair or shaving, are generally observed during the forty-nine-day Omer period between Pesach and Shavuot. On Lag B'Omer, the thirty-third day of Omer, these customs are suspended as is shown in this vignette of a man having his hair cut.

The First Haircut, Lag B'Omer Meron, Israel, 1996

It is customary not to cut a little boy's hair until he reaches three years of age. The first time his hair is cut is at a special celebration called *halake*, which takes place on Lag B'Omer, the anniversary of the death of Rabbi Shimon bar Yohai. Many people come to his tomb in Meron to perform the traditional first haircut (left).

Print and woodcuts on paper
20.2 x 15.5 cm
Photograph: Israel Museum

Photograph
9 x 14 cm
Photograph: Israel Museum/
Rivka Gonen

May | 1 2 3 4 5 6 7 8 9 10 11 12 13 14 15 16 17 18 19 20 21 22 23 24 25 26 **27** 28 29 30 31

א ב ג ד ה ו ז ח ט י יא יב יג יד טו טז יז **יח** יט כ כא כב כג כד כה כו כז כח כט ל   אייר

ARTIST: ELIEZER SUSSMAN OF BRODY
PAINTED WOOD
2.13 X 6.25 X 4.8 M
PERMANENT LOAN OF THE BAMBERG
MUNICIPALITY, GERMANY
RECONSTRUCTED THROUGH A
DONATION FROM JAKOB MICHAEL,
NEW YORK, IN MEMORY OF HIS WIFE,
ERNA SONDHEIMER-MICHAEL
PHOTOGRAPH: ISRAEL MUSEUM

INTERIOR OF THE HORB SYNAGOGUE
HORB, GERMANY, 1735

This painted synagogue from Horb, now reconstructed in The Israel Museum and on permanent display, is the most complete surviving example of Eliezer Sussman's work. It is one of the few painted synagogues that survived World War II. The synagogue originally served a small rural community and was abandoned in the 1860s by the tiny Jewish community that owned it. When rediscovered in 1908, its wall paintings were partly damaged and faded and the synagogue was being used as a hayloft. Eliezer Sussman of Brody (Ukraine) came to southern Germany in the mid-eighteenth century and painted the wooden interiors of at least seven synagogues in a similar style. The walls and ceilings are covered with quotations from prayers alongside animal and floral motifs. Jerusalem is depicted on the west wall of the synagogue, the central motif as seen in this picture is a pair of rampant lions, blowing trumpets and flanking a medallion with an inscription from a prayer recited on Rosh Hashanah and Yom Kippur.

May | 1 2 3 4 5 6 7 8 9 10 11 12 13 14 15 16 17 18 19 20 21 22 23 24 25 26 27 **28** 29 30 31

אייר | א ב ג ד ה ו ז ח ט י״א י״ב י״ג י״ד ט״ו ט״ז י״ז י״ח **י״ט** כ כ״א כ״ב כ״ג כ״ד כ״ה כ״ו כ״ז כ״ח כ״ט ל

"Place of Trumpeting" inscription
Temple Mount, Jerusalem,
Second Temple Period, 1st century bce

Originally a part of the parapet on a building at the southwest corner of the
Temple enclosure, this stone fell down to the street below when the Temple was
destroyed in 70 CE. The Hebrew inscription it bears, "To the place of the
trumpeting to de[clare]," refers to the trumpet blasts sounded by the Temple
priests to announce the times of the daily sacrifices, the opening of the gates,
and the beginning and ending of the Sabbath.

Stone
84 cm (length)
Israel Antiquities Authority
Photograph: Israel Museum

May | 1 2 3 4 5 6 7 8 9 10 11 12 13 14 15 16 17 18 19 20 21 22 23 24 25 26 27 28 **29** 30 31

אייר | א ב ג ד ה ו ז ח ט י יא יב יג יד טו טז יז יח יט כ כא כב כג כד כה כו כז כח כט ל

The Circumcision of the Child on the Eighth Day, 18th Century

Brit milah, the "Covenant of Circumcision," was one of the first commandments made to Abraham before the rest of the Torah was given (Genesis 17:9–12). Through this dramatic rite, a basic tenet of Judaism, the newborn male enters the Jewish fold. According to Kabbalah (the book of the *Zohar*), the circumcision ritual is compared to the offering of a sacrifice on the altar of the Temple, and thus it is endowed with the aura of sublime sanctity. Following the circumcision the infant boy is named. Painter, draftsman, and engraver Bernard Picart studied in France and in 1698 joined the French Calvinist community in Amsterdam, where he worked mainly on book illustrations. Between 1723 and 1738 Picart made over two hundred prints for the *Histoire des Cérémonies et costumes religieuses de tous les peuples du monde* in seven volumes. His prints reproduced here were originally taken from *Cérémonies des Juifs*, part of the large work, and were an attempt to achieve a comprehensive visual documentation of the life of the Jewish community in Amsterdam at the time. The print discussed here is probably taken from an English edition of the *Histoire*. The adjoining text is characterized by its typical inaccuracies; for example, the heading mentions Exodus 17:10, instead of Genesis 17:10.

Anonymous artist after
Bernard Picart (1673,
France–1733), active Holland
Etching on paper
17.5 x 30.5 cm
Printed and sold by
H. Overton & J. Hoole, London
764-6-44
Photograph: Israel Museum

May | 1 2 3 4 5 6 7 8 9 10 11 12 13 14 15 16 17 18 19 20 21 22 23 24 25 26 27 28 29 **30** 31

אייר | א ב ג ד ה ו ז ח ט י יא יב יג יד טו טז יז יח יט כ **כא** כב כג כד כה כו כז כח כט ל

Ossuaries
Jerusalem, Second Temple Period,
1st century bce—1st century ce

Ossuaries are stone containers in which the bones of the deceased were deposited a year after the initial burial. Hundreds have been found in family burial caves in and around Jerusalem. They are frequently decorated with carved floral and geometric designs and sometimes with stylized architectural motifs, such as columns and arches.

May | 1 2 3 4 5 6 7 8 9 10 11 12 13 14 15 16 17 18 19 20 21 22 23 24 25 26 27 28 29 30 **31**

אב ג ד ה ו ז ח ט י יא יב יג יד טו טז יז יח יט כ כא **כב** כג כד כה כו כז כח כט ל | **אייר**

5

1532

צור באחר

בוקעים זה לקבר(?) ... חבו כל המכסה התקמרות

והמרקפלפה ומאחו בארה מסת וחברבורת מק הדורות

בחוס משושה תקמורו... רש בתשפורת דגום חטופים על בדות

כוסו מטוע

84-549

Sarcophagus from

Binyanei HaUma Street, Jerusalem

1st century BCE – 1st century CE

This ossuary is lavishly decorated with floral and geometric
patterns of the Department of Antiquities and Museums

2

1552

Zur-Baher

הקברעות, דר הזיתים

מצע כל לקבר?ל... מצע כל לקבר

הלדסוקמ מחו נאתה מסו דוכרות?רם-הריה שהדלת

הראשי מת מקבל... רש מפורות דגום חטופים על בדות

כ?ות ?רם

71-434

Botanical Garden, Mount Scopus

1st century BCE – 1st century CE

Found in one of many burial caves discovered on the
grounds of the Botanical Garden, this ossuary is
decorated with the typical pattern of framed rosettes.

Courtesy of the Department

7

1526

מאשר זאל לקבר... בקמרות במאתי כפולות

עיטורים מוסף מונמנטליות, נמראה של קבר, מעל לפתוח

חיזות מקמרות כהמקבל עגו רקיע ד אניה מקתורת

יהוזת כאואז לקראי אניה חמקה

MARAMA

באחותבת המון לארבאטחו האוצינ העכרות

13

1529

Provenance unknown

Between the two rosettes in double frames adorning this
ossuary, a monumental entrance, apparently of a tomb,
is depicted. Above the frame is an

Calendar for counting the Omer
Poland, 1871

The period of forty-nine days from the second night of Passover until Shavuot is known as the Omer period. According to Jewish law, each day of this period has to be counted off. In order to keep track of and count the days, a variety of special calendars were produced in different Jewish communities. This Omer calendar is made by papercut, a very popular technique in Europe in the nineteenth century, and signed by its maker, Moshe Zelmans.

Papercuts; watercolor
60 x 53 cm
Photograph: Israel Museum

June | I 2 3 4 5 6 7 8 9 10 11 12 13 14 15 16 17 18 19 20 21 22 23 24 25 26 27 28 29 30

אב ג ד ה ו ז ח ט י יא יב יג יד טו טז יז יח יט כ כא כב **כג** כד כה כו כז כח כט | **אייר**

בָּרוּךְ

אתה יי אלהינו מלך העולם אשר
קדשנו במצותיו וצונו על ספירת
העומר
היום יום אחד לעומר

AMONG THE SABRA PLANTS, 1920S

The colors and style of this work place it firmly within the "Eretz Israel" artistic style of the 1920s. The three elongated figures are wearing Yemenite dress; the bearded men sport side locks, and the black stripes on their clothing represent prayer shawls. The figures are thus identified as Jews and not as local Arabs, despite the similarity of dress. Dotted around the landscape are sabra cactus plants. It is the height of summer and they are bearing fruit. The symbolism of this work is clear, with the plants representing the growth of a nation rooted in the soil of Eretz Israel.

ARIE EL-HANANI
(1898, RUSSIA–1985, ISRAEL)
WATERCOLOR AND PENCIL ON PAPER
38 X 31.5 CM
PURCHASE, AMERICA-ISRAEL
CULTURAL FOUNDATION
B95.0831
PHOTOGRAPH: ISRAEL MUSEUM/
DAVID HARRIS

June | 1 **2** 3 4 5 6 7 8 9 10 11 12 13 14 15 16 17 18 19 20 21 22 23 24 25 26 27 28 29 30

אייר א ב ג ד ה ו ז ח ט י יא יב יג יד טו טז יז יח יט כ כא כב כג **כד** כה כו כז כח כט

CHILD'S DRAWING OF JERUSALEM, 1996

Happy Singaporean children—the only children the artist (a nine-year-old girl from Singapore) knows—live behind the high walls of Jerusalem in this picture. When children around the world were asked to draw pictures of the city to celebrate Jerusalem 3000, the results were a blend of the real and the imaginary, memories and dreams, landscapes and symbols. Some of the artists had seen the ancient city with their own eyes, but many others had to use their imagination.

OIL PASTEL ON PAPER
50 X 35 CM
PHOTOGRAPH: ISRAEL MUSEUM

June | 1 2 **3** 4 5 6 7 8 9 10 11 12 13 14 15 16 17 18 19 20 21 22 23 24 25 26 27 28 29 30

א ב ג ד ה ו ז ח ט י י"א י"ב י"ג י"ד ט"ו ט"ז י"ז י"ח י"ט כ כ"א כ"ב כ"ג כ"ד **כ"ה** כ"ו כ"ז כ"ח כ"ט | אייר

GREAT SYNAGOGUE
ALEPPO, SYRIA, PRIOR TO 1927

From the Middle Ages until the beginning of the nineteenth century, Aleppo was a prominent center of Jewish studies. Maimonides cited Aleppo and its scholars as a "beacon of light in the darkness." The synagogue, built on Byzantine foundations, was rebuilt over the centuries. It consisted of two large prayer halls, one an outside courtyard used in the summertime, as shown in the postcard, and the other an indoor hall used in winter. This synagogue once housed the Aleppo codex *Keter Aram Zova*, one of the earliest manuscripts of most of the text of the Bible, written in the tenth century in the Land of Israel. Today this rare manuscript is exhibited on loan in The Israel Museum, Jerusalem, by decision of the Manuscript's Board of Trustees.

COLOR POSTCARD
9 X 14 CM
GIFT OF JULIAN AND SERENA
GECELTER, SOUTH AFRICA

June | 1 2 3 **4** 5 6 7 8 9 10 11 12 13 14 15 16 17 18 19 20 21 22 23 24 25 26 27 28 29 30

אייר | א ב ג ד ה ו ז ח ט י י"א י"ב י"ג י"ד ט"ו ט"ז י"ז י"ח י"ט כ כ"א כ"ב כ"ג כ"ד כ"ה **כו** כ"ז כ"ח כ"ט

No 12 - ALEP - Intérieur du Grand Synagogue

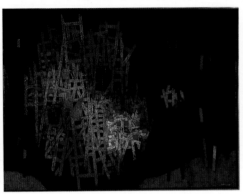

LEFT: *SIGN*;
CENTER: *LADDERS*;
RIGHT: *ROCK*
MORDECAI ARDON
(1896, GERMANY–1992, ISRAEL)
OIL ON CANVAS
194 X 525 CM
GIFT OF THE ARTIST IN HONOR OF
ISRAEL'S 20TH ANNIVERSARY AND THE
UNIFICATION OF JERUSALEM
546.67
PHOTOGRAPH: ISRAEL MUSEUM

AT THE GATES OF JERUSALEM (TRIPTYCH), 1967

Ardon tried to meet the challenge presented by the founding of the new Jewish state by creating a new Israeli art set in the present but with roots in the past. This triptych was painted in 1967, the year of the Six-Day War and the reunification of Jerusalem. The left-hand panel, *Sign*, represents spiritual Jerusalem through the Kabbalistic images of the *sefirot* and shattered vessels. Earthly Jerusalem is portrayed on the right-hand panel, *Rock*, featuring a section of Mt. Moriah. In the central panel ladders of all faiths reach between the earth and the heavens; broken rungs are mended, and rays of light augur the redemption that will lead to the End of Days.

June | 1 2 3 4 **5** 6 7 8 9 10 11 12 13 14 15 16 17 18 19 20 21 22 23 24 25 26 27 28 29 30

אב ג ד ה ו ז ח ט י יא יב יג יד טו טז יז יח יט כ כא כב כג כד כה כו **כז** כח כט | אייר

Aerial View of Jerusalem, 1975

This aerial photograph of Jerusalem taken from the west shows both new, western Jerusalem, and the old, eastern part of the city. In the lower left-hand corner is the YMCA building and soccer field next to the King David Hotel. Above it is a swath of empty land that demarcates the division between West and East Jerusalem that was removed after the 1967 reunification of the city. Clearly visible just to the right of the Temple Mount is the newly cleared plaza in front of the Western Wall. This photograph contrasts the density of the Old City with the spaciousness of the new city.

S. J. SCHWEIG
(1905, AUSTRIA–1984, ISRAEL)
IMMIGRATED TO ERETZ ISRAEL, 1923
GELATIN SILVER PRINT
BEQUEST OF THE ARTIST
PHOTOGRAPH: ISRAEL MUSEUM

June | 1 2 3 4 5 **6** 7 8 9 10 11 12 13 14 15 16 17 18 19 20 21 22 23 24 25 26 27 28 29 30

אייר | א ב ג ד ה ו ז ח ט י י'א י'ב י'ג י'ד ט'ו ט'ז י'ז י'ח י'ט כ כ'א כ'ב כ'ג כ'ד כ'ה כ'ו כ'ז **כח** כט

Farmer in the Field, Kefar Hassidim, 1940s

When the *kibbutz* Kefar Hassidim was founded in 1926 by members of the wave of immigrants known as the Fourth Aliyah, it was only a single hut. The aim was to create a community that combined agricultural and religious ideals. In this photograph we see two members of the community harvesting wheat, which places the season as early summer, before Shavuot. The workers are dressed in traditional Russian work clothes, hinting that although they have made *aliyah* to Eretz Israel, to become part of the new Zionist Israel, they have brought with them many of the traditions, clothes, tools, and farming practices of Eastern Europe.

Yaacov Ben-Dov (1882, Russia–1968, Israel), immigrated to Eretz Israel, 1908
Gelatin silver print
Purchased with the help of Rena (Fisch) and Robert Lewin, London

June | 1 2 3 4 5 6 **7** 8 9 10 11 12 13 14 15 16 17 18 19 20 21 22 23 24 25 26 27 28 29 30

אייר | א ב ג ד ה ו ז ח ט י יא יב יג יד טו טז יז יח יט כ כא כב כג כד כה כו כז כח **כט**

Pouches for medicinal and cooking herbs
Herat, Afghanistan,
early to mid 20th century

These pouches contained dried flowers, nuts, grains, and dried fruits used for treating high temperatures, coughs, stomachaches and even nightmares. Mothers and daughters made these bags out of leftover fabric. They would become part of a young woman's trousseau and would be hung on the walls for decoration.

Silk; cotton
12–18 x 9–12 cm
Photograph: Israel Museum/
David Harris

June | 1 2 3 4 5 6 7 **8** 9 10 11 12 13 14 15 16 17 18 19 20 21 22 23 24 25 26 27 28 29 30

סיון | א ב ג ד ה ו ז ח ט י יא יב יג יד טו טז יז יח יט כ כא כב כג כד כה כו כז כח כט ל

SHAVUOT AT A KINDERGARTEN, 1930S

Shavuot, traditionally one of the three Jewish pilgrim festivals, had always incorporated aspects of a harvest celebration, due to the time of the year at which it is celebrated. In Eretz Israel, with the immigration of secular, socialist Zionists, it became a secular harvest holiday celebrating the first harvest of wheat and other crops. This photograph documents the start of this tradition and the way it is celebrated in kindergartens to this day. The children wear white, put garlands in their hair, and come to kindergarten carrying bunches of flowers to symbolize the spring and the fertility of the land. It is thought that the kindergarten in this photograph, founded by the photographer's daughter, was the first established outside the walls of Jerusalem.

YAACOV BEN-DOV
(1882, RUSSIA–1968, ISRAEL),
IMMIGRATED TO ERETZ ISRAEL, 1908
GELATIN SILVER PRINT
PURCHASED WITH THE HELP OF
RENA (FISCH) AND ROBERT LEWIN,
LONDON

June | 1 2 3 4 5 6 7 8 **9** 10 11 12 13 14 15 16 17 18 19 20 21 22 23 24 25 26 27 28 29 30

סיון | **ב** א ג ד ה ו ז ח ט י י״א י״ב י״ג יד טו טז יז יח יט כ כא כב כג כד כה כו כז כח כט ל

BOAS AND RUTH, 19TH CENTURY

Shavuot, the Feast of Weeks, is one of the three pilgrimage festivals (*Shalosh Regalim*). It is celebrated at the conclusion of the counting of the Omer seven weeks after Passover. In addition to its religious significance as the anniversary of the giving of the Torah to the Children of Israel, it is named in the Bible as *Hag ha-Katzir* (Harvest Festival) as it coincides with the end of the barley harvest and the beginning of the wheat harvest. Another name is *Hag ha-Bikkurim* (Festival of the First Fruits): On this day the first fruits of the season were brought to the Temple in Jerusalem. A custom, dating back to the days of the Talmud, which is universally observed at the synagogue on the morning of Shavuot, is the public reading of the book of Ruth. This seemingly literary work, full of grace and charity, has deep moral, educational, and national meanings. Its relevance to Shavuot is that its story occurs during the barley and wheat harvests. In addition, Ruth is viewed as a proselyte who accepted the Torah, and her conversion was attained through adversity and hardship, as was the knowledge of the Torah, which was received during Shavuot. The Book of Ruth also tells us that King David, who traditionally is said to have died on Shavuot, was a descendant of Ruth and Boas. Moritz Oppenheim discreetly placed his monogram on a clay jar at Ruth's side.

MORITZ DANIEL OPPENHEIM,
GERMAN (1800–1882)
INK AND WASH HEIGHTENED
WITH WHITE ON PAPER
25.5 X 33 CM
GIFT OF RAPHAEL ROSENBERG,
LONDON
M 474-2-55
PHOTOGRAPH: ISRAEL MUSEUM

June | 1 2 3 4 5 6 7 8 9 **10** 11 12 13 14 15 16 17 18 19 20 21 22 23 24 25 26 27 28 29 30

א ב **ג** ד ה ו ז ח ט י יא יב יג יד טו טז יז יח יט כ כא כב כג כד כה כו כז כח כט ל | סיון

THE ROTHSCHILD MISCELLANY MANUSCRIPT
NORTHERN ITALY, CA. 1450–80

The Israel Museum's Rothschild Miscellany, written in Northern Italy in 1479, is a manuscript unrivaled in the richness and quality of its illuminations and marginal texts. It assembles thirty-seven religious and secular units encompassing in minute detail almost every custom of religious and secular Jewish life. The page on the left depicts the blessing of the new moon, recited each month in the open as featured in the decorated vignette; the opening word of the blessing, which is profusely illuminated, is on the right. The Jewish year is calculated according to a lunar/solar system. The beginning of a new month is gauged by the appearance of the moon, while the beginning of the year is determined by the earth's position in relation to the sun.

PEN AND INK, TEMPERA, AND
GOLD LEAF ON VELLUM
21 X 15.9 CM
GIFT OF JAMES A. DE ROTHSCHILD,
LONDON
PHOTOGRAPH: ISRAEL MUSEUM/
DAVID HARRIS

June | 1 2 3 4 5 6 7 8 9 10 **11** 12 13 14 15 16 17 18 19 20 21 22 23 24 25 26 27 28 29 30

סיון | א ב ג ד ה ו ז ח ט י יא יב יג יד טו טז יז יח יט כ כא כב כג כד כה כו כז כח כט ל

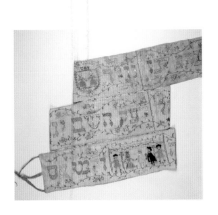

MULTICOLORED SILK THREAD
EMBROIDERY ON LINEN
18.5 X 35.58 CM
THE STIEGLITZ COLLECTION WAS
DONATED TO THE ISRAEL MUSEUM,
JERUSALEM WITH THE
CONTRIBUTION OF ERICA AND
LUDWIG JESSELSON, NEW YORK,
THROUGH THE AMERICAN FRIENDS
OF THE ISRAEL MUSEUM
PHOTOGRAPH: ISRAEL MUSEUM/
AVI GANOR

TORAH BINDER (*WIMPEL*)
GERMANY, 1777

After the circumcision ceremony, the linen spread on which the baby had been circumcised was cut into four pieces and sewn together in a long strip to form a Torah binder. It would be embroidered or painted with the names of the child and his father, the child's birth date, and the blessing that he may be raised in the Torah, to the marriage canopy, and to a life of good deeds. The cloth was dedicated to the synagogue during the child's first visit there, and the Torah scroll from which he read at his bar mitzvah was wrapped with it. This custom, originating in Northern Italy in the sixteenth century, was widespread among the communities of Germany and Central Europe until the late eighteenth or early nineteenth century.

June | 1 2 3 4 5 6 7 8 9 10 11 **12** 13 14 15 16 17 18 19 20 21 22 23 24 25 26 27 28 29 30

סיון | א ב ג ד ה ו ז ח ט י יא יב יג יד טו טז יז יח יט כ כא כב כג כד כה כו כז כח כט ל

TORAH SHIELD
POLAND, 18TH CENTURY

The breastplate (or shield) is usually placed over the mantle, which covers the Torah scrolls. Interchangeable plaques engraved with the names of the different holidays or Torah portion to be read are slid into the center of the shield. This breastplate bears the plaque for Shavuot, the festival of the Giving of the Law. The griffins that flank the crown on the upper area appear widely in Jewish art in Poland, carved on wooden Torah Arks, Torah Ark curtains, Torah crowns, and shields.

REPOUSSÉ, ENGRAVED,
AND PARTLY GILT SILVER
25.2 X 26 X 62 CM
THE STIEGLITZ COLLECTION WAS
DONATED TO THE ISRAEL MUSEUM,
JERUSALEM WITH THE CONTRIBU-
TION OF ERICA AND LUDWIG
JESSELSON, NEW YORK,
THROUGH THE AMERICAN FRIENDS
OF THE ISRAEL MUSEUM
PHOTOGRAPH: ISRAEL MUSEUM/
AVI GANOR

June | 1 2 3 4 5 6 7 8 9 10 11 12 **13** 14 15 16 17 18 19 20 21 22 23 24 25 26 27 28 29 30

סיון | א ב ג ד ה ו ז ח ט י יא יב יג יד טו טז יז יח יט כ כא כב כג כד כה כו כז כח כט ל

MIZRAH
SOUTHERN GERMANY, 18TH CENTURY

The mizrah (east) is a sheet hung on the eastern wall of the Jewish home indicating the direction of prayer. The vignettes decorating this sheet depict typical features of each holiday and the name of the festival: Sukkot (Festival of Tabernacles), Pesach (Passover), Shavuot (Feast of Weeks), Rosh Hashanah (New Year), Yom Kippur (Day of Atonement), Hanukkah, and Purim.

PEN AND INK AND
WATERCOLORS ON PAPER
23 X 34.5 CM
THE FEUCHTWANGER COLLECTION
PURCHASED AND DONATED TO THE
ISRAEL MUSEUM BY BARUCH AND
RUTH RAPPAPORT OF GENEVA
PHOTOGRAPH: ISRAEL MUSEUM/
DAVID HARRIS

June | 1 2 3 4 5 6 7 8 9 10 11 12 13 **14** 15 16 17 18 19 20 21 22 23 24 25 26 27 28 29 30

סיון | א ב ג ד ה ו ז ח ט י יא יב יג יד טו טז יז יח יט כ כא כב כג כד כה כו כז כח כט ל

WEDDING
SAFED, ERETZ ISRAEL, LATE 19TH CENTURY

This old photograph shows a traditional Jewish wedding, held in a courtyard under the open sky, as is customary in many Ashkenazi communities. According to the Rema (Rabbi Moshe Israels) this conveys the hope that the offspring of this couple may be as numerous as the stars in heaven. The bride and bridegroom stand under the canopy, which symbolizes the household they are about to establish. The guests' clothes reflect their different backgrounds and cultural affiliations.

BLACK AND WHITE PHOTOGRAPH
20.5 X 24.5 CM
GIFT OF CHAIM VINITZKY,
JERUSALEM

June | 1 2 3 4 5 6 7 8 9 10 11 12 13 14 **15** 16 17 18 19 20 21 22 23 24 25 26 27 28 29 30

סיון | א ב ג ד ה ו ז **ח** ט י יא יב יג יד טו טז יז יח יט כ כא כב כג כד כה כו כז כח כט ל

Bridal jewelry set
San'a, Yemen, early 20th century

Yemenite Jewish women wore much jewelry at their wedding. The bride's face would be completely framed by gold, pearls, and coral—she herself was barely distinguishable. Rows of necklaces with amulet cases covered her chest, her arms were covered with bracelets, and her fingers with rings. On her head she wore a conical headdress of pearls framed by fragrant flowers. A woman who specialized in preparing brides for the wedding would come to the house, bringing most of the bridal jewelry with her.

RECONSTRUCTION MADE AFTER A
PHOTOGRAPH OF YIHYEH HAYBI; PART
OF THE JEWELRY WAS RECONSTRUCTED
BY THE ZADOK JEWELERS
BROCADED TEXTILE; SILVER AND GILT
SILVER JEWELRY; CORAL; PEARLS
PHOTOGRAPH: ISRAEL MUSEUM/
DAVID HARRIS

June | 1 2 3 4 5 6 7 8 9 10 11 12 13 14 15 **16** 17 18 19 20 21 22 23 24 25 26 27 28 29 30

סיון | א ב ג ד ה ו ז ח ט י יא יב יג יד טו טז יז יח יט כ כא כב כג כד כה כו כז כח כט ל

338

Kiddush wine flask
Syria, 19th century

Special festive dishes and vessels usually decorated the Sabbath table in its honor. This unique red glass wine flask used for the *kiddush* (sanctification over a glass of wine) is inscribed and decorated with the text for the Hebrew blessing over the wine.

Etched red glass
17.2 x 12 cm
Gift in memory of Rabbi
Bernard and Fannie Lissauer
by their children
and grandchildren
Photograph: Israel Museum/
David Harris

June | 1 2 3 4 5 6 7 8 9 10 11 12 13 14 15 16 **17** 18 19 20 21 22 23 24 25 26 27 28 29 30

סיון | א ב ג ד ה ו ז ח ט י יא יב יג יד טו טז יז יח יט כ כא כב כג כד כה כו כז כח כט ל

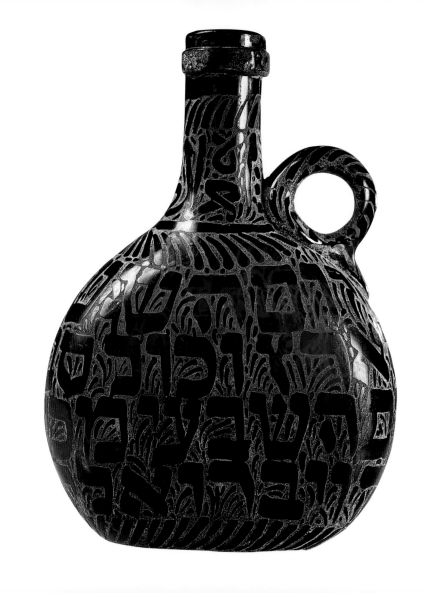

Torah case, crown, and shield
Izmir, Turkey, 1874

After being expelled from Spain in 1492, most Spanish Jews went to live in countries in the Ottoman Empire. There they fashioned their special ceremonial items, borrowing from the local style. This Torah case is covered in velvet and has silver decoration in typical Ottoman style.

Velvet-covered wood;
repoussé and engraved silver
85.5 x 22.5 cm
Photograph: Israel Museum/
Nahum Slapak

June | 1 2 3 4 5 6 7 8 9 10 11 12 13 14 15 16 17 **18** 19 20 21 22 23 24 25 26 27 28 29 30

א ב ג ד ה ו ז ח ט י **י'א** י'ב י'ג י'ד ט'ו ט'ז י'ז י'ח י'ט כ כ'א כ'ב כ'ג כ'ד כ'ה כ'ו כ'ז כ'ח כ'ט ל | **סיון**

Torah binder *(wimpel)* (detail)
Germany, 1728

After the circumcision ceremony the linen spread on which the child was circumcised was cut into pieces which were then sewn together into a long strip to form a Torah binder decorated with part of the blessing for the circumcision ceremony. Either embroidered or painted with the child's name, it would be presented to the synagogue, probably on his first visit, in a special ceremony called *Die Mappe Schultragen*. When the boy celebrated his bar mitzvah, he would read the prescribed portion from the Torah scroll that had been wrapped with the Torah binder he had donated. This detail is elaborately embroidered with the wish for the child to grow up "to the marriage canopy," the blessing said over marriage.

Linen; silk thread embroidery
20 x 392 cm
Gift of Irena Schwabacher
and Marianna Einstein,
Binyamina, Israel
Photograph: Israel Museum/
Peter Lanyi

June | 1 2 3 4 5 6 7 8 9 10 11 12 13 14 15 16 17 18 **19** 20 21 22 23 24 25 26 27 28 29 30

סיון | א ב ג ד ה ו ז ח ט י יא **י'ב** יג יד טו טז יז יח יט כ כא כב כג כד כה כו כז כח כט ל

Marriage contract (*KETUBBAH*)
Rotterdam, Holland, 1648

This *ketubbah* is the work of the well-known Jewish artist Shalom Italia, born in Mantua, Italy, and active in Holland, especially producing engraved Esther scrolls, book illustrations, portraits, and decorated *ketubbah* forms. This *ketubbah* includes vignettes from the life of different biblical couples—Adam and Eve, Abraham and Sarah, Jacob and Rachel, Ruth and Boaz, Rebekah and Eliezer—and a portrayal of the newly married couple in the dress of wealthy seventeenth-century Dutch Jews. The date of this *ketubbah* is the thirteenth of Sivan.

ARTIST: SHALOM ITALIA
GROOM: ISAAC PEREIRA, SON OF
ABRAHAM PEREIRA
BRIDE: RACHEL, DAUGHTER OF
ABRAHAM DE PINTO
HAND-COLORED ETCHING AND
ENGRAVING, PEN AND INK ON
PARCHMENT
37.5 X 33.7 CM
GIFT OF M. H. GANS, AMSTERDAM
PHOTOGRAPH: ISRAEL MUSEUM/
NAHUM SLAPAK

June | 1 2 3 4 5 6 7 8 9 10 11 12 13 14 15 16 17 18 19 **20** 21 22 23 24 25 26 27 28 29 30

סיון | א ב ג ד ה ו ז ח ט י י'א י'ב **ג'** יד טו טז יז יח יט כ כא כב כג כד כה כו כז כח כט ל

והתקדשתם והייתם קדשים

Henna ceremony (*MEHENDI*)
Bene Israel community
Magen Hassidim synagogue,
Bombay, India, 1983

In many countries, Jews adopted the local custom of holding a henna ceremony a few evenings before the wedding, accompanied by music and song. Henna is the sweet, pungent flowering plant whose roots and leaves yield a much-prized dye, believed to ward off evil forces. In India among the Bene Israel, henna paste is put on the ring finger of both the bride and the bridegroom. This ceremony took place simultaneously the night before the wedding in two separate synagogues or in the homes of members of the two engaged families. During the ceremony, some of the groom's henna paste was brought by a messenger to be mixed with some of the bride's. The bride was dressed in a green sari with jasmine wreaths and silver chains tied to her forehead to ensure her fertility and wealth. The henna ceremony exists in many other forms and is practiced by Yemenite Jews and in communities in North Africa and in America.

PHOTOGRAPH: ISRAEL MUSEUM/
ORPA SLAPAK

June | 1 2 3 4 5 6 7 8 9 10 11 12 13 14 15 16 17 18 19 20 **21** 22 23 24 25 26 27 28 29 30

סיון | א ב ג ד ה ו ז ח ט י א יב יג **י'** טו טז יז יח יט כ כא כב כג כד כה כו כז כח כט ל

Man's sash
Taroudant, Morocco,
first half of 20th century

These brightly colored belts woven in stripes and rectangles were commonly worn by Jewish men in Morocco, who folded and tied them around their waists. They were also used as Torah decoration in the synagogue, as were women's scarves.

Silk and cotton
280 x 44 cm
Photograph: Israel Museum/
Chanan Sadeh

June | 1 2 3 4 5 6 7 8 9 10 11 12 13 14 15 16 17 18 19 20 21 **22** 23 24 25 26 27 28 29 30

סיון | א ב ג ד ה ו ז ח ט י יא יב יג יד טו טז יז יח יט כ כא כב כג כד כה כו כז כח כט ל

THE BIBLICAL SPIES
ERETZ ISRAEL, CA. 1925

These tiles were intended for use on the facades of Eretz Israel houses during the 1920s. They were produced in Jerusalem, at the Bezalel ceramics workshop, where objects for personal and public use were created bearing images that would increase the user's identification with the Zionist concept that the modern return to Eretz Israel was a link to the greatness and beauty of the Jewish people's independent life in biblical Eretz Israel. These tiles were meant to inspire passersby with their Zionist message. The biblical story in Numbers 13:17–33, which tells of the spies who surveyed Eretz Israel in preparation for the people of Israel's return to their land after escape from Egypt, symbolizes the promise of redemption and the start of settlement—clearly a Zionist message. It is also a symbol of the fertility of the Land of Milk and Honey, seen as an object of desire and yearning for thousands of years by the people of the Jewish Diaspora. The figures of the spies carrying bunches of fruit was a popular symbol for the agricultural workers in Eretz Israel. They often appeared on the labels of agricultural produce marketed by Jewish Eretz Israel companies and as a central image in ceremonies and processions.

GLAZED TILES
15 X 13.5 CM
4711
PHOTOGRAPH: ISRAEL MUSEUM

June | 1 2 3 4 5 6 7 8 9 10 11 12 13 14 15 16 17 18 19 20 21 22 **23** 24 25 26 27 28 29 30

סיון | א ב ג ד ה ו ז ח ט י יא יב יג יד טו **טז** יז יח יט כ כא כב כג כד כה כו כז כח כט ל

וַיְסַפְּרוּ לוֹ וַיֹּאמְרוּ בָּאנוּ אֶל הָאָרֶץ

אֲשֶׁר שְׁלַחְתָּנוּ וְגַם זָבַת חָלָב

וּדְבַשׁ הִיא וְזֶה פִּרְיָהּ:

Porcelain set
Berlin, Germany, 18th century

This set comprises three pieces: a coffeepot, a teapot, and a bowl, which probably formed part of a larger set once given as a wedding present. The Hebrew inscription on each piece probably indicates the names of the bride and the groom. Such porcelain, called *Judenporzellan*, was subject to an eighteenth-century decree commanding Jews to buy up surplus unsold German porcelain at exorbitant prices. This decree was officially revoked in 1809.

June | 1 2 3 4 5 6 7 8 9 10 11 12 13 14 15 16 17 18 19 20 21 22 23 **24** 25 26 27 28 29 30

סיון | א ב ג ד ה ו ז ח ט י יא יב יג יד טו טז **יז** יח יט כ כא כב כג כד כה כו כז כח כט ל

Torah crown
Padua, Italy, 17th–18th century

A ghetto—a closed, delimited area where Jews were forced to live—was established in Venice in 1516. Paradoxically, it proved to be a catalyst for the development of Jewish ceremonial art, most of which was created in Christian workshops due to the restrictions placed on Jews at the time. This Torah crown is lavishly decorated with scrolling floral motifs and temple implements including the Tablets of the Law, incense utensils, and the Ark of the Covenant. The style of the object combines a traditional design with the fashion of Italian silversmithing of the time.

Repoussé, pierced, chiseled, punched, cast and partly gilt silver
225 x 260 cm
The Stieglitz Collection was donated to the Israel Museum, Jerusalem with the contribution of Erica and Ludwig Jesselson, New York, through the American Friends of the Israel Museum
Photograph: Israel Museum/ Avi Ganor

June | 1 2 3 4 5 6 7 8 9 10 11 12 13 14 15 16 17 18 19 20 21 22 23 24 **25** 26 27 28 29 30

סיון | א ב ג ד ה ו ז ח ט י יא יב יג יד טו טז יז **יח** יט כ כא כב כג כד כה כו כז כח כט ל

MULTICOLORED SILK EMBROIDERED TOWELS OTTOMAN EMPIRE, LATE 19TH CENTURY

Towels and embroideries in a variety of floral and other patterns formed part of a bride's trousseau, which she would display to family and friends a few days before the wedding. Girls learned to embroider in childhood, when they began to prepare their trousseau, but there were also domestic workshops that specialized in embroidering articles for the trousseau. In Izmir several workshops were run by Jewish women.

LINEN; REVERSIBLE MULTICOLORED
SILK AND METAL-THREAD
EMBROIDERIES
112–240 CM (LENGTH)
21–50 CM (WIDTH)
PHOTOGRAPH: ISRAEL MUSEUM/
NAHUM SLAPAK

June | 1 2 3 4 5 6 7 8 9 10 11 12 13 14 15 16 17 18 19 20 21 22 23 24 25 **26** 27 28 29 30

סיון | א ב ג ד ה ו ז ח ט י יא יב יג יד טו טז יז יח **יט** כ כא כב כג כד כה כו כז כח כט ל

Bird ring
Meknes, Morocco, 18th or 19th century

Jewish craftsmen produced most of the jewelry in Morocco, using a variety of techniques and styles. The bird motif, one of the most popular, reflects ancient symbolic myths in many communities and was believed to have the ability to protect against evil.

Engraved gold set with
garnets, emerald, and quartz
2 cm (diameter)
Photograph: Israel Museum/
David Harris

June | 1 2 3 4 5 6 7 8 9 10 11 12 13 14 15 16 17 18 19 20 21 22 23 24 25 26 **27** 28 29 30

סיון | א ב ג ד ה ו ז ח ט י יא יב יג יד טו טז יז יח יט כ כא כב כג כד כה כו כז כח כט ל

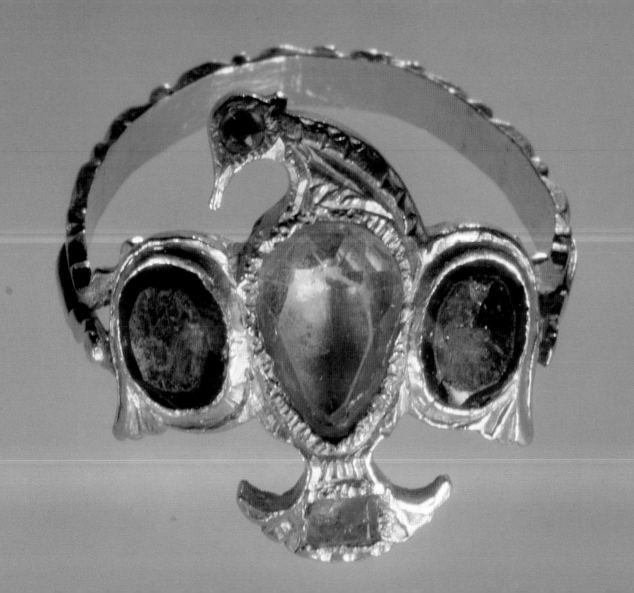

Ornaments to be Worn on the Temples
Bukhara, Uzbekistan, end of 19th century

These ornaments falling on either side of the temples are part of the Bukharan bride's jewelry. The two-headed bird in the center and the tree of life above are some of the most popular patterns in the jewelry of Central Asia. This jewelry contains real peacock feathers, relating to the popular belief in the peacock as the Iranian mythological bird *simurgh*, which can cure, protect, and assure fertility and even eternal life.

Embossed gold set with
tourmaline; pearls
6.5 x 2.7 cm
Photograph: Israel Museum/
Peter Lanyi

June | 1 2 3 4 5 6 7 8 9 10 11 12 13 14 15 16 17 18 19 20 21 22 23 24 25 26 27 **28** 29 30

סיון | א ב ג ד ה ו ז ח ט י י״א י״ב י״ג י״ד ט״ו ט״ז י״ז י״ח י״ט כ **כ״א** כ״ב כ״ג כ״ד כ״ה כ״ו כ״ז כ״ח כ״ט ל

Marriage contract (*KETUBBAH*)
Istanbul, Turkey, 1853

The general decoration of this marriage contract is reminiscent of Turkish textile and embroidery work, with its characteristic foliage and flowers motif. A scene in the upper part of the marriage contract shows the banks of the Bosphorus River with buildings, gardens, shrubs, and large trees. The three buildings are reminiscent of the typical Ottoman kiosk used by the Turkish nobility for special occasions and for receiving guests.

GROOM: SHABBETAI HAYYIM,
SON OF YOSEF HAYYIM
BRIDE: KADEN, DAUGHTER OF
NISSIM AVRAHAM ALKOLUMBRI
GOUACHE AND
GOLD POWDER ON PAPER
108 X 73 CM
PHOTOGRAPH: ISRAEL MUSEUM/
NAHUM SLAPAK

June | 1 2 3 4 5 6 7 8 9 10 11 12 13 14 15 16 17 18 19 20 21 22 23 24 25 26 27 28 **29** 30

סיון | א ב ג ד ה ו ז ח ט י יא יב יג יד טו טז יז יח יט כ כא **כב** כג כד כה כו כז כח כט ל

Miniature phylacteries (*tefillin*) with bag
Meshed, Iran, mid 19th century

In 1839 the Jewish community in Meshed, Iran, was forced to convert to Islam en masse but many continued to practice Judaism in secret. These miniature *tefillin* belonged to Mattityahu ben Aharonov, also forced to convert to Islam, who used them on his Muslim pilgrimage to Mecca in the early twentieth century. He hid them beneath his turban and under the left sleeve of his coat.

Leather and parchment;
printed cotton
Gift of the Nuriel Cohen-
Aharonov Family, Jerusalem
Photograph: Israel Museum/
Peter Lanyi

June │ 1 2 3 4 5 6 7 8 9 10 11 12 13 14 15 16 17 18 19 20 21 22 23 24 25 26 27 28 29 **30**

סיון │ א ב ג ד ה ו ז ח ט י יא יב יג יד טו טז יז יח יט כ כא כב **כג** כד כה כו כז כח כט ל

WEDDING RINGS
GERMANY AND ITALY, 17TH (?) CENTURY

Since the Middle Ages, the ring became a central part of the Jewish marriage rite, as it was for Christians. Most of the rings are surmounted by a tiny architectural structure, which has been interpreted as symbolizing the Temple or the household to be established by the new couple. The rings are usually quite large, are inscribed with the Hebrew *mazal tov* (good luck), and bear a tiny loop so they can be worn on a chain.

ENGRAVED, FILIGREE,
AND ENAMELED GOLD
LEFT TO RIGHT: 31 X 21 X 16 MM;
38 X 24 X 17 MM;
46 X 25 X 19 MM; 26 MM (DIAMETER)
THE STIEGLITZ COLLECTION WAS
DONATED TO THE ISRAEL MUSEUM,
JERUSALEM WITH THE CONTRIBUTION
OF ERICA AND LUDWIG JESSELSON,
NEW YORK, THROUGH THE AMERICAN
FRIENDS OF THE ISRAEL MUSEUM
PHOTOGRAPH: ISRAEL MUSEUM/
AVI GANOR

July 1 2 3 4 5 6 7 8 9 10 11 12 13 14 15 16 17 18 19 20 21 22 23 24 25 26 27 28 29 30 31

סיון | א ב ג ד ה ו ז ח ט י יא יב יג יד טו טז יז יח יט כ כא כב כג כד כה כו כז כח כט ל

SABBATH LAMPS
SA'DAH, YEMEN,
LATE 19TH–EARLY 20TH CENTURY

The saucer-shaped stone oil lamp was lit at the beginning of the Sabbath, as one of the three main duties of the Jewish wife. The saucer was filled with sesame or mustard oil and the wicks were placed in the indentations on the rim. Star-shaped lamps with eight spouts were not only used for the Sabbath but served as Hanukkah lamps in the northern areas of Yemen.

MARBLE ONYX; SOAPSTONE
6–12 CM (HEIGHT)
17.5–20 CM (DIAMETER)
PERMANENT LOAN BY
SALMAN SCHOCKEN, TEL AVIV
PHOTOGRAPH: ISRAEL MUSEUM/
DAVID HARRIS

July | 1 **2** 3 4 5 6 7 8 9 10 11 12 13 14 15 16 17 18 19 20 21 22 23 24 25 26 27 28 29 30 31

סיון | א ב ג ד ה ו ז ח ט י י'א י'ב י'ג י'ד ט'ו ט'ז י'ז י'ח י'ט כ כ'א כ'ב כ'ג כ'ד **כה** כו כז כח כט ל

Inscribed Hebrew seals
Various sites, Iron Age,
8th–6th century bce

In ancient times, when only a small minority of people could read and write, the seal impression was a mark of ownership and a means of authenticating documents, just as a signature is today. In the Bible the seal was the symbol of the king's authority, appearing on all royal edicts (I Kings 21:8).

Stone
0.5–2 cm (height)
Gifts of Norman P. Schenker,
Geneva, Dr. Reuben Hecht,
Haifa, Esther Lamport,
Herzliya, and
Shoshana Richman, Haifa
Photograph: Israel Museum

July | 1 2 **3** 4 5 6 7 8 9 10 11 12 13 14 15 16 17 18 19 20 21 22 23 24 25 26 27 28 29 30 31

סיון | א ב ג ד ה ו ז ח ט י יא יב יג יד טו טז יז יח יט כ כא כב כג כד כה **כו** כז כח כט ל

Epitaph of King Uzziah
Jerusalem, Second Temple Period,
1st century bce(?)

When King Uzziah died in the eighth century BCE, he was buried outside Jerusalem, since he was a leper. More than six centuries later, when the city expanded, his bones were moved to another location. This plaque marked the new burial site. The Aramaic inscription reads: "To this place were brought the bones of Uzziah King of Judah and do not open!"

Stone
35 cm (height)
Photograph: Israel Museum

July │ 1 2 3 **4** 5 6 7 8 9 10 11 12 13 14 15 16 17 18 19 20 21 22 23 24 25 26 27 28 29 30 31

א ב ג ד ה ו ז ח ט י יא יב יג יד טו טז יז יח יט כ כא כב כג כד כה כו **כז** כח כט ל │ סיון

Nose ring
Bene Israel community,
Bombay region, India,
early–mid 20th century

The women of the Bene Israel community, one of the three main Jewish groups in India, wore distinctive jewelry including heavy silver anklets, and silver and gold chains around their neck. They also wore silver and gold nose rings set with pearls. As Jews migrated to the cities and were exposed to British culture, the nose ring disappeared.

Gold; pearls; glass beads
3 cm (diameter)
Photograph: Israel Museum/
Avraham Hay

July | 1 2 3 4 **5** 6 7 8 9 10 11 12 13 14 15 16 17 18 19 20 21 22 23 24 25 26 27 28 29 30 31

סיון | א ב ג ד ה ו ז ח ט י יא יב יג יד טו טז יז יח יט כ כא כב כג כד כה כו כז **כח** כט ל

Capital decorated with a menorah
Synagogue at Caesarea, Byzantine Period, 5th century ce

The city of Caesarea was the capital of Judea during the Roman and Byzantine periods, and one of the greatest harbors on the Eastern Mediterranean. This marble capital, adorned with a menorah, decorated one of the synagogues of this multicultural city.

Marble
40 cm (height)
Israel Antiquities Authority
Photograph: Israel Museum

July | 1 2 3 4 5 **6** 7 8 9 10 11 12 13 14 15 16 17 18 19 20 21 22 23 24 25 26 27 28 29 30 31

ל **כט** כח כז כו כה כד כג כב כא כ יט יח יז טז טו יד יג יב יא י ט ח ז ו ה ד ג ב א | סיון

Amulet
Persia, 18th century

The magical power of this gold amulet lies in the inscription invoking the name of God. Traditional belief holds that general protection is found in the power of the names of God. These are written on amulets in various formulas. Here the forty-two-letter name is used; it consists of the acronyms of the *Ana be-koah* prayer attributed to R. Nehunyah ben Hakana, written in seven words of six letters each.

Gold; turquoise; ruby
6 x 4.8 cm
The Stieglitz Collection was donated to the Israel Museum, Jerusalem with the contribution of Erica and Ludwig Jesselson, New York, through the American Friends of the Israel Museum
Photograph: Israel Museum/ Avi Ganor

July | 1 2 3 4 5 6 **7** 8 9 10 11 12 13 14 15 16 17 18 19 20 21 22 23 24 25 26 27 28 29 30 31

ל כט כח כז כו כה כד כג כב כא כ יט יח יז טז טו יד יג יב יא י ט ח ז ו ה ד ג ב א | סיון

Alms boxes
Austria, 1843, and Reggio, Italy, 1830

Alms boxes were used to collect money that would be distributed to the city's poor. They were found in many Jewish homes and in every Jewish community, either fixed to the wall of the synagogue or built into it. In one of these alms boxes the name of a woman is inscribed as a member of the Burial Society, which testifies to her social involvement in the community. The double charity box was designed with a hinged lid for coins and another section for additional money.

LEFT: REPOUSSÉ, CAST, AND ENGRAVED SILVER HANDLE AT BACK
FIRM: IKPAL
14 X 14 CM
GIFT: IRCO

RIGHT: ENGRAVED AND SOLDERED BRASS
17.4 X 11.1 CM
GIFT OF MR. AND MRS. SIEGFRIED KREMSKY

PHOTOGRAPH: ISRAEL MUSEUM

July | 1 2 3 4 5 6 7 **8** 9 10 11 12 13 14 15 16 17 18 19 20 21 22 23 24 25 26 27 28 29 30 31

תמוז א | ב ג ד ה ו ז ח ט י יא יב יג יד טו טז יז יח יט כ כא כב כג כד כה כו כז כח כט

PEN AND INK, TEMPERA, AND GOLD
LEAF ON PARCHMENT; HANDWRITTEN
18.5 X 14.5 CM
PHOTOGRAPH: ISRAEL MUSEUM/
NAHUM SLAPAK

PRAYER BOOK OF THE RABBI OF RUZHIN
EASTERN EUROPE, LATE 15TH CENTURY

The personal *siddur* (prayer book) of the Rabbi of Ruzhin contains daily, Sabbath, and festival prayers. The prayer book was known to have been in the possession of the Hasidic leader Rabbi Israel Friedman of Ruzhin in the nineteenth century. As the manuscript has no signature (scribal colophon) its exact date and place of origin are unknown, although it is known that the prayer book originated in Eastern Europe. Written in square Ashkenazi script, the *siddur* is lavishly decorated with initial-word panels for the different prayers.

July │ 1 2 3 4 5 6 7 8 **9** 10 11 12 13 14 15 16 17 18 19 20 21 22 23 24 25 26 27 28 29 30 31

תמוז │ א **ב** ג ד ה ו ז ח ט י יא יב יג יד טו טז יז יח יט כ כא כב כג כד כה כו כז כח כט

Plaiting the bride's hair
In the tradition of Habban, Yemen

Most of the Habban community from southeast Yemen immigrated to a rural area near Tel Aviv after the State of Israel was created. Since then its members have maintained their age-old traditions, such as the plaiting of multiple braids, which was one of the preparations a bride had to undergo before her wedding. An experienced elderly woman, a so-called "bridal caretaker," traditionally fulfilled this task, as seen in the picture.

Moshav Bareket, Israel, 1980s
Photograph: Israel Museum/
Douglas Guthry, Jerusalem

July | 1 2 3 4 5 6 7 8 9 **IO** 11 12 13 14 15 16 17 18 19 20 21 22 23 24 25 26 27 28 29 30 31

תמוז | א ב **ג** ד ה ו ז ח ט י יא יב יג יד טו טז יז יח יט כ כא כב כג כד כה כו כז כח כט

Dowry chest for the wedding of Regina Karo
Izmir, Turkey, 1940

The bridal chest was an important part of the dowry. It was used to store the bride's clothing and bed linen, and then to carry it from her home to the groom's. It was later used to store the household textiles. This large box, made for the wedding of a woman named Regina Karo, is decorated with red fabric and metal foil, with star and plant decorations. The bride's initials, R. K., appear on the back of the chest.

Wood covered with cloth
and metal foil
101 x 54 x 62 cm
Photograph: Israel Museum/
David Harris

July | 1 2 3 4 5 6 7 8 9 10 **11** 12 13 14 15 16 17 18 19 20 21 22 23 24 25 26 27 28 29 30 31

תמוז | א ב ג **ד** ה ו ז ח ט י יא יב יג יד טו טז יז יח יט כ כא כב כג כד כה כו כז כח כט

PREPARATION OF THE BRIDE IN THE TRADITION OF AFGHANISTAN

On her wedding day, the bride underwent various cosmetic treatments. Her hair was combed and plaited in many thin braids. Gilt paper was rolled on the two front locks of hair. Then she was heavily powdered, and her eyebrows were blackened and joined, creating a frame for the gilt paper placed on her forehead, on which sequins were glued.

RECONSTRUCTION BY
MALKA YAZDI, TEL AVIV, 1979
PHOTOGRAPH: ISRAEL MUSEUM/
NO'AM BAR'AM-BEN YOSSEF

July | 1 2 3 4 5 6 7 8 9 10 11 **12** 13 14 15 16 17 18 19 20 21 22 23 24 25 26 27 28 29 30 31

תמוז | א ב ג ד **ה** ו ז ח ט י יא יב יג יד טו טז יז יח יט כ כא כב כג כד כה כו כז כח כט

BRIDE ADORNED WITH JEWELRY
IN THE TRADITION OF HERAT, AFGHANISTAN

In Herat, the bride was bedecked with jewelry and several scarves. Undoubtedly the most outstanding element in her adornment were the sequins and gilt-paper cutouts glued to her forehead, in perfect harmony with the jewels. In order to enlarge the forehead, the bride's hair would be plucked from her forehead in a painful cosmetic process.

RECONSTRUCTED BY ALIA BEN-AMI
AND BRACHA ASHEROV, ISRAEL
MUSEUM, 1997
PHOTOGRAPH: ISRAEL MUSEUM/
NAHUM SLAPAK

July | 1 2 3 4 5 6 7 8 9 10 11 12 **13** 14 15 16 17 18 19 20 21 22 23 24 25 26 27 28 29 30 31

תמוז | א ב ג ד ה ו ז ח ט י יא יב יג יד טו טז יז יח יט כ כא כב כג כד כה כו כז כח כט

"BLESSINGS OF THE HOUSE" TILES
NORTH AFRICA, 19TH–20TH CENTURY

These tiles, welcoming visitors and blessing the household, were attached to the walls at the entrance of the house. They are inscribed: "Blessed be you when you come in, and blessed be you when you go out" (Deuteronomy 28:6).

July | 1 2 3 4 5 6 7 8 9 10 11 12 13 **I4** 15 16 17 18 19 20 21 22 23 24 25 26 27 28 29 30 31

א ב ג ד ה ו **ז** ח ט י יא יב יג יד טו טז יז יח יט כ כא כב כג כד כה כו כז כח כט | תמוז

TOMBSTONE
ZOAR, BYZANTINE PERIOD, 508 CE

Found in the cemetery of Zoar, a flourishing Jewish village south of the Dead Sea, this tombstone bears an Aramaic epitaph and is decorated with Jewish symbols: the menorah, *lulav*, shofar, and the Temple facade. The epitaph reads:

> This is the tombstone of Hannah,
> daughter of Ha[nie]l the *Kohen*,
> who died on the Sabbath,
> the first festival day
> of Passover, on the fifteenth day of the month of Nisan,
> in the fifth year
> of the sabbatical cycle, which is the year
> three hundred and sixty-
> nine after the destruction
> of the Temple. Peace.
> May (her) soul rest. Peace.

SANDSTONE
45 CM (HEIGHT)
PHOTOGRAPH: ISRAEL MUSEUM/
PETER LANYI

July | 1 2 3 4 5 6 7 8 9 10 11 12 13 14 **15** 16 17 18 19 20 21 22 23 24 25 26 27 28 29 30 31

תמוז | א ב ג ד ה ו ז **ח** ט י יא יב יג יד טו טז יז יח יט כ כא כב כג כד כה כו כז כח כט

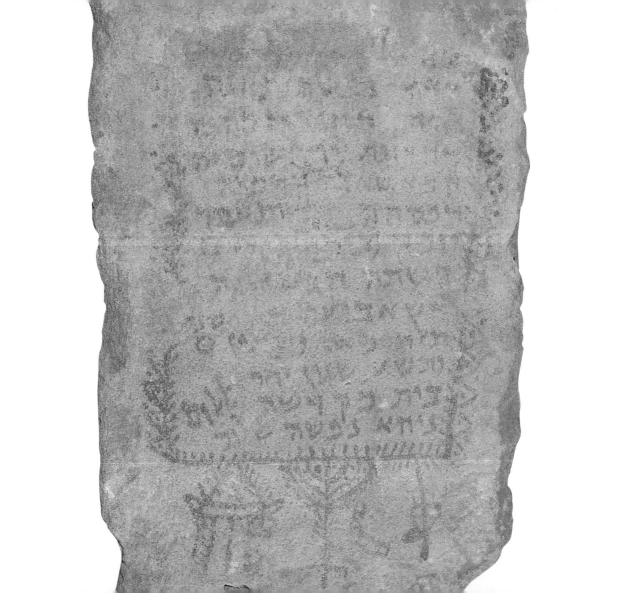

Torah binder (*wimpel*) (detail)
Halberstadt, Germany, 1737

This Torah binder was made from the linen spread on which the child was circumcised. It was later cut into pieces that were then sewn together in a long strip and decorated with the names of the child and his father, the child's birth date, and part of the blessing from the circumcision ceremony "to the Torah, to the marriage canopy and a life of good deeds." This binder records that it was donated by the child Yankel (Jacob), son of Aaron Katz in Halberstadt, born on Thursday, ninth of Tammuz in the Hebrew year 5497 (1737). The elaborately embroidered letters in this detail express the wish for the child to grow up with the Torah.

LINEN, WITH SILK THREAD
EMBROIDERY
18 X 340 CM
PHOTOGRAPH: ISRAEL MUSEUM/
PETER LANYI

July | 1 2 3 4 5 6 7 8 9 10 11 12 13 14 15 **16** 17 18 19 20 21 22 23 24 25 26 27 28 29 30 31

תמוז | א ב ג ד ה ו ז ח **ט** י יא יב יג יד טו טז יז יח יט כ כא כב כג כד כה כו כז כח כט

PLAQUE AGAINST THE EVIL EYE
PROVENANCE UNKNOWN, BYZANTINE PERIOD,
5TH CENTURY CE

This plaque is in the shape of a gabled architectural facade, with two menorahs flanking a central niche and a frieze with three birds as a base. The four circular hollows were originally inlaid with mirrors, intended to ward off the evil eye. This type of plaque is a common find in tombs and houses of this period. Plaques bearing pagan or Christian symbols are also known.

LIMESTONE AND GLASS
31.5 CM (HEIGHT)
INSTITUTE OF ARCHAEOLOGY,
THE HEBREW UNIVERSITY
OF JERUSALEM
PHOTOGRAPH: ISRAEL MUSEUM/
DAVID HARRIS

July | 1 2 3 4 5 6 7 8 9 10 11 12 13 14 15 16 **17** 18 19 20 21 22 23 24 25 26 27 28 29 30 31

תמוז | א ב ג ד ה ו ז ח ט י יא יב יג יד טו טז יז יח יט כ כא כב כג כד כה כו כז כח כט

Child's Drawing of Jerusalem, 1996

For Jerusalem 3000, a ten-year-old Argentine child made this drawing, depicting the inner life of the city, with its inhabitants—Arabs and Orthodox Jews—and hodgepodge of architectural styles. Children from Israel and around the world were asked to draw pictures of the city to commemorate this anniversary. Some had seen the city with their own eyes, but others had only heard stories and seen pictures. The images the children created were displayed at the Museum.

Felt-tip pen on paper
50 x 35 cm
Photograph: Israel Museum

July │ 1 2 3 4 5 6 7 8 9 10 11 12 13 14 15 16 17 **18** 19 20 21 22 23 24 25 26 27 28 29 30 31

תמוז │ א ב ג ד ה ו ז ח ט י **י״א** י״ב י״ג י״ד ט״ו ט״ז י״ז י״ח י״ט כ כ״א כ״ב כ״ג כ״ד כ״ה כ״ו כ״ז כ״ח כ״ט

Shammash's hat
Wolfisheim, Alsace, 19th–20th century

Jews of Alsace became French citizens with equal rights after the decree of emancipation was issued in 1791 by the Assemblée Constituante of the First French Republic. Grateful for finally being made equal members of French society, the Alsatian Jews were always loyal to the French government. This two-horned hat, whose ribbon bears the colors of the French flag, was typical for French officials. It was also worn by the *shammash*, a synagogue official, and can be seen as a gesture of loyalty toward the French.

Felt; silk ribbon
Gift of the Community of
Wolfisheim
Photograph: Israel Museum/
Nahum Slapak

July | 1 2 3 4 5 6 7 8 9 10 11 12 13 14 15 16 17 18 **19** 20 21 22 23 24 25 26 27 28 29 30 31

א ב ג ד ה ו ז ח ט י **י'א** י'ג י'ד ט'ו ט'ז י'ז י'ח י'ט כ כ'א כ'ב כ'ג כ'ד כ'ה כ'ו כ'ז כ'ח כ'ט | תמוז

MEMORIAL PAGE COMMEMORATING THE FIFTH ZIONIST CONGRESS AT BASEL, 1902

This is a sketch for a poster intended as a souvenir for participants in the Zionist Congress. Lilien, who was then considered one of the great Jewish illustrators in Europe, incorporated a number of the characteristic motifs from the array of Zionist symbols that he created during those years. An old Jew in traditional dress trapped in a thornbush represents the generation of the Diaspora and slavery. An angel shows him the Zionist vision: a Jew plowing the land of Eretz Israel, which represents the transformation of Jews into active and productive workers of the land. The sun shines and expels the darkness—a symbol of a new dawn and hope. Sheaves of wheat symbolize the blessed result of tilling the land, a complete contrast to the dry thorns symbolizing death, evil, and aridity.

EPHRAIM MOSES LILIEN
AUSTRIAN (1874–1925)
PENCIL, PEN, BRUSH, WASH,
AND GOUACHE ON PAPER
44 x 66 CM
PHOTOGRAPH: ISRAEL MUSEUM/
D. HARRIS

July | 1 2 3 4 5 6 7 8 9 10 11 12 13 14 15 16 17 18 19 **20** 21 22 23 24 25 26 27 28 29 30 31

תמוז | א ב ג ד ה ו ז ח ט י יא יב **ג'** יד טו טז יז יח יט כ כא כב כג כד כה כו כז כח כט

Bernard Picart (1673, France–1733),
active Holland
Etching, slightly hand-colored on
paper, 18th century
16.6 x 22.2 cm
From: *Cérémonies des Juifs* in
*Cérémonies et costumes religieuses
de tous les peuples du monde*,
delineated by Picart in 1722,
published 1723–1738
Gift of Mrs. Erika Elizabeth Mauer,
New York,
in memory of her parents,
Georg and Renee Holänder
B 95.0873
Photograph: Israel Museum

Ceremonie nuptiale des Juifs Portugais (Wedding Ceremony of Portuguese Jews)

Matrimony occupies a unique place in Jewish life both as a condition of spiritual and mental well being, and as a means to the fulfillment of the commandment "Be fruitful and multiply" (Genesis 1:28). Its importance means that marriage is an elaborate ceremony, which abounds in more customs than any other religious observance. In Hebrew, the ceremony of marriage is called *kiddushin* (sanctification), and its consummation—when the bride is received into the house of the husband—is called *nissuin* (elevation). The wedding is signified by the *huppah* (the bridal canopy) and performed in the presence of witnesses. Aside from the main elements of the wedding, as the groom's placing a ring on the bride's finger while declaring the new bond between them, and reading of the *ketubbah* (marriage contract), there is a special commemoration of the destruction of the Temple: to fulfill the verse "If I fail to elevate Jerusalem above my greatest joy" (Psalms 137:6), the groom smashes a glass. Picart illustrated this dramatic and joyful moment celebrated by aristocratic Portuguese Jews in eighteenth-century Amsterdam.

July | 1 2 3 4 5 6 7 8 9 10 11 12 13 14 15 16 17 18 19 20 **21** 22 23 24 25 26 27 28 29 30 31

תמוז | א ב ג ד ה ו ז ח ט י יא יב יג **י"ד** טו טז יז יח יט כ כא כב כג כד כה כו כז כח כט

INTERIOR OF THE PORTUGUESE SYNAGOGUE IN AMSTERDAM, NO DATE

EMANUEL DE WITTE, DUTCH
(1618–1692)
OIL ON CANVAS
108 X 123 CM
ACQUISITION, 1953
4450/5/53
PHOTOGRAPH: ISRAEL MUSEUM

Emanuel de Witte was born in Alkmaar, Holland. During the course of a fruitful career he lived in Rotterdam, Delft (where he was admitted into the Guild of St. Luke in 1642), and finally Amsterdam, where he settled in 1652. Although he also produced genre scenes and landscapes, de Witte came to specialize in architectural subjects and in his own lifetime was already considered a leading architectural painter. The works from his mature period (1650–60) include depictions of the interiors of churches and private homes, as well as three known versions of the interior of the Portuguese Synagogue in Amsterdam, depicting the main congregation center of the Sephardic Jews who came to live in the city after the 1492 expulsion from Spain. Throughout his rather unstable life de Witte was plagued by debts, which robbed him of economic independence and may have led him to take his own life.

July │ 1 2 3 4 5 6 7 8 9 10 11 12 13 14 15 16 17 18 19 20 21 **22** 23 24 25 26 27 28 29 30 31

תמוז │ א ב ג ד ה ו ז ח ט י יא יב יג יד **טו** טז יז יח יט כ כא כב כג כד כה כו כז כח כט

Spice boxes
Central and Eastern Europe,
18th–19th century

The Havdalah ceremony takes place on Saturday evening, marking the end of the Sabbath and the beginning of the new week. The ceremony performed at home includes blessings recited over wine, spices, and a lit candle. The aromatic spices were often kept in beautifully decorated containers such as these, which are passed around to be smelled by each member of the family after the blessing over the spices. The sage and philosopher Maimonides noted that spices are used to revive the souls saddened by the end of the Sabbath.

FILIGREE SILVER AND
SEMIPRECIOUS STONES
10–45 CM (HEIGHT)
PHOTOGRAPH: ISRAEL MUSEUM/
YORAM LEHMANN

July | 1 2 3 4 5 6 7 8 9 10 11 12 13 14 15 16 17 18 19 20 21 22 **23** 24 25 26 27 28 29 30 31

תמוז | א ב ג ד ה ו ז ח ט י יא יב יג יד טו **טז** יז יח יט כ כא כב כג כד כה כו כז כח כט

THE DESTRUCTION OF JERUSALEM, 1493

This imaginary depiction of the destruction of Jerusalem is one of a pair printed by Schedel in his book, which is richly illustrated with woodcuts, including many faithful, realistic depictions of cities. Unhampered by methodical historical research, the fifteenth-century imagination was free to create "historic" depictions of Jerusalem and the Holy Land rife with fanciful anachronisms. Alongside ruined walls and towers, and the blazing Holy Temple shaped like the Dome of the Rock, the Church of the Holy Sepulchre and a mosque stand firm. Wohlgemut was the teacher of Albrecht Dürer (1471–1528). His workshop, including Dürer, most likely worked with him on the woodcuts that appear in the book. This day, the seventeenth of Tammuz, is one of the four fast days held in memory of the destruction of the temple in Jerusalem.

HARTMANN SCHEDEL,
GERMAN (1440–1514)
HAND-COLORED WOODCUT ON PAPER,
BY MICHAEL WOHLGEMUT
25.8 x 54.3 CM (IMAGE)
FROM: HARTMANN SCHEDEL,
LIBER CHRONICARUM,
ANTON KOBERGER, NURENBERG, 1493
NORMAN BIER SECTION
FOR MAPS OF THE HOLY LAND
GIFT OF KARL AND LI HANDLER,
VIENNA
P1154-5-61
PHOTOGRAPH: ISRAEL MUSEUM/
ILAN STZULMAN

July | 1 2 3 4 5 6 7 8 9 10 11 12 13 14 15 16 17 18 19 20 21 22 23 **24** 25 26 27 28 29 30 31

תמוז | א ב ג ד ה ו ז ח ט י יא יב יג יד טו טז **יז** יח יט כ כא כב כג כד כה כו כז כח כט

verwundert.vnd bekant das solche vberwindung nicht auß menschlicher kraft sunder auß götlichen gnaden ge
schehen wer.in der zerstörung ist solcher todschlag geschehen.hunger vnd tödliche not.so du das alles wissen wilt
liese Josephum der mit gehöite sunder geschehen hat vnd anderń wissend geschriben hat.Do also Titus mit sei
nem vater Vespasiano in die stat kome do ließ er Symonê(der der zerstörung vrsach wz)in triumph füre mit
stricken durch die gantze stat schlaffen.sein leib verwundet vnd darnach tötten.Vespasianus pawt einen tempel
des frids vñ ließ darein legen die iuden heiligkait.als die tafeln des gesetz vnd ander ding.Die stat ist dozumal ge
wesen ein behawsing der tawber vnd möider piß auff die zeit Adriani.auch bey.l.iarn vngepawt belyben.die
selbigen darnach Adrianus der keyser mit mawr vnd gepew verneüet vnd hat sie nach seinem namen Heliam ge
haissen.vñ als der heilig Jeronimus zu Paulino schreibt so ist vö der zeit Adriani piß auff Constantinum bey dcc.
vnd.lxx.iarn an der stat der vrstend die abgot Jouis.vnd auff dem berg des kreüz ein steyne sewl auff der der
abgot Venus vö den hayden angepet in maynung das die iuden solche vneren den heiligen stette bewysen de
glawben der vrstende vnd des kreüz entmennen möchten.Es haben auch vnser fürsten die ieruzalem lang
besessen vnd darnach wider verloÿ.Der groß Karolus hat sie zum ersten mit großer arbeit erobert.darnach wi
der verloÿ.Godfridus hat sie zum andern gewunnen.do mit sie auch behalten wurde biß ist keyser Conrad vnnd
Ludwicus ein kúnig zu fanckreich mit macht piß in Asia gezogen.do aber vnser fürste darnach treg sind worde so
ist weder Jerusalem noch Anthiochia in vnserm gewalt belÿben.Der sinaheit vnd des iamers das alle dr vr
sprung vnsers anfangs abgenomen hat das die feind des kreüz den hohberümbten tempel Salomonis in dem
schlössel den der vrstend Christ in der er gepein warde.Caluariam do der herr gekreuzigt ist.die Sarracen die
zierlich grab in dem der herr vö vnsern wegen geschlaffen hat besitzen süllen.das die cristen(wo sie selbst mit wol
ten)nit vnbedacht möchten lassen.Seht die stat die lebendigen gots.die ampt vnserer erlösung.die stat die vns
got mit wunderwerck erleücht vnd mit seinem plůt geheiligt hat.in der die plůmen der erste vrstend erschine sein
vber die ritterschafft Machmeti gewalt haben vnd dem süntlichen volck vntterworffen ist.

Hie hebt sich an das fünft alter der werlt.vnd hat anfang von dem als die iuden gefangen gefürt wurde in Ba
bilonam.vnd werdt biß auff die gepurt vnsers herrn Jhesu cristi bey.v⁰.rc.iarn.wiewol etlich in d̄ rechnũg
anders vermaynen dy die iar der rechten gefencknus zeln wöllen.von dê.rl.iar.des reichs Sedechie.als Eusebius
setzt.als dań haben dy.lxx.iar der gefencknus in andern iar Darij ein ende.Josephus aber vnd der heilig Jhero
nimus rechen vö dem.xiij.iar.Josie des königs biß auff das dritt iar des königs Ciri.Etlich vö dem letzst iar des kö
nigs Joachim biß auff das letzst iar Ciri.Damit man aber das recht verstee.die lxx.iar die sich in dritten oder letzste
iare Ciri enden sind aygentlich die iar iüdischer gefencknus.die iar sich aber enden in den andern Darij sein aygen
lich was geschehen vö dem iar des anfangs der werlt.iiij.M.v⁰.r.vö der sintfluss.iiij.M.lxx.Vö d̄ gepurt Abra
he.tausent.iiij.M.xxviij.Do vö dem.xxviij.iar des reichs Tarquini des Römischen königs.als auch bey d̄ Medeern
Astyage.bey den Macedones Europe.bey den Lidos Alyacte.bey den Egypcios Vaphre.vnd bey den Caldeos Na
buchodonosor der erst geregirt haben.

Hie hebt sich an die gefencknus der hebreyschen die da ist gewesen in zerstörung des volcks Jherusalem vnd we
ret.lxx.iar.Als das volck vö istahel yetzo lang zeit den abgöttern gedient auch das plůt der vnschuldige vergos
sen hat.Do wolt got dyß geschlecht vertilgen vnd verderget So wz diß volck in dem reich Caldeorum.lxx.iar.gefan
geweret.auff das.das nach disen.lxx.iaren ein news volck mit solchen sünden vnbeladen gein Jherusalem die zupawen
komen solt.

Jerusalem zerstörung

DESTRVCCIO IHEROSOLIME

COIN OF THE BAR KOKHBA REVOLT
PROVENANCE UNKNOWN, ROMAN PERIOD, 132 CE

The musical instruments appearing on the Bar Kokhba coins symbolize the desire to rebuild the Temple in Jerusalem, which was destroyed by the Romans in 70 CE. This coin depicts a harp surrounded by the legend: "Year One of the Redemption of Israel."

BRONZE
2.3 CM (DIAMETER)
PHOTOGRAPH: ISRAEL MUSEUM

July | 1 2 3 4 5 6 7 8 9 10 11 12 13 14 15 16 17 18 19 20 21 22 23 24 **25** 26 27 28 29 30 31

תמוז | א ב ג ד ה ו ז ח ט י יא יב יג יד טו טז יז **י'ח** י'ט כ כא כב כג כד כה כו כז כח כט

NECKLACES
SOUS REGION, MOROCCO, EARLY 20TH CENTURY

These necklaces are typical of jewelry worn by the Jewish women of the Sous region in the Anti-Atlas mountains. They are decorated with coins, cloisonné enamel, semiprecious stones, and pieces of coral. This technique was introduced into the region by Jewish jewelers expelled from Spain at the end of the fifteenth century.

July | 1 2 3 4 5 6 7 8 9 10 11 12 13 14 15 16 17 18 19 20 21 22 23 24 25 **26** 27 28 29 30 31

תמוז | א ב ג ד ה ו ז ח ט י יא יב יג יד טו טז יז יח **יט** כ כא כב כג כד כה כו כז כח כט

The Temple Scroll (columns 52–57)
Qumran, Cave 11, Roman Period, late 1st
century bce–early 1st century ce

The Temple Scroll—the longest and one of the most important Dead Sea Scrolls—
was discovered in Cave 11 at Qumran in 1956. The scroll was written while the
Second Temple still stood in Jerusalem. It describes an ideal and different type of
Temple that, according to the Qumran sectarians' beliefs, would someday replace
the existing one.

Parchment
19 x 815 cm
Photograph: Israel Museum/
David Harris

July | 1 2 3 4 5 6 7 8 9 10 11 12 13 14 15 16 17 18 19 20 21 22 23 24 25 26 **27** 28 29 30 31

א ב ג ד ה ו ז ח ט י יא יב יג יד טו טז יז יח יט כ כא כב כג כד כה כו כז כח כט | תמוז

אות נפש

Column 3 (right)

לוא תקום
ולוא תקום לנד רע ד
כה בכול ארצכה לה שתה אלוה ולוא
אשר יהוה ט כול מים רע ט ות עבת חלל
רושה ועו והבא עליאות נו ות עבד הלמה אל
עבע לוא תובה פרוס אחר ולוא תעבד אל
טל הדבור אשר ולוא בפחרינה ובמו אנטו
אתעטר בבטר שוויכה ולואתמאן בגור
לו שנא בשנה במצוות אשר אבחר ואת יהוה
או טל מום רע לוא תובחנו לו בשעריכה
חר בנה וחאמר כי נבר ובאול רק חדם לואתאכל
נמים ונסות בשער ולוא תחמטום שונע על ירטו
יחאמר וחומו לוא תאכל שרו ושה ועו טהורים
למראשא דרך של ישת ובום ט ואם בתוך
עשות אות עולה או זבח שלמים ואנלתה
קום אשר אבא לשום שמו עלוו ובל הבזהמה
ט בא מום בשעריכה תואכלנה רחוק מק שאויו
לוא תובה קריב למקרשו נו בשר נו אול
ושה אשר שור ועז בתוך שרו אשר אענו מקראמם
ש אשר לוא ובוא לתוך מקראשי וזבחו שמה
לסוד מזבח העולה ואת חלבו וקטורו

Column 2 (center)

וחה נעשנה לאטל

תו אנרל די מעו הענה ובפקרונה נברכ א הסד יאטר
לחה והבלתה בשעריכה ר טהור וחטמא בבה וזוי נעבו
וכאול רק ט ט לבי עו אבו עו על הארץ תשופכנו כמים ונסות
בעבר ט הדרך הוא הנפש ולוא תאכל את חנפש עם הבשר למש
וטוב לכה ולבניכה אחריכה עד שלק ועשותה הישר והטוב
לפב אה ט וה זה אלוה הנכה
רק קושיכה ובו ובל צרינכה תשא ובאתה אל המקום אשר אשטו
שפו עלו ובחהתה שמא לבט כאשר הקרשתה או נרדתה בגובה
ובו זאם תרוו ער לוא תאחר לשלמו נ דרוש ארורשט מדרטד
יהודה בבה לחטאד ואם תחדל ולוא תריר לוא יהוה בבה חטואה
פרא שמחובה תשמור כאשר צרתה נדבה בפונה לעשות
כאשר נרתה
שבועה לאטור אסר על נפשו ולואאחל דבריו נבל דוינא כמוחו
ואשר ט תרוו נדר לו או אסרה אסר עלנפשה
בבות אבוה כשבטי בנעוריה ושמע אבוה את נרדה או
את האסר אשר אסרה על נפשה והחריש לה אבוה וקמו
על נרוה ובל אסרה אשר אסרה עלנפשה וקמו
ואם
נא ואם הניד אבוה או נה ביום שומע טל נרוה ואסרוה
אשר אסרה על נפש לוא עשה ויחומו ואונו אסלה לה טהנואא

Column 1 (left)

או טל שביעות
אשיבה או פס ם
ט ביום שומע ואנ
ובל נדר אלמנו וגרושה כול אי
וש אשר יצא מפות
אטנ נ תטמור לעשות לואתוכ
תא מחמה
אם ט ח בי בת צבוא אחולך חלום ונת
תונה בא אלוה ואת ונהפות אשר דבר
ט נעבודה יט ט טם אחרינ אשר לוא
תשמ אלאבו הדוא או לחולם הז
וכ אטטו ארבבה לרטעת הושבנכ אוזב
אלוהו אבותו נפא בבול לבבכם ובול נעשכ
אלוהי נבא חלטו ואות תעבודן ואותא
ובו תד בקון וזהצבוא הדוא או חולם הל
על ואן אלוה אשר חוענאטד בארץ
פבות עבדין לר ויחבה מן הדרך אשר
חרע מקרבכה
ואם ט
א אשת חקכה או ט עוכה אשר בעשכ
נלוד ונעבוד אלוהי אחרינ אשר לו

Plaque with a menorah carved in high relief
Horvat Qoshet, Lower Galilee,
Late Byzantine–Early Umayyad Period,
6th–8th century ce

Reconstructed from several fragments, this menorah relief is richly ornamented between the branches. The decorations include acanthus leaves, pomegranates, and birds.

Marble
64 cm (height)
Israel Antiquities Authority
Reconstructed in the Israel
Museum Laboratories through
a donation by Janis and
Harold Cooper, Florida
Photograph: Israel Museum

July | 1 2 3 4 5 6 7 8 9 10 11 12 13 14 15 16 17 18 19 20 21 22 23 24 25 26 27 **28** 29 30 31

א ב ג ד ה ו ז ח ט י יא יב יג יד טו טז יז יח יט כ **כא** כב כג כד כה כו כז כח כט | תמוז

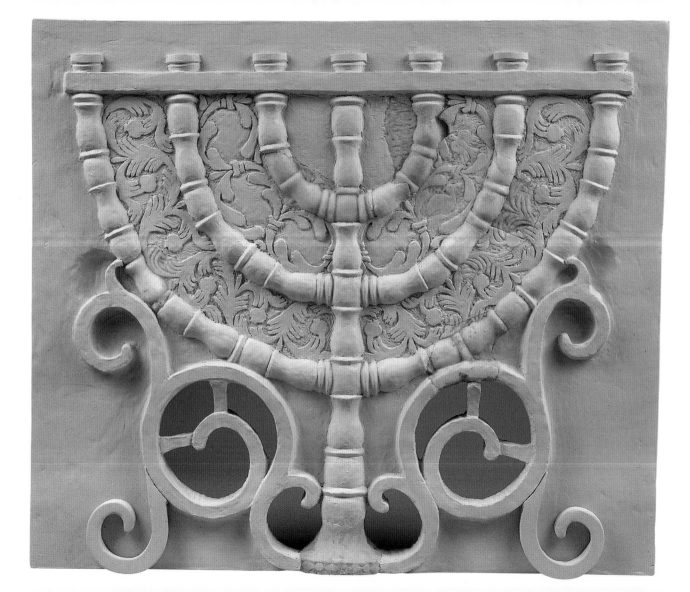

Cooking pot with silver hoard
Ein Gedi, Iron Age,
late 8th–7th century BCE

The silver ingots found in the pot had been chipped off larger chunks of silver
and weighed so they could be used as means of payment.

POTTERY AND SILVER
POT: 10.5 CM (HEIGHT)
ISRAEL ANTIQUITIES AUTHORITY
PHOTOGRAPH: ISRAEL MUSEUM/
AVRAHAM HAY

July | 1 2 3 4 5 6 7 8 9 10 11 12 13 14 15 16 17 18 19 20 21 22 23 24 25 26 27 28 **29** 30 31

תמוז | א ב ג ד ה ו ז ח ט י יא יב יג יד טו טז יז יח יט כ כא **כב** כג כד כה כו כז כח כט

424

Bridal casket
Northern Italy,
second half of 15th century

This casket (*cofanetto*) was probably intended as a wedding gift for a Jewish bride in which she could keep keys to the linen cases, as is indicated by the Italian inscription in Hebrew letters found below the clock dials on the lid. The numerical Hebrew dials are probably for inventory purposes. The three scenes in the front depict the duties usually undertaken by Jewish women: *hallah* (setting aside a portion of the dough), *niddah* (ritual immersion at the end of the menstrual cycle), and *hadlakat ha'ner* (kindling of the Sabbath lights).

Cast and engraved silver;
niello; partly gilt
6.6 x 13 x 6 cm
Gift of Astorre Mayer
Photograph: Israel Museum/
Yoram Lehmann

July | 1 2 3 4 5 6 7 8 9 10 11 12 13 14 15 16 17 18 19 20 21 22 23 24 25 26 27 28 29 **30** 31

תמוז | א ב ג ד ה ו ז ח ט י יא יב יג יד טו טז יז יח יט כ כא כב **כג** כד כה כו כז כח כט

Dome-shaped weights
Arad and Ein Gedi, Iron Age,
7th century bce

Many stone weights, on which the amount of the weight is incised, have been discovered in the area of the southern kingdom of Judah. They were used together with sets of scales for weighing silver and gold.

Stone
1.4–7.1 cm (diameter)
Israel Antiquities Authority
Photograph: Israel Museum

July | 1 2 3 4 5 6 7 8 9 10 11 12 13 14 15 16 17 18 19 20 21 22 23 24 25 26 27 28 29 30 **31**

תמוז | א ב ג ד ה ו ז ח ט י יא יב יג יד טו טז יז יח יט כ כא כב כג **כד** כה כו כז כח כט

THE WAILING WALL, 1920S

Although the angle in Ben-Dov's depiction of the Western Wall seems to copy nineteenth-century photographs, it is in fact the result of the constrictions of the place. Up until 1967, when the plaza in front of the Wall was cleared, there was only a narrow passage between the buildings in front of the Wall and the Wall itself, which limited the possible angles of view. During those years there were strong disagreements between the Arabs and the Jews (with the British arbitrators in the middle) about the options for Jewish prayer rituals at the Western Wall. Although the Jews were forbidden to erect a division (*mehitzah*) between the men and women, this photograph captures only women praying.

YAACOV BEN-DOV
(1882, RUSSIA–1968, ISRAEL),
IMMIGRATED TO ERETZ ISRAEL, 1908
GELATIN SILVER PRINT
PURCHASED WITH THE HELP OF
RENA (FISCH) AND ROBERT LEWIN,
LONDON

August | 1 2 3 4 5 6 7 8 9 10 11 12 13 14 15 16 17 18 19 20 21 22 23 24 25 26 27 28 29 30 31

תמוז | א ב ג ד ה ו ז ח ט י י"א י"ב י"ג י"ד ט"ו ט"ז י"ז י"ח י"ט כ כ"א כ"ב כ"ג כ"ד **כה** כו כז כח כט

NAMING A BABY GIRL (*BARSA*)
IN THE TRADITION OF
BENE ISRAEL COMMUNITY, INDIA

This ceremony usually takes place on the twelfth day after birth. The baby girl's cradle is placed in the middle of the house and decorated with flowers and colored paper. Cooked chickpeas, peeled coconut, and cookies are placed inside the cradle, along the edges of the sheet. These will be "stolen" later by the children of the family as part of a traditional game. The infant's aunt has the honor of giving the baby her name. She holds the baby in her arms, blesses her, whispers her new name in her ear, and then places her back in the cradle. Then the women, standing around the cradle, sing her to sleep.

August | 1 **2** 3 4 5 6 7 8 9 10 11 12 13 14 15 16 17 18 19 20 21 22 23 24 25 26 27 28 29 30 31

תמוז | א ב ג ד ה ו ז ח ט י יא יב יג יד טו טז יז יח יט כ כא כב כג כד כה **כו** כז כח כט

Cosmetics palette
Provenance unknown, Iron Age,
8th–7th century bce

This small, decorated palette was used for grinding and mixing cosmetics, such as kohl, an eye makeup.

Stone
8 cm (height)
Photograph: Israel Museum/
Avraham Hay

August | 1 2 **3** 4 5 6 7 8 9 10 11 12 13 14 15 16 17 18 19 20 21 22 23 24 25 26 27 28 29 30 31

תמוז | א ב ג ד ה ו ז ח ט י יא יב יג יד טו טז יז יח יט כ כא כב כג כד כה **כו** כז כח כט

A MAP OF THE LAND OF CANAAN, 1757

WILLEM ALBERT BACHIENE,
DUTCH (1712–1783)
AFTER ADRIAN RELAND,
DUTCH (1676–1718)
HAND-COLORED ENGRAVING AND
ETCHING ON PAPER
BY O. LINDEMAN IN ALMELO
36.3 X 44.4 CM
FROM: WILLEM ALBERT BACHIENE,
HEILIGE GEOGRAPHIE…
UTRECHT,
G.T. AND A. VAN PADDENBURG,
1765–68, BOUND IN A
COMPOSITE ATLAS
NORMAN BIER SECTION FOR
MAPS OF THE HOLY LAND
GIFT OF LEOPOLD LEOB,
SAO PAOLO, 1975
473.76A
PHOTOGRAPH: ISRAEL MUSEUM/
ILAN STZULMAN

In 1765–68 the Dutch priest, astronomer, and geographer Willem Albert Bachiene published a series of twelve maps of the Holy Land, which were compiled into a kind of complete historical atlas called "Sacred Geography." These maps are distinguished by their fine etching and delicate coloration, as well as their artistic illustrations and cartouches, typical of the Netherlands in that period. This map corrects many of the errors found in its predecessors, rendering it fairly reliable. The coastline extends from Sidon in the north to the Nile delta in the south. It stresses the topography of Canaan prior to the conquest of the Israelites. In the lower right, Abraham banishes Hagar and Ishmael from his tent.

August | 1 2 3 **4** 5 6 7 8 9 10 11 12 13 14 15 16 17 18 19 20 21 22 23 24 25 26 27 28 29 30 31

תמוז | א ב ג ד ה ו ז ח ט י יא יב יג יד טו טז יז יח יט כ כא כב כג כד כה כו כז **כח** כט

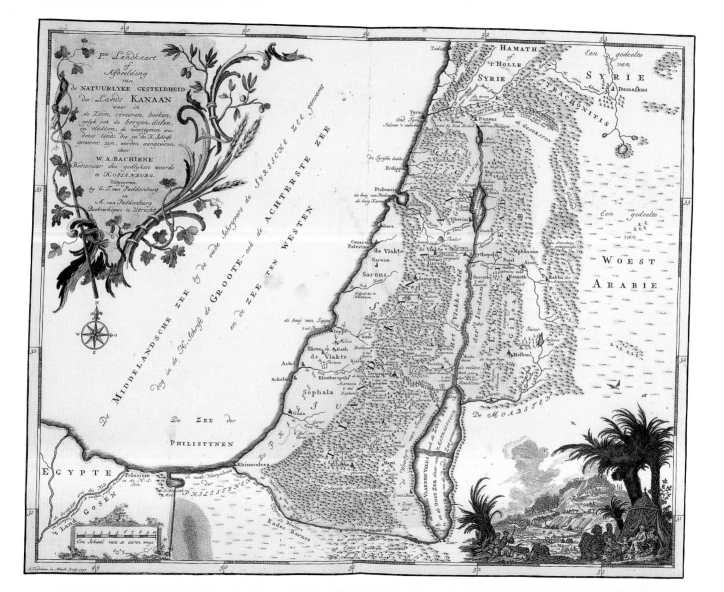

Iste Landkaart of Afbeelding van de NATUURLYKE GESTELDHEID des Lands KANAAN waar in de Zeen, rivieren, beeken, gelyk ook de bergen, dalen, en vlakten, de woestynen enz. dezes lands, die in de H. Schrift genoemt zyn, worden aangewezen. door W. A. BACHIENE Bedienaar des godlyken woords te KUILENBURG. Uitgegeven by G. T. van Paddenburg en A. van Paddenburg Boekverkopers te Utrecht

Menorah and goblet
Synagogue at Ein Gedi, Dead Sea shore,
Byzantine Period, 6th century CE

Ein Gedi was a prosperous village on the western shores of the Dead Sea.
This menorah and goblet were found among the ruins of its lavishly decorated
synagogue, next to the Torah Ark. We may therefore assume that the objects had
a ceremonial function.

BRONZE
MENORAH: 14.5 CM (HEIGHT)
GOBLET: 11 CM (HEIGHT)
ISRAEL ANTIQUITIES AUTHORITY
PHOTOGRAPH: ISRAEL MUSEUM

August | 1 2 3 4 **5** 6 7 8 9 10 11 12 13 14 15 16 17 18 19 20 21 22 23 24 25 26 27 28 29 30 31

תמוז | א ב ג ד ה ו ז ח ט י יא יב יג יד טו טז יז יח יט כ כא כב כג כד כה כו כז כח **כט**

BREAD (*HALLAH*) COVER
JERUSALEM, 1876

Sabbath and festival breads are always covered with a special cloth, often decorated, at the beginning of the festive meal. This richly colored embroidered cover depicts the Patriarchs' Tomb in Hebron surrounded by a fish. Maybe the fish is the mythical leviathan, a recurrent motif of Jewish art painted on ceilings of wooden synagogues in Eastern Europe. According to the Talmud it will be given as a reward to the righteous in the Time to Come. The *hallah* cover is dedicated to R. Akiva Lehrer of the Clerks and Treasurers of Amsterdam, who dispersed funds from the society to needy Jews living in Palestine.

EMBROIDERED BY
HANNA RIVKA HERMAN
WOOL THREAD ON TULLE;
EMBROIDERY; BEADS; SEQUINS
78 X 81 CM
PHOTOGRAPH: ISRAEL MUSEUM

August | 1 2 3 4 5 **6** 7 8 9 10 11 12 13 14 15 16 17 18 19 20 21 22 23 24 25 26 27 28 29 30 31

ל כט כח כז כו כה כד כג כב כא כ יט יח יז טז טו יד יג יב יא י ט ח ז ו ה ד ג ב **א** | אב

Figurines of musicians
Achziv, Iron Age, 8th–7th century bce

Music was an integral part of life in the ancient world: "And David and all the
House of Israel danced before the Lord to [the sound of] all kinds of cypress wood
[instruments], with lyres, harps, timbrels, sistrums, and cymbals" (II Samuel 6:5).
One of the musicians shown here plays a timbrel and the other a double-pipe.

Pottery
16, 20 cm (height)
Israel Antiquities Authority
Photograph: Israel Museum/
Avraham Hay

August | 1 2 3 4 5 6 **7** 8 9 10 11 12 13 14 15 16 17 18 19 20 21 22 23 24 25 26 27 28 29 30 31

א ‫ב‬ ג ד ה ו ז ח ט י יא יב יג יד טו טז יז יח יט כ כא כב כג כד כה כו כז כח כט ל   אב | ‫ב‬ א

TALLITH BAG
MOROCCO, 19TH–20TH CENTURY

This bag for the prayer shawl is decorated on all sides with floral patterns, birds, and Stars of David in pierced and engraved silver, as well as biblical inscriptions in Hebrew: "Honor your father and your mother" (Exodus 20:12) and verses from Proverbs (7:1, 23:25, 23:15).

PIERCED AND ENGRAVED SILVER;
VELVET; CARDBOARD
26 X 20.5 CM
THE FEUCHTWANGER COLLECTION,
PURCHASED AND DONATED BY
BARUCH AND RUTH RAPPAPORT,
GENEVA
PHOTOGRAPH: ISRAEL MUSEUM

August | 1 2 3 4 5 6 7 **8** 9 10 11 12 13 14 15 16 17 18 19 20 21 22 23 24 25 26 27 28 29 30 31

אב | א ב ג ד ה ו ז ח ט י יא יב יג יד טו טז יז יח יט כ כא כב כג כד כה כו כז כח כט ל

SUNDIAL (?)
KHIRBET QUMRAN
HELLENISTIC-ROMAN PERIOD,
1ST CENTURY BCE–1ST CENTURY CE

This sundial is believed to have been used by members of the Qumran sect for determining the hours of the day. The sectarians had a solar calendar, with a 364-day year. Since this calendar was not used by the bulk of the Jewish people at that time, the Qumran sectarians did not observe the festivals on the same days as the rest of the Jewish population.

LIMESTONE
14.5 CM (DIAMETER)
ISRAEL ANTIQUITIES AUTHORITY
PHOTOGRAPH: ISRAEL
MUSEUM/AVRAHAM HAY

August | 1 2 3 4 5 6 7 8 **9** 10 11 12 13 14 15 16 17 18 19 20 21 22 23 24 25 26 27 28 29 30 31

אב | א ב ג **ד** ה ו ז ח ט י יא יב יג יד טו טז יז יח יט כ כא כב כג כד כה כו כז כח כט ל

MAP OF THE HOLY LAND—THE PROMISED LAND, CA. 1630

GERARDUS MERCATOR, FLEMISH
(1512–1594)
AFTER ABRAHAM ORTELIUS,
FLEMISH (1527–1598)
AFTER LAICSTAIN-SCHROTT MAP
HAND-COLORED ENGRAVING
ON PAPER
36 X 50.2 CM
FROM: *GERARDUS MERCATOR,
ATLAS SIVE COSMOGRAPHICAE
MEDITATIONES,* JODOCUS HONDIUS,
LATIN EDITION, AMSTERDAM,
CA. 1630
NORMAN BIER SECTION FOR
MAPS OF THE HOLY LAND
M 795-3-55
PHOTOGRAPH: ISRAEL MUSEUM/
ILAN STZULMAN

This map exists in numerous variations. In 1556, the Dutch astronomer and cartographer Peter Laicstain visited the Holy Land and recorded what he saw; the Dutch cartographer Christian Schrott designed a map according to Laicstain's verbal description; and Abraham Ortelius copied the map shown here from Schrott's version, adding his own alterations. Ortelius was the student and heir of Mercator, who was considered the most prominent cartographer of the sixteenth century. The map, oriented to the east, depicts the Land of Israel on both sides of the Jordan. The craggy, indented coastline stretching from Beirut to Gaza is a product of the artist's imagination, as are the bends and curves in the river Jordan. The map cites places by their biblical and modern names, in a variety of types of script. The geographical symbols, too, integrate old and new. This is particularly so for the cities, which are drawn with different sizes and numbers of towers in accordance with their size, as was customary in ancient maps; alongside the towers are dots of different sizes, common in maps to this day. Sodom and Gomorrah, Adama and Seboim (Genesis 14 and 19) are indicated on the Dead Sea. The story of Jonah and the whale is depicted on the lower left.

August | 1 2 3 4 5 6 7 8 9 **10** 11 12 13 14 15 16 17 18 19 20 21 22 23 24 25 26 27 28 29 30 31

אב | א ב ג ד ה **ו** ז ח ט י יא יב יג יד טו טז יז יח יט כ כא כב כג כד כה כו כז כח כט ל

SYRIÆ
PARS

TERRA SANCTA
quæ in Sacris
Terra Promissionis ol:
PALESTINA

Moab

Desertum

PHILADELPHIA.

Moabitarum
Regio.

TERRA MACCES

PERÆA

Bazor
desert.

rhai

Bamoth vallis

MARE MORTUUM, SALSUM
sive SALIS, LACUS ASPHALTITIS

Olim vallis Salinarum, prædicatæ fæcunditatis & amænitatis.
Post autem Sodoma eversa, mutata est in illam sterilitatis
qua hodie conspicitur. Divinæ ultionis admiranda vestigia.

ITURÆA

REGNUM

TERRA · HUS.

GERASAEORUM

TRACHONITIS
REGIO

Gaulanitæ

Galilæa

Mare Galilææ vel
Tiberiadis quod
efferkin et Stagnu Gene-
zareth

Dimidia Tri-
bus Manasses

Acraba-
Topar chia
tenæ

Gomorra

Desertum Maon

Magnus campus Sa-
mariæ

CHA

NANÆI

GA

Neptalim

LI

GALILÆA SUPERIOR SEU
GENTI
UM

Tribus Zabu

lon

Tribus Ascr

PHOENI CIA

GALILÆA
INFERIOR

HEVAEI

Narbathæ toparchia

Isach ar.

A S A

MA

RI bus A

IUDAEA

Tribus Desertum Adomin

Benjamin

Vallis
Iosaphat

Sinæi

Tribus Iuda

Hierusalem

Iebusæi

Enachim

Tribus Simeon

IDUMÆA
RIOR

Solitudo

Bersabe

Desertum
arenosum

Vallis benedictio-
nis

MARIS

Mare Syriacum

ME

DI
TER

RA

NEI

PARS

Campus Capharsaba

Thamnatica

IDUMÆA

Philis

thijm

Statuette of a Bull
Dothan, Iron Age, 12th century bce

The bull is an ancient symbol of virility. This bronze statuette of a young
bull recalls the golden calf made by the Israelites in the desert (Exodus 32).

Bronze
12.4 cm (height)
Staff Archaeological Officer
in the Civil Administration
of Judea and Samaria
Photograph: Israel Museum/
David Harris

August | 1 2 3 4 5 6 7 8 9 10 **11** 12 13 14 15 16 17 18 19 20 21 22 23 24 25 26 27 28 29 30 31

א ב ג ד ה ו | ז ח ט י יא יב יג יד טו טז יז יח יט כ כא כב כג כד כה כו כז כח כט ל | **אב**

Sabbath candlesticks
Israel, 1988

Zelig Segal, a contemporary Israeli Judaica artist, creates original designs for traditional ritual objects in an innovative manner. According to tradition a Jewish woman lights two Sabbath lights every Friday night. Segal's candlesticks, entitled *In memory of the destruction of the Temple*, consist of three bent cylinders, one of them truncated and without a socket, giving expression to both religious and spiritual ideas.

Designer: Zelig Segal
Bent and fabricated silver
17.5 x 3.8 cm
Purchased through the
Eric Estorick Fund
Photograph: Israel Museum/
Nahum Slapak

August | 1 2 3 4 5 6 7 8 9 10 11 **12** 13 14 15 16 17 18 19 20 21 22 23 24 25 26 27 28 29 30 31

אב ‏| א ב ג ד ה ו **ז** ח ט י יא יב יג יד טו טז יז יח יט כ כא כב כג כד כה כו כז כח כט ל

De Castro Pentateuch, *Haftarot* and Five *Megillot* manuscript, Germany, 1344

Pen and ink, tempera, and silver leaf on parchment
Scribes: Levi ben David HaLevi and Netanel (ben) Daniel
46 x 31 cm
Acquired on the advice of Joseph and Caroline Gruss and with the assistance of friends of the Israel Museum at the Sassoon Collection Auction, Zurich, 1978
Photograph: Israel Museum/David Harris

The De Castro Pentateuch, completed in 1344, is a splendid example of a decorated and illustrated medieval Jewish manuscript, written in square Ashkenazi script. The decorative style and vivid colors are typical of Ashkenazi manuscripts of this period in their use of pen and ink and depiction of human, animal, and grotesque figures. This page, the first in the book of Deuteronomy, with its decorated initial word panel and silver leaf decoration, is framed by animals and grotesque figures and incorporates a commentary by Rashi on the text. The exact date of its completion is noted on the final page of the manuscript by the grammarian Levi ben David HaLevi, along with the name of the intended owner, Joseph ben Ephraim, who commissioned and paid for its preparation. The manuscript was in the possession of David Henriques de Castro of Amsterdam until 1899, when it was acquired by David Solomon Sassoon. One of the *megillot* contained in this manuscript is the Book of Lamentations read on this night in memory of the destruction of the Temple in Jerusalem.

August | 1 2 3 4 5 6 7 8 9 10 11 12 **13** 14 15 16 17 18 19 20 21 22 23 24 25 26 27 28 29 30 31

אב | א ב ג ד ה ו ז **ח** ט י יא יב יג יד טו טז יז יח יט כ כא כב כג כד כה כו כז כח כט ל

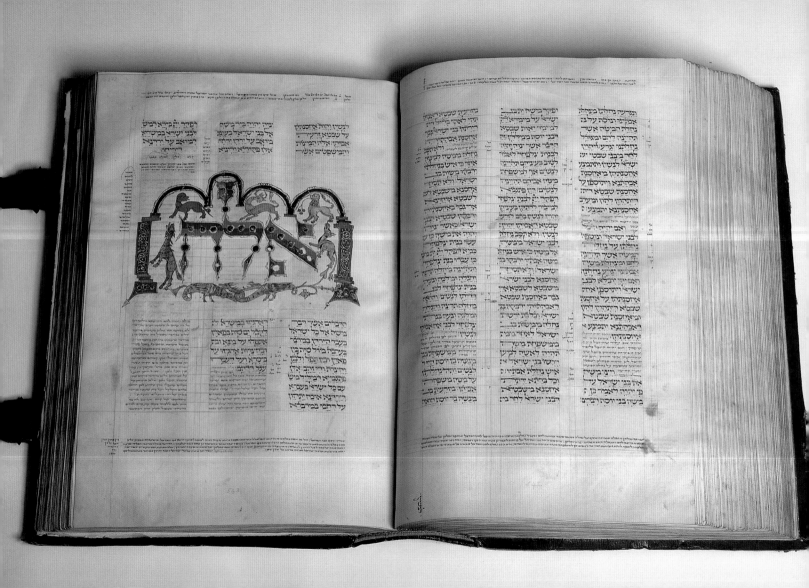

FIVE SCROLLS IN MICROGRAPHY
VIENNA, AUSTRIA, 1748

The master Jewish scribe Aaron Wolf Herlingen, born in Gewitch, Moravia, is known to have been employed as a calligrapher and scribe at the Imperial and Royal Library in Vienna. This single sheet is a masterpiece of micrography (minute script) and illustrated with vignettes of biblical scenes. It contains the Book of Ruth written in German in Gothic script, the Song of Songs in Latin, the Books of Ecclesiastes and Esther in Hebrew square and cursive scripts, and Lamentations in French. Herlingen's style belongs to the school of eighteenth-century Moravian manuscript illumination. On this day, the ninth of Av, a fast day, the Book of Lamentations is read in the synagogue in memory of the destruction of both Jerusalem Temples and the exile of the people of Israel (586 BCE and 70 CE).

August | 1 2 3 4 5 6 7 8 9 10 11 12 13 **14** 15 16 17 18 19 20 21 22 23 24 25 26 27 28 29 30 31

אב | א ב ג ד ה ו ז ח **ט** י יא יב יג יד טו טז יז יח יט כ כא כב כג כד כה כו כז כח כט ל

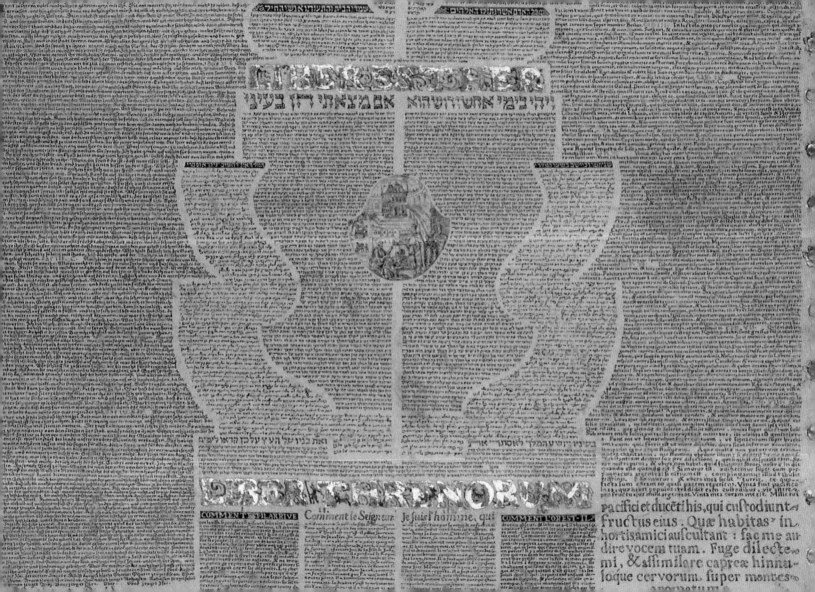

The Holy Land, known in the Scriptures as the Promised Land, formerly Palestine, 1629

WILLEM JANSZOON BLAEU,
DUTCH (1571–1638)
AFTER JODOCUS HONDIUS, JR.,
DUTCH, AFTER
LAIKSAIN-SGROOTEN MAP
HAND-COLORED ENGRAVING
ON PAPER
38.6 x 50.3 CM
FROM: THE FRENCH EDITION OF THE
ATLAS: *LE THÉÂTRE DU MONDE OU
NOUVEL ATLAS*, AMSTERDAM, 1640
NORMAN BIER SECTION FOR
MAPS OF THE HOLY LAND
GIFT OF KARL AND LI HANDLER,
VIENNA
P 1178-5-61
PHOTOGRAPH: ISRAEL MUSEUM/
ILAN STZULMAN

This west-oriented map depicts the Land of Israel on both banks of the river Jordan; the coastline extends from Tripoli in the north to the Nile delta in the south. Pharaoh and his armies are seen drowning in the parted Red Sea. Hatched lines trace the route of the Israelites' wanderings in the desert. The Jordan Valley and the Dead Sea are distorted and imaginary. A further common error is the Kishon River, which erroneously connects the Sea of Galilee and the Mediterranean. At the lower right, Moses and Aaron flank the cartouche, which is composed of Italian Renaissance–style ornamentation, imitating a stone plaque decorated with fruit and a globe. The compass rose, sea monsters, and the story of Jonah and the whale are shown in the sea.

August | 1 2 3 4 5 6 7 8 9 10 11 12 13 14 **15** 16 17 18 19 20 21 22 23 24 25 26 27 28 29 30 31

אב | א ב ג ד ה ו ז ח ט י יא יב יג יד טו טז יז יח יט כ כא כב כג כד כה כו כז כח כט ל

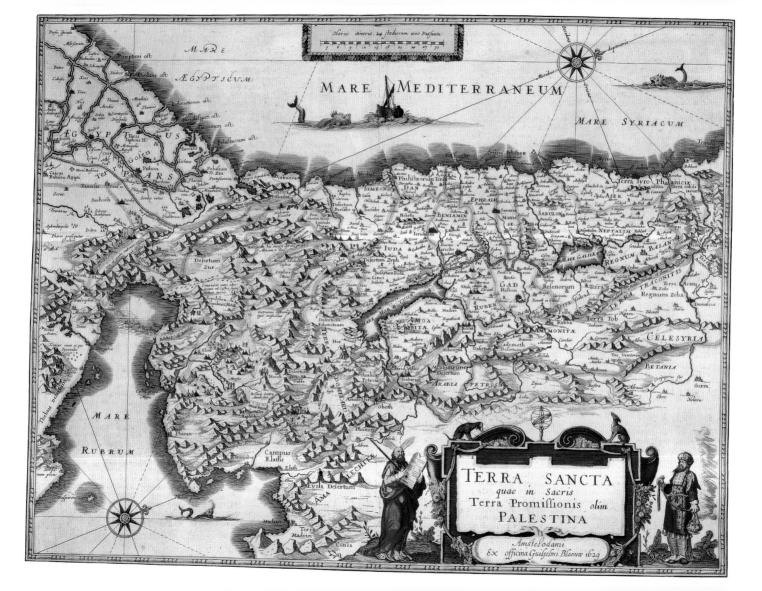

TERRA SANCTA
quae in Sacris
Terra Promissionis olim
PALESTINA

Amstelodami
Ex officina Guilielmi Blaeuw 1629

NECKLACE
SOUTHERN YEMEN,
LATE 19TH–EARLY 20TH CENTURY

This necklace, typical of southern Yemen, consists of seven strings of alternating silver and coral beads worn only on special occasions. Coral was very popular in Yemen because of its red color, considered to be a symbol of beauty, youth, and wealth. The small, tubular filigree charm cases with delicate pendants ensure the wearer's magical protection. The Austrian and Indian coins are an additional sign of wealth.

SILVER; CORAL; COINS;
GRANULATION; FILIGREE
45 X 34 CM
PHOTOGRAPH: ISRAEL MUSEUM/
ODED LOEBL

August | 1 2 3 4 5 6 7 8 9 10 11 12 13 14 15 **16** 17 18 19 20 21 22 23 24 25 26 27 28 29 30 31

אב | א ב ג ד ה ו ז ח ט **י׳** י׳ב י׳ג י׳ד ט׳ו ט׳ז י׳ז י׳ח י׳ט כ כ׳א כ׳ב כ׳ג כ׳ד כ׳ה כ׳ו כ׳ז כ׳ח כ׳ט ל

Planting a Young Orange Tree, 1930s

Citrus fruit became one of the main agricultural products produced by the many agricultural communities, *kibbutzim* and *moshavim*, that were established during the early twentieth century. Oranges and grapefruit fast became symbols of the successful Zionist agricultural program. In this photograph from the 1930s, we can see two young men planting a grove of young orange trees.

Yaacov Ben-Dov
(1882, Russia–1968, Israel),
immigrated to Eretz Israel, 1908
Gelatin silver print
Purchased with the help of
Rena (Fisch) and Robert Lewin,
London

August | 1 2 3 4 5 6 7 8 9 10 11 12 13 14 15 16 **17** 18 19 20 21 22 23 24 25 26 27 28 29 30 31

462

אב | א ב ג ד ה ו ז ח ט י יא **י'** יג יד טו טז יז יח יט כ כא כב כג כד כה כו כז כח כט ל

OSSUARY OF "JOSEPH SON OF CAIAPHAS"
JERUSALEM, SECOND TEMPLE PERIOD,
1ST CENTURY CE

Joseph Caiaphas, high priest in Jerusalem from 18 to 36 CE, is chiefly known for his involvement in the arrest of Jesus as described in the Gospels. This elaborately decorated ossuary was found in the burial cave of the Caiaphas clan in Jerusalem. The name "Joseph son of Caiaphas" is inscribed on it twice.

STONE
74 CM (LENGTH)
ISRAEL ANTIQUITIES AUTHORITY
PHOTOGRAPH: ISRAEL MUSEUM/
AVRAHAM HAY

August | 1 2 3 4 5 6 7 8 9 10 11 12 13 14 15 16 17 **18** 19 20 21 22 23 24 25 26 27 28 29 30 31

אב | א ב ג ד ה ו ז ח ט י י'א י'ב **ג'** יד טו טז יז יח יט כ כא כב כג כד כה כו כז כח כט ל

A World Map, 1571

The Spanish theologian, philosopher, and scientist Arias Montanus edited a polyglot edition of the Bible in Hebrew, Greek, Latin, and Syrian. Commissioned by King Philip II, this Bible was considered one of the most exquisite typographical documents of the Renaissance. The eighth and final volume, published in 1572, contained this map, two maps of the Holy Land, and a plan of Jerusalem in antiquity. Headed "A Biblical Geographical Map intended to facilitate explaining sacred texts," the map aims to illustrate, for example, the locations of Noah's descendants (Genesis 10). Most of the inscriptions are in Hebrew and Latin, including those accompanying the personified heads of the four winds.

August | 1 2 3 4 5 6 7 8 9 10 11 12 13 14 15 16 17 18 **19** 20 21 22 23 24 25 26 27 28 29 30 31

אב | א ב ג ד ה ו ז ח ט י יא יב יג **י'** טו טז יז יח יט כ כא כב כג כד כה כו כז כח כט ל

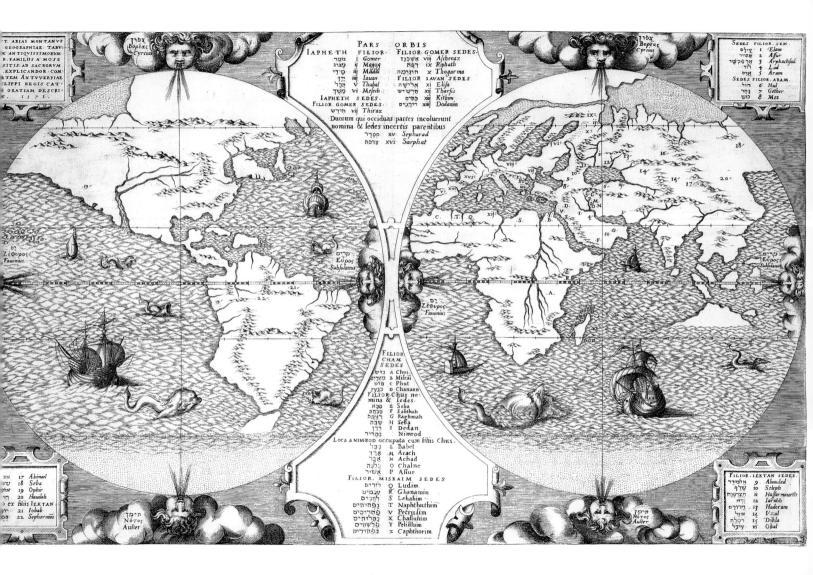

HOUSEHOLD POTS
CAUCASUS, 20TH CENTURY

The agricultural lifestyle of the peoples of the Caucasus forced them to prepare ahead for the harsh winters of the region. The whole community worked together to preserve meat, fruits, and vegetables using such pots. These clay water jars, plates, and vessels were used for various household tasks including warming food on the Sabbath, since they held heat for a long time.

CLAY
18.5–31 CM (HEIGHT)
PHOTOGRAPH: ISRAEL MUSEUM

August | 1 2 3 4 5 6 7 8 9 10 11 12 13 14 15 16 17 18 19 **20** 21 22 23 24 25 26 27 28 29 30 31

א ב ג ד ה ו ז ח ט י יא יב יג יד **טו** טז יז יח יט כ כא כב כג כד כה כו כז כח כט ל | **אב**

UNTITLED, 1930S

This unidentified photograph shows a group of children standing outside a building in the blinding sun. They are taking part in a ceremony and hold palm fronds in their hands. The occasion that has been eternalized by this photograph is not clear. It could be a harvest festival, end-of-year ceremony or play, or Sukkot, when palm fronds are used to make a roof for the *sukkah*.

YAACOV BEN-DOV
(1882, RUSSIA–1968, ISRAEL),
IMMIGRATED TO ERETZ ISRAEL, 1908
GELATIN SILVER PRINT
PURCHASED WITH THE HELP OF
RENA (FISCH) AND ROBERT LEWIN,
LONDON

August   1 2 3 4 5 6 7 8 9 10 11 12 13 14 15 16 17 18 19 20 **21** 22 23 24 25 26 27 28 29 30 31

אב ‎א ב ג ד ה ו ז ח ט י יא יב יג יד טו **טז** יז יח יט כ כא כב כג כד כה כו כז כח כט ל

Circumcision set
Prague, Bohemia, 1681

Circumcision is one of the basic precepts of the Jewish religion, recalling God's covenant with Abraham. A qualified circumciser (*mohel*) performs the ceremony (*brit milah*) on eight-day-old boys, using special implements. This flask and the knife, designed in a late-Renaissance style, bear a Hebrew inscription indicating the name of the owner, the year, and a verse of Psalms (119:162). The design, workmanship, and inscription indicate that the set was created by a master craftsman to "embellish the commandment" (Exodus 15:2).

REPOUSSÉ AND ENGRAVED GOLD;
ENGRAVED, CHASED, PIERCED,
AND CAST SILVER; STEEL
12.7 X 4.7 CM (FLASK)
17.5 X 2.3 CM (KNIFE)
THE STIEGLITZ COLLECTION WAS
DONATED TO THE ISRAEL MUSEUM,
JERUSALEM WITH THE
CONTRIBUTION OF ERICA AND
LUDWIG JESSELSON, NEW YORK,
THROUGH THE AMERICAN FRIENDS
OF THE ISRAEL MUSEUM
PHOTOGRAPH: ISRAEL MUSEUM/
AVI GANOR

August | 1 2 3 4 5 6 7 8 9 10 11 12 13 14 15 16 17 18 19 20 21 **22** 23 24 25 26 27 28 29 30 31

אב | א ב ג ד ה ו ז ח ט י יא יב יג יד טו טז **יז** יח יט כ כא כב כג כד כה כו כז כח כט ל

CHAIR OF ELIJAH
DERMBACH, GERMANY, 1768

The Chair of Elijah is a basic component of the circumcision ceremony throughout the Jewish world. These chairs are mostly tall and wide, and some have a double seat. On one of the two seats sat the *sandaq* (godfather), who held the child on his lap; the other seat was reserved for Elijah the prophet, traditionally believed to be present at every circumcision. On the back of the chair is a Hebrew inscription bearing the name of the person who commissioned it, Zelig Hendel Fach.

CARVED AND PAINTED WOOD
1100 X 1120 X 550 CM
THE FEUCHTWANGER COLLECTION
PURCHASED AND DONATED TO THE
ISRAEL MUSEUM BY BARUCH AND
RUTH RAPPAPORT OF GENEVA
PHOTOGRAPH: ISRAEL MUSEUM/
DAVID HARRIS

August | 1 2 3 4 5 6 7 8 9 10 11 12 13 14 15 16 17 18 19 20 21 22 **23** 24 25 26 27 28 29 30 31

אב | א ב ג ד ה ו ז ח ט י יא יב יג יד טו טז יז **יח** יט כ כא כב כג כד כה כו כז כח כט ל

Lintel decorated in relief
Synagogue(?) at Kokhav Hayarden, Byzantine Period, 4th–5th century ce

This is the left half of a large lintel that may have adorned the entrance to a synagogue. The drawing shows the reconstruction of the missing section. The lintel is decorated with a menorah flanked by two architectonic facades and two blank frames for dedicatory inscriptions. The facades symbolize the Temple and the synagogue Torah Ark.

Basalt
112 cm (length)
Israel Antiquities Authority
Photograph: Israel Museum
Drawing: Israel Museum/
Pnina Arad

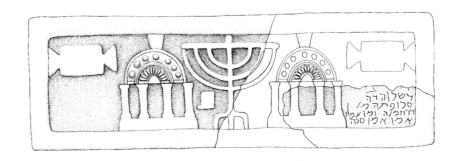

August | 1 2 3 4 5 6 7 8 9 10 11 12 13 14 15 16 17 18 19 20 21 22 23 **24** 25 26 27 28 29 30 31

אב | א ב ג ד ה ו ז ח ט י יא יב יג יד טו טז יז **יח** יט כ כא כב כג כד כה כו כז כח כט ל

Bulla of Berechiah, son of Neriah the Scribe
Provenance unknown, Iron Age, late 7th century BCE

This bulla (seal impression) once sealed a papyrus document. It bears the name of a scribe mentioned in the Bible (Jeremiah 36:4), who lived in Jerusalem and was the confidant of the prophet Jeremiah.

Clay
1.7 cm (height)
Gift of the Reuben and
Edith Hecht Trust
Photograph: Israel Museum/
Avraham Hay
Drawing: Israel Museum/
Pnina Arad

August | 1 2 3 4 5 6 7 8 9 10 11 12 13 14 15 16 17 18 19 20 21 22 23 24 **25** 26 27 28 29 30 31

א ב ג ד ה ו ז ח ט י יא יב יג יד טו טז יז יח יט **כ** כא כב כג כד כה כו כז כח כט ל | אב

478

THE JUDEAN HILLS, CA. 1970

Of her first impressions of Eretz Israel, Anna Ticho said, "When I speak of Israel, I really mean Jerusalem.... When I came to Israel I was impressed by the grandeur of the scenery, the bare hills, the large, ancient olive trees and the cleft slopes.... I was dumbfounded and overcome with emotion." The harsh landscape burned yellow by the blazing sun and the colors flattened and bleached in the strong light had a paralyzing effect on the artist, who returned to painting only after many years of living in Jerusalem. This charcoal and pastel drawing depicts the hills around the city at the height of summer, with scorched and dry vegetation dotting the rolling slopes empty of all signs of habitation. The only color other than browns and yellows, is the pale blue of the cloud resting low in the sky.

ANNA TICHO
(1894, BRNO–1980, ISRAEL)
CHARCOAL AND PASTEL ON PAPER
67 X 90.2 CM
BEQUEST OF ANNA TICHO,
JERUSALEM
1157.85
PHOTOGRAPH: ISRAEL MUSEUM

August | 1 2 3 4 5 6 7 8 9 10 11 12 13 14 15 16 17 18 19 20 21 22 23 24 25 **26** 27 28 29 30 31

ל כט כח כז כו כה כד כג כב **כא** כ יט יח יז טז טו יד יג יב יא י ט ח ז ו ה ד ג ב א | אב

PRAYER STAND
SAN'A, YEMEN, 18TH CENTURY

This portable Yemenite prayer stand (*tevah*) on which the Torah scrolls were placed to be read in the synagogue usually stood next to the Ark in a niche in the northern wall oriented in the direction of Jerusalem. The *tevah* was moved to the center of the synagogue when the Torah was read. This is the older of only two known surviving decorated *tevot* from San'a. The style of this *tevah* is reminiscent of Islamic prayer stands, and also similar to the style of doorways and lattice balconies in San'a.

CARVED AND PAINTED WOOD
100 X 34 X 30 CM
PURCHASED WITH THE HELP
OF FLORENCE AND
SYLVAIN J. STEINBERG, JERUSALEM
PHOTOGRAPH: ISRAEL MUSEUM/
DAVID HARRIS

August | 1 2 3 4 5 6 7 8 9 10 11 12 13 14 15 16 17 18 19 20 21 22 23 24 25 26 **27** 28 29 30 31

א ב ג ד ה ו ז ח ט י יא יב יג יד טו טז יז יח יט כ כא **כב** כג כד כה כו כז כח כט ל ‎ אב

Mosaic floor featuring rabbinic laws Synagogue at Rehov, Beth Shean Valley, Byzantine Period, 6th century ce

Exceptional in size and unique in content, this mosaic inscription covered the floor of the narthex (entrance room) of the synagogue at Rehov, south of Beth Shean. Written in Hebrew and Aramaic, it is a compilation of rabbinic laws from the Palestinian Talmud regarding the sabbatical year, tithes, and priestly dues. These obligations had to be kept within the "boundaries of the Land of Israel." Thus the inscription specifies these boundaries in great detail and lists the other places with Jewish populations where the laws had to be followed. It also records the agricultural products to which the laws apply.

Stone
430 cm (width)
Israel Antiquities Authority
Photograph: Israel Museum

August 1 2 3 4 5 6 7 8 9 10 11 12 13 14 15 16 17 18 19 20 21 22 23 24 25 26 27 **28** 29 30 31

אב א ב ג ד ה ו ז ח ט י יא יב יג יד טו טז יז יח יט כ כא כב **כג** כד כה כו כז כח כט ל

Stone table and bowl
Jerusalem, Second Temple Period,
1st century BCE–1st century CE

The stone-carving industry that flourished in Jerusalem in the late Second Temple period produced a wide range of furniture and vessels of different shapes and sizes and varying degrees of elaboration. The widespread use of stoneware may be explained by the fact that stone vessels cannot become impure according to the Jewish laws of purity.

August | 1 2 3 4 5 6 7 8 9 10 11 12 13 14 15 16 17 18 19 20 21 22 23 24 25 26 27 28 **29** 30 31

אב | א ב ג ד ה ו ז ח ט י יא יב יג יד טו טז יז יח יט כ כא כב כג כד כה כו כז כח כט ל

MIZRAH
POLAND, 1882

The *mizrah* (literally: east) is a single sheet or plaque, a drawing on paper or parchment that sometimes bore cut-out work, which was hung on an eastern wall in the house, facing Jerusalem, to indicate the direction of prayer. This papercut *mizrah* signed by the maker Israel Milman is densely illustrated and in the center contains a depiction of the Ten Commandments.

PAPERCUT; PEN AND INK;
WATERCOLORS
34 X 41 CM
GIFT OF ELIEZER BURSTEIN
COLLECTION, LUGANO, SWITZERLAND
PHOTOGRAPH: ISRAEL MUSEUM

August │ 1 2 3 4 5 6 7 8 9 10 11 12 13 14 15 16 17 18 19 20 21 22 23 24 25 26 27 28 29 **30** 31

א ב ג ד ה ו ז ח ט י יא יב יג יד טו טז יז יח יט כ כא כב כג כד **כה** כו כז כח כט ל │ אב

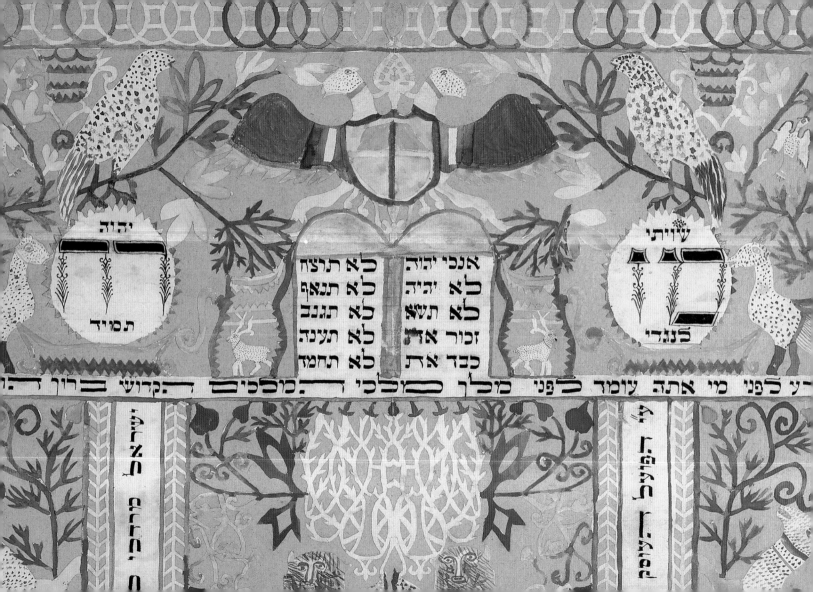

יהוה
תמיד

שׁוּיתִי
לנגדי

לא תרצח · אנכי יהוה
לא תנאף · לא יהיה
לא תגנב · לא תשא
לא תענה · זכור את
לא תחמד · כבד את

...ע לפני מי אתה עומד לפני מלך מלכי המלכים הקדוש ברוך ה...

Model shrine
Mount Nebo, Iron Age,
9th–8th century bce

The facade of this miniature shrine brings to mind the entrance to Solomon's Temple in Jerusalem, which according to the Bible was flanked by two columns, named Jachin and Boaz (I Kings 7:21).

Pottery
29 cm (height)
Gift of the Reuben and Edith
Hecht Trust, Haifa
Photograph: Israel Museum/
Yoram Lehmann

August | 1 2 3 4 5 6 7 8 9 10 11 12 13 14 15 16 17 18 19 20 21 22 23 24 25 26 27 28 29 30 31

490

אב | א ב ג ד ה ו ז ח ט י יא יב יג יד טו טז יז יח יט כ כא כב כג כד כה כו כז כח כט ל

SCARF
SAN'A, YEMEN, EARLY 20TH CENTURY

A married Jewish woman from San'a would drape a square scarf over her hood
when she went outdoors. It would cover her head, shoulders, and part of her back.
Whenever a man crossed her path she would conceal the lower part of her face
with the scarf, a custom that probably was influenced by the Muslim woman's
veiling of her entire face.

DYED AND BLOCK-PRINTED COTTON
120 X 82 CM
PHOTOGRAPH: ISRAEL MUSEUM/
DAVID HARRIS

September | 1 2 3 4 5 6 7 8 9 10 11 12 13 14 15 16 17 18 19 20 21 22 23 24 25 26 27 28 29 30

אב | א ב ג ד ה ו ז ח ט י יא יב יג יד טו טז יז יח יט כ כא כב כג כד כה כו כז כח כט ל

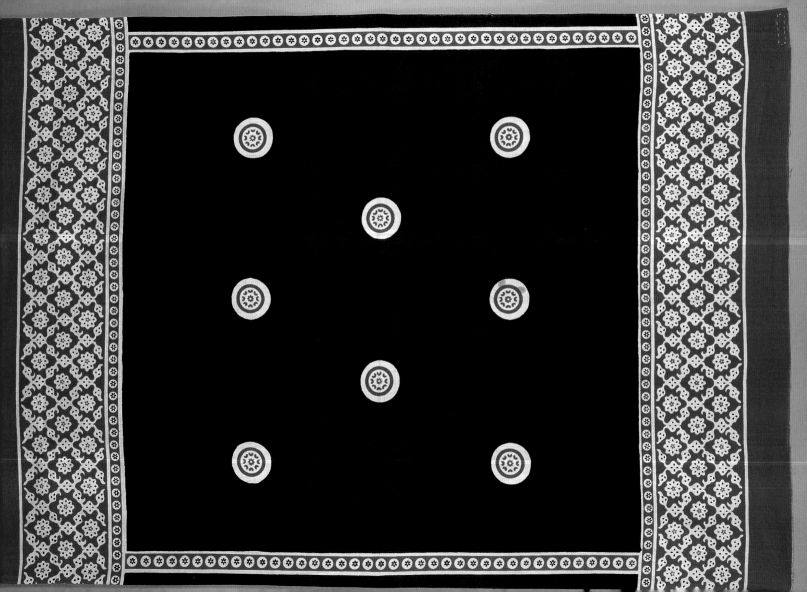

THE FIRST PLOWING OF THE EIN HAROD VALLEY, 1928

Rather than taking a photograph of the agriculture in the Ein Harod Valley during the summer, Schweig waited until autumn, when the clouds gave the image an especially dramatic effect. They sit low and heavy in the sky, building up to the first rains. On the ground, the farm workers race to finish their work before the drops begin to fall.

S. J. Schweig
(1905, Austria–1984, Israel),
immigrated to Eretz Israel, 1923
Gelatin silver print
Bequest of the artist

STONE KITCHENWARE
SA'DAH, YEMEN, EARLY 20TH CENTURY

It was, and partly still is, customary in all parts of Yemen to use stoneware of various shapes for food. Ancient predecessors to these vessels with a similar "prehistoric" look have been uncovered in archaeological sites on the Arabian Peninsula. Besides enhancing the taste of the food cooked in them, they also held the heat for a long time, making them suitable for use on the Sabbath, when the oven could not be rekindled.

GRAY SOAPSTONE
25 CM (HEIGHT), 18 CM (DIAMETER)
5 CM (HEIGHT), 12.5 CM (DIAMETER)
7 CM (HEIGHT), 20.5 CM (DIAMETER)
19.5 CM (HEIGHT), 49 CM (DIAMETER)
PHOTOGRAPH: ISRAEL MUSEUM

September | 1 2 **3** 4 5 6 7 8 9 10 11 12 13 14 15 16 17 18 19 20 21 22 23 24 25 26 27 28 29 30

אב | א ב ג ד ה ו ז ח ט י יא יב יג יד טו טז יז יח יט כ כא כב כג כד כה כו כז כח **כט** ל

Torah shields
Turkey, 19th–20th century

Turkish Torah scrolls were usually covered by a mantle and decorated with crowns, finials, and shields. The shields are of unusual geometric forms and function mainly as decorative objects, often with dedicatory inscriptions, unlike the traditional Ashkenazi shields. The round Torah shield in the center was originally the back of a mirror; when it was donated to the synagogue, a Hebrew inscription was affixed to its front. The practice of reusing everyday objects and converting them into ritual objects is widespread among different Jewish communities.

Repoussé and punched silver
Photograph: Israel Museum/
Yoram Lehmann

September | 1 2 3 **4** 5 6 7 8 9 10 11 12 13 14 15 16 17 18 19 20 21 22 23 24 25 26 27 28 29 30

א ב ג ד ה ו ז ח ט י יא יב יג יד טו טז יז יח יט כ כא כב כג כד כה כו כז כח כט ל | אב

Regensburg Pentateuch manuscript
Bavaria, Germany, ca. 1300

The Regensburg Pentateuch, written in square and cursive Ashkenazi script, was executed for R. Gad ben Peter ha-Levi of Regensburg, who was head of the community. These pages show Aaron the High Priest wearing a long robe lighting the Tabernacle menorah wearing a breastplate inscribed with the names of the twelve tribes together with an array of implements of the Tabernacle. In both the Ashkenazi and Sephardi traditions the seven-branched menorah serves as a symbol of the Temple to be rebuilt in Jerusalem in future days. This depiction of the vessels of the Temple was influenced by similar Sephardi arrangements, although the style of drawings and colors are typical of Southern Germany.

Pen and ink, tempera,
and gold leaf on vellum
24.5 x 18.5 cm
Photograph: Israel Museum/
David Harris

September | 1 2 3 4 **5** 6 7 8 9 10 11 12 13 14 15 16 17 18 19 20 21 22 23 24 25 26 27 28 29 30

אלול | **א** ב ג ד ה ו ז ח ט י יא יב יג יד טו טז יז יח יט כ כא כב כג כד כה כו כז כח כט

יעשׂית יהרו עני שפים ויעקרין יהק יקנ · ויהי קרשים יושו ובמ פאמיעלה כככב בנבהרם עמשׂל
הפרק רעביהכ · איש אל אחזיר אל הכנה זה הכנה · ויעבביהי הם פ... ברב פרישׂים כנב...נ אהל

ברבה ... מחרה מחרה השבע · שליחו נפעכ...ורד
...כבם מיענ... ... ... מאורה כברויה יפרה כן לשׂובתה דקשׂו ...ה...ליב...ן
הכ...זה

Ivory pomegranate
Jerusalem, Iron Age, mid-8th century bce

This thumb-sized pomegranate is the only known relic from Solomon's Temple in Jerusalem. It was probably the head of a ceremonial scepter used by the Temple priests.

4.3 CM (HEIGHT)
ACQUIRED WITH A DONATION BY A
FRIEND OF CULTURE IN ISRAEL,
BASEL, SWITZERLAND
PHOTOGRAPH: ISRAEL MUSEUM/
NAHUM SLAPAK

September | 1 2 3 4 5 **6** 7 8 9 10 11 12 13 14 15 16 17 18 19 20 21 22 23 24 25 26 27 28 29 30

אלול | א **ב** ג ד ה ו ז ח ט י יא יב יג יד טו טז יז יח יט כ כא כב כג כד כה כו כז כח כט

MAP OF ASIA IN THE SHAPE OF A WINGED HORSE (PEGASUS), 1594

Bünting was a senior Protestant clergyman; his book was an Old and New Testament presented as an illustrated travelogue. It opens with the famous clover-leaf map of the world, with Jerusalem at the center, and includes other maps, such as "Europe" in the image of a woman wearing a crown, and two views of the holy Temple. In this imaginary map, Judea and Jerusalem are located on the horse's breast, the Caspian Sea rests between its wings and the saddle, and India is situated on its hind leg. Pegasus was the mythical son of Poseidon and Medusa, and his image was connected with the fountain of the Muses. The map vividly illustrates the artistic aspect of the synthesis of science and art in cartography, representing the genre known as cartographical curiosities.

HEINRICH BÜNTING, GERMAN
(1545–1606)
HAND-COLORED WOODCUT
ON PAPER
26.2 x 36.4 CM
FROM: HEINRICH BÜNTING,
ITINERARIUM SACRAE SCRIPTURAE,
AMBROSII KIRCHNER,
MAGDEBURG, 1594
NORMAN BIER SECTION FOR
MAPS OF THE HOLY LAND
GIFT OF NORMAN AND
FRIEDA BIER, LONDON
B 95.0650D
PHOTOGRAPH: ISRAEL MUSEUM/
ILAN STZULMAN

September | 1 2 3 4 5 6 **7** 8 9 10 11 12 13 14 15 16 17 18 19 20 21 22 23 24 25 26 27 28 29 30

אלול | ג ב א ד ה ו ז ח ט י יא יב יג יד טו טז יז יח יט כ כא כב כג כד כה כו כז כח כט

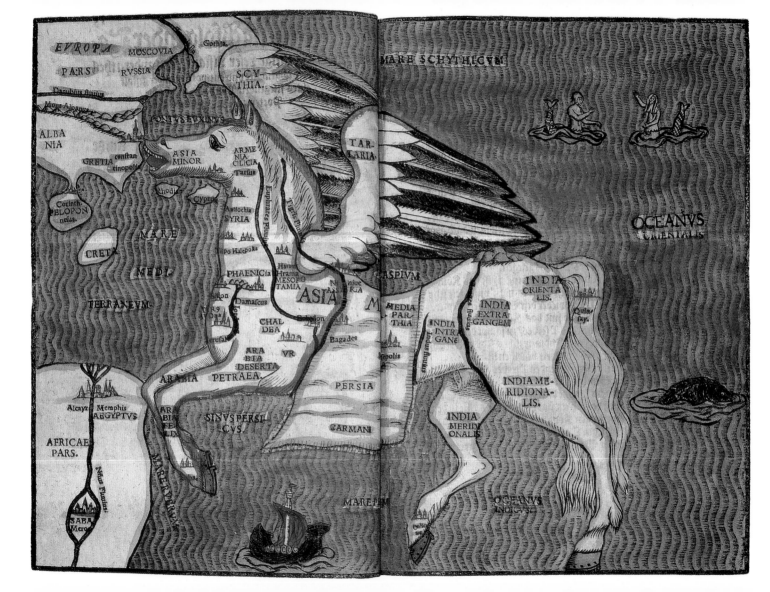

EVROPA
PARS
MOSCOVIA
RVSSIA
Danubius fluuius
Mons Albanus
ALBANIA
GRETIA constantinopolis
CORINTH. PLOPONnesus.
CRETA
MARE MEDI. TERRANEVM
PONTVS EVXINVS
ASIA MINOR
Rhodi
Cypru
ARME NIA CILICIA
Tarsus
Antiochia
SYRIA
Alepo Halepol?
PHAENICIA
Sidon
Damascus
Tyrus?
Ierusale
CHAL DEA
ARA BIA DESERTA
ARABIA PETRAEA.
Alcayr Memphis ABGYPTVS
AFRICAE PARS.
ARA BIA FEE LIX.
SINVS PERSI CVS.
SABA Meroe
Nilus Fluuius
MARE RVBRVM
MARE PM
SCY THIA.
TARTARIA
Euphrates fluuius
Tigris fluuius
Hauan Hram MESOPO TAMIA
Niniue ASSYRIA
ASIA
VR
Bagades
Babilon
Persepolis
PERSIA
CARMANI
MARE SCYTHICVM
OCEANVS ORIENTALIS
CASPIVM
MEDIA PAR THIA
INDIA INTRA GANE
INDIA EXTRA GANGEM
INDIA ORIENTA LIS.
Quinsay.
Bizinga fluuius
Ganges fluuius
INDIA MERIDIONA LIS.
INDIA MERIDIONALIS.
OCEANVS INDICVS

Scale pans
Hebron region, Iron Age,
12th–6th century BCE

Scales are frequently mentioned in the Bible. The silver or gold to be weighed was placed in one pan and balanced by the stone weights in the other.

Bronze
6 cm (diameter)
Photograph: Israel Museum/
Avraham Hay

September | 1 2 3 4 5 6 7 **8** 9 10 11 12 13 14 15 16 17 18 19 20 21 22 23 24 25 26 27 28 29 30

אלול | א ב ג **ד** ה ו ז ח ט י יא יב יג יד טו טז יז יח יט כ כא כב כג כד כה כו כז כח כט

MEMENTO MORI
GERMANY OR POLAND, 19TH CENTURY

Papercut sheets were hung in Jewish homes, serving a variety of purposes connected to religious needs. Although decorative papercuts share similarities, they have a recognizable style and geographic origin. Generally cut with a sharp knife, they were often very elaborate. Their compositions were usually symmetrical (as in this example). This papercut has a Hebrew inscription in the central medallion evoking the inevitability of death:

> If you seek in the world a place to settle,
> And even tie yourself to it with a rope,
> Know that all is for nought
> If to your soul you would give direction,
> Do not do evil to anyone
> For there is no man whose hour will not come.

PAPERCUT; PEN AND INK; WATERCOLORS
145 X 189 CM
THE FEUCHTWANGER COLLECTION
PURCHASED AND DONATED TO THE
ISRAEL MUSEUM BY BARUCH AND
RUTH RAPPAPORT OF GENEVA.
PHOTOGRAPH: ISRAEL MUSEUM/
DAVID HARRIS

September | 1 2 3 4 5 6 7 8 **9** 10 11 12 13 14 15 16 17 18 19 20 21 22 23 24 25 26 27 28 29 30

אלול ‏| א ב ג ד ‏**ה** ו ז ח ט י יא יב יג יד טו טז יז יח יט כ כא כב כג כד כה כו כז כח כט

אם תבקש
מהתבלי נחלה וחבל
ואת תקשר בה בכבל
דע כי הנה הכל הבל:
אם לנפשך שמה דעה · אל
תעשה עם שום אדם רעה ·
כי אין לך אדם שאין
לו שעה:

FIVE TORAH POINTERS
VARIOUS COUNTRIES, 18TH–EARLY 20TH CENTURY

Torah pointers enable the reader of the Torah scroll to follow the correct reading of the text without touching the parchment because of the Torah's sanctity. These pointers, traditionally fashioned in the shape of a hand, are from different countries and show a wide variety in design and style.

LEFT TO RIGHT:
RHODES, GREECE, 1917
ENGRAVED AND CAST SILVER;
GILT THREAD TASSEL

GERMANY, 18TH CENTURY
ENGRAVED AND CAST SILVER

VIENNA, AUSTRIA-HUNGARY,
19TH CENTURY
REPOUSSÉ AND CAST SILVER

ITALY, 18TH CENTURY
PIERCED SILVER; CORAL

IRAN, LATE 19TH CENTURY
CAST, PIERCED, AND ENGRAVED SILVER
PHOTOGRAPH: ISRAEL MUSEUM

September | 1 2 3 4 5 6 7 8 9 **10** 11 12 13 14 15 16 17 18 19 20 21 22 23 24 25 26 27 28 29 30

אלול | א ב ג ד ה ו | ז ח ט י יא יב יג יד טו טז יז יח יט כ כא כב כג כד כה כו כז כח כט

King David playing the lyre on a mosaic floor fragment
Synagogue at Gaza, Mediterranean coast, Byzantine Period, 6th century CE

This section of the mosaic floor that decorated the synagogue at Gaza depicts King David as Orpheus, the mythological hero whose music surpassed that of all mortals. David is represented seated on a throne, his crowned head encircled by a halo. He holds a lyre in his lap and is surrounded by an audience of animals enchanted by his playing. To the right of his head is the Hebrew legend "David."

Stone
300 cm (height)
Staff Archaeological Officer
in the Civil Administration
of Judea and Samaria
Photograph: Israel Museum

September | 1 2 3 4 5 6 7 8 9 10 **11** 12 13 14 15 16 17 18 19 20 21 22 23 24 25 26 27 28 29 30

אלול | א ב ג ד ה ו **ז** ח ט י יא יב יג יד טו טז יז יח יט כ כא כב כג כד כה כו כז כח כט

Pedestal decorated with a menorah
Synagogue at Ashkelon, Mediterranean coast, Byzantine Period, 5th–6th century ce

Most synagogues of the Byzantine period in Israel had a main hall and two side aisles, separated from the hall by rows of columns. This pedestal was the base of one such column. The menorah is flanked by a shofar and incense shovel.

Marble
70 cm (height)
Israel Antiquities Authority
Photograph: Israel Museum

September | 1 2 3 4 5 6 7 8 9 10 11 **12** 13 14 15 16 17 18 19 20 21 22 23 24 25 26 27 28 29 30

אלול | א ב ג ד ה ו ז **ח** ט י יא יב יג יד טו טז יז יח יט כ כא כב כג כד כה כו כז כח כט

MEZUZAH CASES
VARIOUS PLACES, 19TH AND 20TH CENTURY

LEFT TO RIGHT:
GERMANY, 19TH CENTURY
ENGRAVED, REPOUSSÉ, AND
PIERCED SILVER

CENTRAL EUROPE, 19TH CENTURY
ENGRAVED SILVER

SLOVAKIA, 19TH CENTURY
CARVED WOOD

GERMANY, EARLY 19TH CENTURY
CARVED WOOD

BOMBAY, INDIA, 19TH CENTURY
CAST BRASS

UNITED STATES, 20TH CENTURY
PIERCED SILVER
ARTIST: LUDWIG WOLPERT
11.2–28.5 CM (HEIGHT)

A mezuzah is a piece of parchment inscribed by an expert scribe with biblical verses from Deuteronomy (6:4–11, 13–21). The parchment is rolled up, placed in a case, and fixed to the right-hand doorpost in each room of the house according to the biblical injunction: "And thou shalt write them upon the doorposts of thy house, and on thy gates" (Deuteronomy 6:9). Mezuzah cases are made from various materials, and styles and design vary according to local traditions and taste. The mezuzah is believed to have protective powers because of the Divine name visible on it and the text inside.

GIFT OF E. BURSTEIN COLLECTION, LUGANO, SWITZERLAND
THE STIEGLITZ COLLECTION WAS DONATED TO THE ISRAEL MUSEUM,
JERUSALEM WITH THE CONTRIBUTION OF ERICA AND LUDWIG JESSELSON,
NEW YORK, THROUGH THE AMERICAN FRIENDS OF THE ISRAEL MUSEUM
GIFT OF MR. AND MRS. VICTOR CARTER, LOS ANGELES, USA
GIFT OF MR. AND MRS. ABRAHAM KANOFF, NEW YORK, USA
PHOTOGRAPH: ISRAEL MUSEUM/AVI GANOR

September | 1 2 3 4 5 6 7 8 9 10 11 12 **13** 14 15 16 17 18 19 20 21 22 23 24 25 26 27 28 29 30

אלול | א ב ג ד ה ו ז ח **ט** י יא יב יג יד טו טז יז יח יט כ כא כב כג כד כה כו כז כח כט

AUTUMN LANDSCAPE, 1973

Anna Ticho immigrated to Eretz Israel with her husband, the ophthalmologist Dr. Albert Ticho, in 1912. Although she had painted before coming to live in Jerusalem, the new environment—barren and harsh, in stark contrast to the soft, verdant landscape of central Europe—astounded her, and it took time for her to pick up the brush again. When she did, it was the local landscape that was her inspiration. She drew faithfully from nature in the hills and other areas surrounding Jerusalem, sometimes venturing to Jericho and Tiberias as well.

ANNA TICHO
(1894, BRNO–1980, ISRAEL)
CHARCOAL AND PASTEL ON PAPER
61.5 X 83 CM
BEQUEST OF ANNA TICHO,
JERUSALEM
434.80
PHOTOGRAPH: ISRAEL MUSEUM

September | 1 2 3 4 5 6 7 8 9 10 11 12 13 **14** 15 16 17 18 19 20 21 22 23 24 25 26 27 28 29 30

אלול א ב ג ד ה ו ז ח ט 'י יא יב יג יד טו טז יז יח יט כ כא כב כג כד כה כו כז כח כט

BRACELETS (MANIA DE ČATÓN)
NECKLACE (*OGADÉRO*)
OTTOMAN EMPIRE, LATE 19TH CENTURY

This necklace (*ogadéro*) and pair of *mania de čatón* bracelets formed a set, part of the traditional costume of Jewish women of Izmir, Rhodes, and Jerusalem. A man would give the valuable set of jewelry to his wife, and she would keep it for years, until it was time to sell it in order to purchase a burial plot.

BRACELETS:
STAMPED GOLD WITH LINK CHAINS
LEFT TO RIGHT: 17 X 18.2, 20 X 8.5 CM
PURCHASED BY COURTESY OF
JACQUES LEVY, BARCELONA
PHOTOGRAPH: ISRAEL MUSEUM/
NAHUM SLAPAK

NECKLACE:
STAMPED AND HAMMERED GOLD
40 X 4.7 CM
PURCHASED THROUGH
THE GENEROSITY OF
YOSSI BENYAMINOFF, NEW YORK
PHOTOGRAPH: ISRAEL MUSEUM/
ODED LOEBL

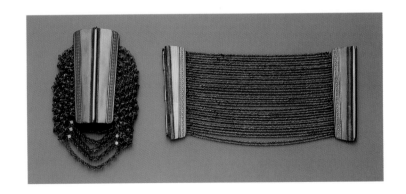

September | 1 2 3 4 5 6 7 8 9 10 11 12 13 14 **15** 16 17 18 19 20 21 22 23 24 25 26 27 28 29 30

אלול | א ב ג ד ה ו ז ח ט י **י״א** י״ב י״ג י״ד ט״ו ט״ז י״ז י״ח י״ט כ כ״א כ״ב כ״ג כ״ד כ״ה כ״ו כ״ז כ״ח כ״ט

Men's skullcaps
Herat, Mazar-e Sharif, and Kabul,
Afghanistan, early 20th century–1970s

According to the Code of Jewish Law, a head covering is the sign of a God-fearing Jew. Although there is no such precept in the Torah, the custom for men to cover their heads developed over time into an obligation. In Afghanistan, the men wore a wide range of silk or colorful cotton skullcaps, embroidered by Uzbek or Turkomen embroiderers. A silk turban was usually wrapped around the cap.

September | 1 2 3 4 5 6 7 8 9 10 11 12 13 14 15 **16** 17 18 19 20 21 22 23 24 25 26 27 28 29 30

אלול | א ב ג ד ה ו ז ח ט י **י"א** י"ב **י"ג** י"ד ט"ו ט"ז י"ז י"ח י"ט כ כ"א כ"ב כ"ג כ"ד כ"ה כ"ו כ"ז כ"ח כ"ט

Decoration for a Torah Ark
Parur, India, 1891

A depiction of a menorah with vegetal motifs on either side is prominent in this detail from the upper part of a Torah Ark. This image is based on the prophet Zechariah's vision of a golden menorah being filled with oil flanked by two olive trees—an allegory of the Temple, thus alluding to the messianic prophecy of its reconstruction. The plants shown here are mistakenly depicted as bunches of grapes, as olive trees were unknown in India. The entire scene is framed by an arch inscribed with a quotation from the book of Zechariah.

Carved teak
480 x 287 cm
Photograph: Israel Museum

September | 1 2 3 4 5 6 7 8 9 10 11 12 13 14 15 16 **17** 18 19 20 21 22 23 24 25 26 27 28 29 30

אלול | ג׳ א ב ג ד ה ו ז ח ט י יא יב׳ יד טו טז יז יח יט כ כא כב כג כד כה כו כז כח כט

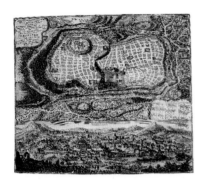

MATTHAEUS SEUTTER,
GERMAN (1678–1757)
HAND-COLORED ETCHING
ON PAPER
50 x 58.2 CM
FROM: MATTHAEUS SEUTTER,
GROSSER ATLAS, AUGSBURG, CA. 1734
NORMAN BIER SECTION FOR
MAPS OF THE HOLY LAND
GIFT OF KARL AND LI HANDLER,
VIENNA
P1165-5-61
PHOTOGRAPH: ISRAEL MUSEUM/
ILAN STZULMAN

ANCIENT JERUSALEM AND MODERN JERUSALEM, CA. 1734

In surprising juxtaposition, an imaginary "historical" map of Jerusalem from above by the Spanish geographer and cleric Juan Bautista Villalpando (1551–1608) is shown above a contemporaneous realistic bird's-eye-view map of the city by the Swiss etcher and publisher Matthäus Merian (1593–1650). Although Villalpando's map is imaginary, it is based in scripture, and particularly on the writings of Josephus Flavius. The city is divided into two sections: the western part, at the left, Mt. Zion with the Citadel at its crest; at the right, the Temple, Ophel, Bezeta, "Stadt Salem," Milo, and the Akra. Only sites of special importance are depicted. The city streets are drawn in a kind of grid. The engraver and publisher Seutter copied most of his maps from Dutch and French cartographers, often neglecting to cite his sources. In printing the two maps together, he apparently intended to present a complete view from two different periods.

September | 1 2 3 4 5 6 7 8 9 10 11 12 13 14 15 16 17 **18** 19 20 21 22 23 24 25 26 27 28 29 30

א ב ג ד ה ו ז ח ט י יא יב יג **י'** טו טז יז יח יט כ כא כב כג כד כה כו כז כח כט ‏אלול

Feld Lager

Der Brunn
vom Berg
Gion

Der Berber
Acker

Die Trappe

Der obere
Weyer

Das
Castell

6

5

Das Haus Asariæ

Haus Euaur

Garten des Königs

Die Burg Maspha

Stat David

Der obere
Marck

Renplatz

Palast vom Berg Sion

Gefängnis

Garten

Der Konigs Weer

Das König Wasser
leitung

Richt Platz

Berg
Calvariæ

Der Pilge
Acker

Palast Herodis

Haus von Anna

Salomons Tempel
Der Saal das Haus Pilati

Bach Kidron

Thal Iosaphat

Berg Horeb

Berg Goliath

DER BERG ACRA

DIE STADT SALEM

Antiog. Schloß

MELCHISEDECHS

Das Roht Meer

Das Spielhaus

Das Haus Herodis

Holtz
Marck

Der Fisch
Marck

Das Fisch
Thor

Jewelry from Burial Caves
Jerusalem, Iron Age, 7th–6th century bce

"I decked you out in finery and put bracelets on your arms and a chain around your neck. I put a ring in your nose and earrings in your ears" (Ezekiel 16:11–12).

Silver; carnelian; glass
Israel Antiquities Authority
Photograph: Israel Museum

Chancel screen
Synagogue at Hammat Gader, Golan Heights, Byzantine Period, 6th century ce

This chancel screen, decorated in relief, features a wreath set within rectangular frames, with a menorah in the center and ivy leaves below. It is interesting to note that some of the chancel screens used in the churches of this period are practically identical to those used in the synagogues, the only difference being that they feature crosses instead of menorahs. Both types were probably manufactured in the same workshops.

Marble
100 cm (width)
Israel Antiquities Authority
Photograph: Israel Museum/
Avraham Hay

September | 1 2 3 4 5 6 7 8 9 10 11 12 13 14 15 16 17 18 19 **20** 21 22 23 24 25 26 27 28 29 30

אלול | א ב ג ד ה ו ז ח ט י יא יב יג יד **טו** **טז** יז יח יט כ כא כב כג כד כה כו כז כח כט

Incense burners
San'a and Sa'dah, Yemen, 19th century

Incense was traditionally used to scent the air in the Middle East, especially in Yemen, where it had been exported to Europe since antiquity. Incense burners were an integral part of every Yemenite household. Certain kinds of incense served specific purposes and were therefore used on certain occasions such as weddings, birth celebrations, and burial rites. Jews have lived in Yemen uninterruptedly for at least two thousand years. Some believe that the first Jews arrived there even as early as the tenth century BCE through King Solomon's commercial ties with southern Arabia and his romantic ties with the Queen of Sheba. The Yemenite Jewish community faithfully maintained its Jewish traditions despite its relative isolation. The community's size has fluctuated greatly throughout history, numbering some sixty thousand at the time of the mass immigration of Yemenite Jews to Israel in 1949–50.

CARVED SOAPSTONE
LEFT TO RIGHT: 20 X 10.5 CM,
12.5 X 7 CM
PERMANENT LOAN BY
SALMAN SCHOCKEN, TEL AVIV
PHOTOGRAPH: ISRAEL MUSEUM/
DAVID HARRIS

September | 1 2 3 4 5 6 7 8 9 10 11 12 13 14 15 16 17 18 19 20 **21** 22 23 24 25 26 27 28 29 30

אלול | א ב ג ד ה ו ז ח ט י יא יב יג יד טו טז **יז** יח יט כ כא כב כג כד כה כו כז כח כט

Mosaic floor
Synagogue at Beth Shean, Byzantine Period, 6th century ce

This panel, belonging to a mosaic floor, was located near the apse of a sixth-century ce synagogue at Beth Shean—an important city at that time, inhabited by Jews, Christians, and Samaritans. In the center is a representation of a shrine within a shrine. It probably depicted the synagogue's Torah Ark and served as a symbol of the Temple. The menorahs, *shofarot* (ram's horns), and incense shovels that flank the central motif also symbolize the Temple and the hope for redemption. Similar representations have been found in many other Jewish and Samaritan synagogues of this period.

STONE AND GLASS
429 CM (WIDTH)
ISRAEL ANTIQUITIES AUTHORITY
PHOTOGRAPH: ISRAEL MUSEUM

September | 1 2 3 4 5 6 7 8 9 10 11 12 13 14 15 16 17 18 19 20 21 **22** 23 24 25 26 27 28 29 30

אלול | א ב ג ד ה ו ז ח ט י יא יב יג יד טו טז יז **יח** יט כ כא כב כג כד כה כו כז כח כט

KIBBUTZ MA'OZ CHAIM, 1937

In the center of the photograph a tower and stockade can be seen. This type of structure defined settlements established during the bloody years 1936–39, when the British government tried to freeze immigration and settlement in Eretz Israel. A wooden tower crowned by a searchlight for observation and signaling was surrounded by a few huts; a wall, built of two wooden fences between which gravel was filled to shield the settlers from bullets, enclosed the entire area. The design of the tower-and-stockade settlement answered several major needs: it could be assembled in one day (and made permanent over time) and it enabled a small group of defenders to withstand an attack until the arrival of reinforcements.

DR. NAHUM TIM GIDAL
(1909, GERMANY–1996, ISRAEL),
IMMIGRATED TO ERETZ ISRAEL, 1936
GELATIN SILVER PRINT

September | 1 2 3 4 5 6 7 8 9 10 11 12 13 14 15 16 17 18 19 20 21 22 **23** 24 25 26 27 28 29 30

אלול | א ב ג ד ה ו ז ח ט י יא יב יג יד טו טז יז יח **יט** כ כא כב כג כד כה כו כז כח כט

Torah binders
Turkey, 19th–20th century

Torah binders, usually made from a long, narrow strip of simple fabric, are used to wrap and hold the closed Torah scrolls. Some of these examples from Turkey, called *mitpahat* or *fasa*, are richly embroidered in gold thread. In the Ottoman Empire many of the binders were donated to the synagogue in conjunction with childbirth. Mothers of newborn babies would bring a binder to the synagogue on their first visit after giving birth.

Brocade; silk; linen; satin
113–117 cm (length)
15–19 cm (width)
Photograph: Israel Museum/
Nahum Slapak

September | 1 2 3 4 5 6 7 8 9 10 11 12 13 14 15 16 17 18 19 20 21 22 23 **24** 25 26 27 28 29 30

אלול | א ב ג ד ה ו ז ח ט י יא יב יג יד טו טז יז יח יט **כ** כא כב כג כד כה כו כז כח כט

JERUSALEM FROM THE MOUNT OF OLIVES, 1834–35

Over the centuries, the city of Jerusalem has captured the hearts and minds of many poets and painters. Although J. M. W. Turner never visited the Holy Land, he was nevertheless strongly attracted to its topography, which he knew through the Bible and paintings and prints of the region made by nineteenth-century Romantic artists. Turner painted this watercolor from a sketch drawn in situ by Sir Charles Barry (1795–1860), who made the Grand Tour in 1817–20. Turner's view shows the city from the east looking west, with the Dome of the Rock dominating the center of the picture. A rainbow arches across the left-hand side of the work, touching a landscape dotted with olive trees and slabs of stone that appear to be old graves, indicating that the painting was executed from the Mount of Olives.

JOSEPH MALLORD WILLIAM TURNER,
ENGLISH (1775–1851)
WATERCOLOR ON PAPER
13.7 X 25 CM
GIFT OF ALAN FLACKS, LONDON
B87.993
PHOTOGRAPH: ISRAEL MUSEUM/
AVSHALOM AVITAL

September │ 1 2 3 4 5 6 7 8 9 10 11 12 13 14 15 16 17 18 19 20 21 22 23 24 **25** 26 27 28 29 30

אלול │ א ב ג ד ה ו ז ח ט י יא יב יג יד טו טז יז יח יט כ **כא** כב כג כד כה כו כז כח כט

Tiberias, 1920s

The ancient city of Tiberias is situated on the western shore of the Sea of Galilee, known in Hebrew as Lake Kinneret. The site has been inhabited for centuries, with one city being built on the ruins of an earlier one. The large size of the lake is clear from the sweep of the coastline, seen here from a hill above Tiberias.

Yaacov Ben-Dov
(1882, Russia–1968, Israel),
immigrated to Eretz Israel, 1908
Gelatin silver print
Gift of Rena (Fisch) and
Robert Lewin, London

September | 1 2 3 4 5 6 7 8 9 10 11 12 13 14 15 16 17 18 19 20 21 22 23 24 25 **26** 27 28 29 30

אלול ‏א ב ג ד ה ו ז ח ט י יא יב יג יד טו טז יז יח יט כ כא **כב** כג כד כה כו כז כח כט

"Tomb" bracelets
San'a, Yemen,
late 19th–early 20th century

This pair of gilt silver bracelets with their triangular shapes are reminiscent of tombs, a sobering reminder of the inevitability of death. The bracelets were worn by Jewish women from San'a at such special occasions as their wedding and after-birth celebrations.

Gilt silver; pearls; semiprecious
stones; filigree; granulation
9 x 2.5 cm
Photograph: Israel Museum/
David Harris

September | 1 2 3 4 5 6 7 8 9 10 11 12 13 14 15 16 17 18 19 20 21 22 23 24 25 26 **27** 28 29 30

אלול | א ב ג ד ה ו ז ח ט י יא יב יג יד טו טז יז יח יט כ כא כב **כג** כד כה כו כז כח כט

La Sepoltura/La Sépulture (Burial Ceremony), mid 18th century

"Then shall the dust return to the earth as it was: and the spirit shall return unto God who gave it." (Ecclesiastes 12:7)

The citation accompanying this etching is from the book of Ecclesiastes, and describes the Jewish attitude to death: "God gives God takes may the Lord be blessed." This approach is well reflected in the *Kaddish*, the ancient Aramaic prayer glorifying God's name, in memory of the deceased. According to Jewish custom, the dead are not embalmed or cremated; following ritual washing, immersion, and wrapping in shrouds, the body is buried in the earth as soon as possible (to this day, coffins are usually used outside of Israel). Traditionally, the *Hevra Kadisha*, the voluntary association responsible for supervising these rituals, was one of the most important in the Jewish community. After the funeral, different customs correspond to specific periods of mourning that reflect the immediacy of the loss; for example, during the first seven days after burial (the *shiv'ah*) the mourners do not leave their house, but are visited and cared for by other members of the community.

PIETRO ANTONIO NOVELLI AFTER
BERNARD PICART
(1673, FRANCE–1733),
ACTIVE HOLLAND
ETCHING ON PAPER,
29 X 35.6 CM
144-2-43
PHOTOGRAPH: ISRAEL MUSEUM

September | 1 2 3 4 5 6 7 8 9 10 11 12 13 14 15 16 17 18 19 20 21 22 23 24 25 26 27 **28** 29 30

אלול א ב ג ד ה ו ז ח ט י יא יב יג יד טו טז יז יח יט כ כא כב כג **כד** כה כו כז כח כט

BURIAL SOCIETY PLAQUE
NORTH ITALY, 1776

This decorated eighteenth-century Burial Society plaque lists the names and duties of the members of the local Burial Society, *Hevra Kadisha*. This is one of the few objects showing how members of the society carried out their work in preparing the dead for burial. Members of the Burial Society took on the honor voluntarily. It was customary to hold an annual banquet on the anniversary of the traditional date of death of Moses, when society members were elected to office and other matters were discussed.

PEN AND INK AND TEMPERA ON
PARCHMENT AND PAPER
84 x 55 CM
ACQUIRED THROUGH THE VIKTORIA
WITLIN-VINRICA BEQUEST
PHOTOGRAPH: ISRAEL MUSEUM/
RONY TERRY

September │ 1 2 3 4 5 6 7 8 9 10 11 12 13 14 15 16 17 18 19 20 21 22 23 24 25 26 27 28 **29** 30

א ב ג ד ה ו ז ח ט י יא יב יג יד טו טז יז יח יט כ כא כב כג כד **כה** כו כז כח כט │ אלול

כמרדכיש | כ שבתי חיים | כ חנניא | כ' יצחק | כ' אברהם שוחט | ב'
פונטיקורוב | מודיליאני | בר מ' עזרא | בולבב | מ"ע הזקן יחי' יהוד' | מ"ע הזקן יחי' יהוד'
יצ"ו | יצ"ו | יצ"ו | יצ"ו | אלמטיורי יצ"ו | אלמטיורי יצ"ו

Tetradrachm of the Bar Kokhba revolt
Provenance unknown,
Roman Period, 135 ce

The aim of the Bar Kokhba revolt (132–135 ce) was to retake Jerusalem and to restore its Temple. Thus the silver tetradrachms, the most valuable coins minted by Bar Kokhba, the leader of the revolt, all depict the facade of the Temple.

Silver
2.6 cm (diameter)
Photograph: Israel Museum

September | 1 2 3 4 5 6 7 8 9 10 11 12 13 14 15 16 17 18 19 20 21 22 23 24 25 26 27 28 29 **30**

אלול | א ב ג ד ה ו ז ח ט י יא יב יג יד טו טז יז יח יט כ כא כב כג כד כה **כו** כז כח כט

Prayer book cover
Derbent Dagestan,
Caucasus, mid 19th century

The isolated community of Jews in the Caucasus lived in the northern part of the Muslim state of Azerbaijan and in southern Russia. They are traditionally thought to have settled in the Caucasus in the first millennium BCE, and in the face of centuries of oppression and hardship managed to retain strong Zionist yearnings and create objects and artifacts reflecting their unique brand of Judaism. This woven prayer book cover in the style of the region's rugs once belonged to the Abramov family of rabbis.

WOVEN WOOL
47 X 30 CM
PHOTOGRAPH: ISRAEL MUSEUM/
AVSHALOM AVITAL

October | 1 2 3 4 5 6 7 8 9 10 11 12 13 14 15 16 17 18 19 20 21 22 23 24 25 26 27 28 29 30

אלול | א ב ג ד ה ו ז ח ט י יא יב יג יד טו טז יז יח יט כ כא כב כג כד כה כו כז כח כט

Jews Going to Selichot Prayer, 1921

The *selichot* prayers are said during the period leading up to Rosh Hashanah (New Year) and Yom Kippur (Day of Atonement)—the *Yamim Hanoraim* (Days of Awe). During the prayers, which are held before dawn, Jews traditionally ask for forgiveness for any wrongs they may have committed in the past year, in preparation for Yom Kippur. In this painting one can see the men leaving their homes in the predawn darkness. The northern European shtetl is already covered in snow and the haggard, drawn old men show the signs of the harshness of shtetl life after World War I.

Jakob Steinhardt
(1887, Germany–1968, Israel)
Oil on canvas
79 x 90.3 cm
Gift of Ora and Moshe Yavnai,
Tel Aviv, in memory of their
parents Esther and
Pinchas Yevnoson
1225.77
Photograph: Israel Museum/
Avraham Hay

October | 1 **2** 3 4 5 6 7 8 9 10 11 12 13 14 15 16 17 18 19 20 21 22 23 24 25 26 27 28 29 30 31

אלול | א ב ג ד ה ו ז ח ט י יא יב יג יד טו טז יז יח יט כ כא כב כג כד כה כו כז **כח** כט

Decorative Rosh Hashanah plate
Delft, Holland, 1672

Rosh Hashanah is the festival of the Jewish New Year, a time in which divine judgment is made for the coming year. This blue-and-black glazed ceramic plate decorated with flowers and birds has the Hebrew words *Has[t]ima Tova* on it, meaning "a good sealing," a greeting exchanged with friends. It refers to the traditional belief that the divine decree is inscribed on Rosh Hashanah and one's fate for the coming year is sealed ten days later, on Yom Kippur.

MAKER: JACOBUS AYNACKEN
PORCELAIN
23.5 X 3.5 CM
GIFT OF MAXIM PIHAR, 1942
PHOTOGRAPH: ISRAEL MUSEUM/
DAVID HARRIS

October | 1 2 **3** 4 5 6 7 8 9 10 11 12 13 14 15 16 17 18 19 20 21 22 23 24 25 26 27 28 29 30 31

אלול | א ב ג ד ה ו ז ח ט י יא יב יג יד טו טז יז יח יט כ כא כב כג כד כה כו כז כח **כט**

Shofar
Germany, 1681

This shofar (ram's horn) bears a Hebrew inscription from Psalms 81:4–5 commanding that the shofar be blown on the New Year. Sounding the ram's horn is a principal precept and feature of the High Holidays (the New Year and the Day of Atonement). Jewish tradition links the ram's horn to the Binding of Isaac and the ram caught in the thickets by its horns. The shofar is not usually decorated.

Engraved horn
42 x 6.2 cm
The Stieglitz Collection was
donated to the Israel Museum,
Jerusalem with the contribution
of Erica and Ludwig Jesselson,
New York, through the
American Friends
of the Israel Museum
Photograph: Israel Museum/
Avi Ganor

October | 1 2 3 **4** 5 6 7 8 9 10 11 12 13 14 15 16 17 18 19 20 21 22 23 24 25 26 27 28 29 30 31

תשרי א | ב ג ד ה ו ז ח ט י יא יב יג יד טו טז יז יח יט כ כא כב כג כד כה כו כז כח כט ל

Book of customs (*Sefer ha-Minhagim*)
Amsterdam, Holland, 1713

Illustrated books describing customs and holidays for the year were written as guides to Jewish practice and reflect Jewish life in different places in Europe from the end of the Middle Ages to the beginning of the nineteenth century. This vignette from the Amsterdam customs book shows the blowing of the ram's horn (shofar) during the Rosh Hashanah holiday.

PRINT AND WOODCUTS ON PAPER
20.2 X 15.5 CM
PHOTOGRAPH: ISRAEL MUSEUM

October | 1 2 3 4 **5** 6 7 8 9 10 11 12 13 14 15 16 17 18 19 20 21 22 23 24 25 26 27 28 29 30 31

תשרי | א **ב** ג ד ה ו ז ח ט י יא יב יג יד טו טז יז יח יט כ כא כב כג כד כה כו כז כח כט ל

THE TASCHLICH CEREMONY,
LATE 19TH–EARLY 20TH CENTURY

According to tradition, one's individual and collective fate is decreed on Rosh Hashanah (the Jewish New Year) and sealed on Yom Kippur (the Day of Atonement). In this context, there is a custom, which originated probably in late medieval Germany, called *Taschlich*. It calls for Jews to approach a body of water, even a well, on the first day of Rosh Hashanah after the afternoon liturgy and before sunset. There they recite psalms in addition to the verses "You shall cast all their sins into the depths of the sea" (Micha 7:18–19) and shake out their pockets, symbolically ridding themselves of all their sins by casting them into the water. This colored lithograph depicts a group of Jewish men and boys in East European dress performing the *Taschlich* ceremony at the edge of a lake. The provenance of this lithograph, and its relation to Jewish history is particularly interesting since a stamp of a German Reich library is found on the lower right margin. This lithograph was probably stolen from Jews by the Nazis, and returned to Jewish hands through IRSO (Jewish Restitution Successor Organization) after World War II.

KARL FELSENHARDT
(1824, POLAND–1903),
ACTIVE GERMANY
COLORED LITHOGRAPH ON PAPER
26.2 X 37.5 CM
ACQUIRED THROUGH THE
JEWISH RESTITUTION
SUCCESSOR ORGANIZATION
(IRSO),1952
M 4016-6-52
PHOTOGRAPH: ISRAEL MUSEUM

October | 1 2 3 4 5 **6** 7 8 9 10 11 12 13 14 15 16 17 18 19 20 21 22 23 24 25 26 27 28 29 30 31

תשרי | א ב **ג** ד ה ו ז ח ט י יא יב יג יד טו טז יז יח יט כ כא כב כג כד כה כו כז כח כט ל

Verlag: Wolf Topilowsky, Cöln a. Rh.

תשליך Taschlich.

Topilowsky u. Schapiro, London, 9 Commercial Street.

GROOM: ELIAHU HAYYIM, SON OF
EL'AZAR MULLA ELIYAHU HACOHEN
BRIDE: RAHMAH MATTANEH,
DAUGHTER OF REFAEL HAYYIM
MULLA ELIYAHU HACOHEN
GOUACHE AND PEN AND
INK ON PARCHMENT
50 X 40 CM
PHOTOGRAPH: ISRAEL MUSEUM/
AVRAHAM HAY

MARRIAGE CONTRACT (KETUBBAH)
CALCUTTA, INDIA, 1898

This marriage contract comes from India's Baghdad Jewish community, one of
the three Jewish communities there. Baghdadi *ketubbot* are usually decorated with
animal and vegetal motifs. In addition to the tigers portrayed here, Baghdadi
ketubbot contain exotic birds, pairs of peacocks in luxuriant colors, and lush multicolored flowers, which decorate the border. The pair of fish facing each other in the
middle of the *ketubbah* may symbolize fertility and protection against the evil eye.

October | 1 2 3 4 5 6 **7** 8 9 10 11 12 13 14 15 16 17 18 19 20 21 22 23 24 25 26 27 28 29 30 31

תשרי | א ב ג **ד** ה ו ז ח ט י יא יב יג יד טו טז יז יח יט כ כא כב כג כד כה כו כז כח כט ל

לס"י

מלא רחמים
אשר לו הגדול'
כסימנא טבא ובסימנא מעלי'
חדוה וגילה שמחה וצהל'
שה לחתן ולכלה ולכל
יציצו ויפרחו יפרו וירבו יכנו ויצליחו
מה בית והון נחלת אבות ומה אש'
ביתך בניך כשתילי זיתים סביב לשלחנך
וראה בנים לבניך שלום על ישרא'

לכ'

בשם הרחמן
יברך שמו בשם
ומרומים על כל ברכה ותהלה
בשעה מעולה ועונה מהוללה
פדות ישע וגאולה ומלוי כל
הקהלה הנקהלה ישישו וישמחו
מצא אשה מצא טוב ויפק רצון
משכלת אשתך כגפן פוריה בירכתי
הנה כי כן יבורך גבר ירא ה'

בשלושה בטבת חמישה ישיש נחום קעיר שנת תשמ"ח שלום ושפע טובה וברכה ורפואה לבריאות טובה נ"ע לב"ט אמנת שץ לה ש"ץ כלכתה יש
כי נהיה נעבא ישיש נ"א וכא צורפא מ"ץ רחתן נ"ך כה"ר אליהו חיים ל"ע ב"ן נ"ד אלעזר מולא צלירהו הכהן

SABBATH AFTERNOON, 1866

From 1865 on Oppenheim devoted himself almost solely to Jewish themes, creating the series "Scenes from Traditional Jewish Family Life." On the eve of modernity, he devoted himself to portraying the Jewish family and community as a haven of comfort, warmth, and tradition, as can be seen in this serene and cozy Shabbat scene.

MORITZ DANIEL OPPENHEIM,
GERMAN (1800–1882)
OIL (GRISAILLE) ON CANVAS
52.5 X 63 CM
ACQUISITION, 1942
76/3/42
PHOTOGRAPH: ISRAEL MUSEUM

October │ 1 2 3 4 5 6 7 **8** 9 10 11 12 13 14 15 16 17 18 19 20 21 22 23 24 25 26 27 28 29 30 31

תשרי │ א ב ג ד **ה** ו ז ח ט י יא יב יג יד טו טז יז יח יט כ כא כב כג כד כה כו כז כח כט ל

Plate for the redemption of the firstborn (*Pidyon Ha-Ben*)
Lvov (Lemberg), Austria-Hungary, 1838

When a firstborn son is thirty days old, his father symbolically redeems him from a *cohen* (descendant of the priestly tribe) for five silver coins. The ceremonial redemption of the son derives from the biblical idea that a mother's firstborn male child is sanctified to God and is redeemed through a priest. These plates were probably used to hold the coins.

Repoussé silver
37 x 26.2 x 2 cm
The Stieglitz Collection was donated to the Israel Museum, Jerusalem with the contribution of Erica and Ludwig Jesselson, New York, through the American Friends of the Israel Museum
Photograph: Israel Museum/ Avi Ganor

October | 1 2 3 4 5 6 7 8 **9** 10 11 12 13 14 15 16 17 18 19 20 21 22 23 24 25 26 27 28 29 30 31

תשרי | א ב ג ד ה | ז ח ט י יא יב יג יד טו טז יז יח יט כ כא כב כג כד כה כו כז כח כט ל

Book cover
Poland, 18th century

The inscription on the cover reads, "Five Books of Moses," indicating its use. It is decorated with floral motifs with a depiction of the biblical story of the Binding of Isaac, with a Hebrew inscription "Do not raise your hands against the boy" (Genesis 22:12).

Pierced and engraved silver;
niello; enamel
14.7 x 31 x 6 cm
The Stieglitz Collection was
donated to the Israel Museum,
Jerusalem with the contribution
of Erica and Ludwig Jesselson,
New York, through the American
Friends of the Israel Museum
Photograph: Israel Museum/
Avi Ganor

October | 1 2 3 4 5 6 7 8 9 **10** 11 12 13 14 15 16 17 18 19 20 21 22 23 24 25 26 27 28 29 30 31

תשרי | א ב ג ד ה ו ז ח ט י יא יב יג יד טו טז יז יח יט כ כא כב כג כד כה כו כז כח כט ל

TOMB OF RACHEL, 1920S

According to the teachings, Jacob the patriarch buried Rachel at the side of the road. A tradition developed of pilgrimage to Rachel's tomb to pray for healing and aid. Women would walk around the tomb, winding a red thread around it; it was believed the blessing was transmitted through the thread. During the month of Elul and the ten days of repentance before Rosh Hashanah, the tomb was open at all times of day and night, and thousands would come to pray. Many photographed it as one of the holy sites in Eretz Israel, and Ben-Dov's image became one of the best-known photographs in the Jewish world. Horses and carriages can be seen in the foreground, emphasizing the closeness of the tomb to the road.

YAACOV BEN-DOV
(1882, RUSSIA–1968, ISRAEL),
IMMIGRATED TO ERETZ ISRAEL, 1908
GELATIN SILVER PRINT
GIFT OF RENA (FISCH) AND
ROBERT LEWIN, LONDON

October | 1 2 3 4 5 6 7 8 9 10 **11** 12 13 14 15 16 17 18 19 20 21 22 23 24 25 26 27 28 29 30 31

תשרי | א ב ג ד ה ו ז ח ט י יא יב יג יד טו טז יז יח יט כ כא כב כג כד כה כו כז כח כט ל

PARENTS' BLESSING ON YOM KIPPUR EVE
VILNA, RUSSIA, 1902

The depiction illustrates an intimate festive event in a Russian Jewish family home in the early twentieth century. The atmosphere of the period is reflected in the modern clothes worn by the younger generation, while the parents are still wearing the traditional *kittel*, the white gown. The walls are hung with pictures of prominent rabbis and Jewish philanthropists, a popular custom in Eastern Europe in that time. The traditional blessing of parents over their children is:

> May the Lord bless you and keep you
>> May He make his face to shine upon you
> And be gracious unto you
>> May the Lord turn his countenance unto you
> And give you peace.

CHROMOLITHOGRAPH ON PAPER
PRINTED BY PUBLISHER
MORDEHAI KATZENELENBOGEN
39 X 61 CM
PHOTOGRAPH: ISRAEL MUSEUM/
PETER LANYI

October | 1 2 3 4 5 6 7 8 9 10 11 **12** 13 14 15 16 17 18 19 20 21 22 23 24 25 26 27 28 29 30 31

תשרי | א ב ג ד ה ו ז ח **ט** י יא יב יג יד טו טז יז יח יט כ כא כב כג כד כה כו כז כח כט ל

CLOTH: PRINTED COTTON
70 x 68 CM
THE FEUCHTWANGER COLLECTION
PURCHASED AND DONATED TO THE
ISRAEL MUSEUM BY BARUCH AND
RUTH RAPPAPORT OF GENEVA
PHOTOGRAPH: ISRAEL MUSEUM/
DAVID HARRIS

BELT BUCKLES: REPOUSSÉ AND
ENGRAVED SILVER;
GILT COTTON THREAD
13 x 6.9 CM (TOP)
12 x 6.7 CM (BOTTOM)

YOM KIPPUR BELT BUCKLES
POLAND, 19TH CENTURY

The traditional white garment called *kittel* is usually worn in Ashkenazi communities on both Yom Kippur and the Seder night. It is fastened in the middle with a belt and decorative buckle. Both belts have a central inscription exhorting the keeping of the Day of Atonement.

COMMEMORATIVE CLOTH DEPICTING YOM KIPPUR PRAYERS IN METZ, GERMANY, 1870

After the Franco-Prussian War, an anonymous artist drew a commemorative depiction of the Yom Kippur services held for 1,200 Jewish soldiers of the Germany army outside the besieged city of Metz (left).

THE STIEGLITZ COLLECTION WAS DONATED TO THE ISRAEL MUSEUM,
JERUSALEM WITH THE CONTRIBUTION OF ERICA AND LUDWIG JESSELSON,
NEW YORK, THROUGH THE AMERICAN FRIENDS OF THE ISRAEL MUSEUM
PHOTOGRAPH: ISRAEL MUSEUM/AVI GANOR

October | 1 2 3 4 5 6 7 8 9 10 11 12 **13** 14 15 16 17 18 19 20 21 22 23 24 25 26 27 28 29 30 31

תשרי | א ב ג ד ה ו ז ח ט י יא יב יג יד טו טז יז יח יט כ כא כב כג כד כה כו כז כח כט ל

Plaque for a synagogue memorial lamp
Rissani, Morocco,
early 20th century

This memorial plaque, made of carved and painted wood, originally held an oil-filled cup, serving as a memorial lamp. It is inscribed along the arch at the top, in memory of Baba Hana ben Yosef, and has a seven-branched candelabrum in the center with the verse "Blessed be you in your coming in and blessed be you in your going out" (Deuteronomy 28:6).

Carved and painted wood; metal
67 x 33 cm
Israel Museum Collection
Gift of the Zeyde Schulmann
Collection, Paris
Photograph: Israel Museum/
David Harris

October | 1 2 3 4 5 6 7 8 9 10 11 12 13 **14** 15 16 17 18 19 20 21 22 23 24 25 26 27 28 29 30 31

תשרי | א ב ג ד ה ו ז ח ט **י"א** י"ב י"ג י"ד ט"ו ט"ז י"ז י"ח י"ט כ כ"א כ"ב כ"ג כ"ד כ"ה כ"ו כ"ז כ"ח כ"ט ל

Prayer shawl (TALLITH)
Venice, Italy, 18th century

The ritual prayer shawl known as the *tallith* has been worn by Jewish men since ancient times. At the four corners (*arba kanfot*), fringes (*tzitzit*) are attached in fulfillment of the biblical commandment (Numbers 15:38–41). A smaller prayer shawl (*tallith katan*) is traditionally worn daily under the shirt, while the larger shawl is worn only during prayer. Made of wool, cotton, or silk, the *tallith* may be decorated with silk and metal embroidery or brocade appliqué. This festive example, adorned with blue and gold stripes and gold-thread embroidery, was probably worn on special occasions.

Silk; gold- and
silk-thread embroidery
186 x 116 cm
Gift of Jakob Michael,
New York, in memory of his wife,
Erna Sondheimer-Michael
Photograph: Israel Museum/
David Harris

October | 1 2 3 4 5 6 7 8 9 10 11 12 13 14 **15** 16 17 18 19 20 21 22 23 24 25 26 27 28 29 30 31

תשרי | א ב ג ד ה ו ז ח ט י י"א **י"ב** י"ג י"ד ט"ו ט"ז י"ז י"ח י"ט כ כ"א כ"ב כ"ג כ"ד כ"ה כ"ו כ"ז כ"ח כ"ט ל

AMULETS
YEMEN, EARLY 20TH CENTURY

In Yemen, as in most traditional societies, amulets functioned as a means of warding off evil spirits and invoking beneficial forces. A special triangular amulet was worn by the Jewish bridegroom and a baby boy wore a smaller version at his circumcision. The pouchlike triangle, usually hanging from an iron ring, was believed to have special protective properties, as did the various materials, such as mercury, salt, and grains, which were kept inside.

TEXTILE; SILVER; COINS; CORAL;
GLASS; MOTHER-OF-PEARL
IRON RING: 13 CM
LARGE AMULET: 16 X 11.5 CM
PERMANENT LOAN BY
SALMAN SCHOCKEN, TEL AVIV
PHOTOGRAPH: ISRAEL MUSEUM/
DAVID HARRIS

October | 1 2 3 4 5 6 7 8 9 10 11 12 13 14 15 **16** 17 18 19 20 21 22 23 24 25 26 27 28 29 30 31

תשרי | א ב ג ד ה ו ז ח ט י י'א י'ב **י'ג** יד טו טז יז יח יט כ כא כב כג כד כה כו כז כח כט ל

Sukkah, 1953

Jewish motifs and depictions of synagogues are common in Arie Aroch's oeuvre. In this work he paints the *sukkah* and its furniture schematically, flattening the features into two-dimensionality. This creates the feeling that they are hovering, not quite secured to the ground. The painting's composition is a horizontal rectangle, yet all of its elements are composed of vertical lines, which, with the foreshortened structure and table, adds to the floating, temporary atmosphere of the work. The deceptively simple format and naive style bring to mind the children's drawings that often decorate family *sukkahs*.

Arie Aroch
(1908, Russia–1974, Israel)
Oil on canvas
63.5 x 79 cm
Lent by Jonathan Aroch,
Tel Aviv
L86.27
Photograph: Israel Museum/
Avraham Hay

October | 1 2 3 4 5 6 7 8 9 10 11 12 13 14 15 16 **17** 18 19 20 21 22 23 24 25 26 27 28 29 30 31

תשרי | א ב ג ד ה ו ז ח ט י יא יב יג **י׳** טו טז יז יח יט כ כא כב כג כד כה כו כז כח כט ל

SUKKAH
SOUTHERN GERMANY, CA. 1837

Sukkot (Feast of the Tabernacles) is the festival that commemorates the wanderings of the Israelites in the desert following the Exodus from Egypt, during which time they lived in booths. The central biblical commandment relating to the holiday is to "dwell" in the *sukkah*, a temporary outdoor structure with a roof made of branches, for seven days. This *sukkah* was used by the Deller family until the beginning of the twentieth century, when it was stored in the attic to prevent further deterioration. It was smuggled out of Germany in 1935. This painted *sukkah* is a unique example of Jewish folk art in Germany, combining motifs inspired by traditional German folk art showing everyday scenes, as well as biblical and Holy Land themes.

WOOD; OIL PAINT
2 X 2.9 X 2.9 M
GIFT OF THE DELLER FAMILY
WITH THE HELP OF
DR. HEINRICH FEUCHTWANGER
PHOTOGRAPH: ISRAEL MUSEUM/
AVRAHAM HAY

October | 1 2 3 4 5 6 7 8 9 10 11 12 13 14 15 16 17 **18** 19 20 21 22 23 24 25 26 27 28 29 30 31

תשרי | א ב ג ד ה ו ז ח ט י יא יב יג יד **טו** טז יז יח יט כ כא כב כג כד כה כו כז כח כט ל

ETROG BOX
GERMANY, 1860

This special *etrog* container is unusually decorated with colorful beads. It is used during the autumn Sukkot festival to hold the *etrog* citrus fruit, one of the four prescribed species for the benediction. The Hebrew inscription formed by the beads commands, "You shall take for yourselves on the first day (of the festival) the fruit of the tree hadar (myrtle), branches of palm trees and the boughs of thick leaved trees and the willows of the brook." The box is inscribed: "In honor of my forefather on behalf of Gershon Pieta."

GLASS BEADS ON CARDBOARD
8.3 x 8.8 x 13.9 CM
GIFT OF THE E. BURSTEIN
COLLECTION, LUGANO
PHOTOGRAPH: ISRAEL MUSEUM/
DAVID HARRIS

October | 1 2 3 4 5 6 7 8 9 10 11 12 13 14 15 16 17 18 **19** 20 21 22 23 24 25 26 27 28 29 30 31

תשרי | א ב ג ד ה ו ז ח ט י יא יב יג יד טו **טז** יז יח יט כ כא כב כג כד כה כו כז כח כט ל

588

ETROG BOX
UNITED STATES, 1918

This *etrog* container has a Hebrew dedication that indicates that the box was given as a wedding gift. The sides are carved with scenes connected to Sukkot (Feast of Tabernacles) and to marriage. The box was made in the United States and sent to Slovakia in 1918, eventually arriving back in the States when the groom—Rabbi Gelbman—and his family arrived in New York on November 30, 1937.

CARVED AND PAINTED WOOD;
PLATED COPPER AND BRASS
12.6 x 10.8 x 18.1 CM
GIFT OF MR. AND MRS. JOHN WILCOX,
NEW YORK, TO AMERICAN FRIENDS
OF THE ISRAEL MUSEUM
PHOTOGRAPH: ISRAEL MUSEUM

October | 1 2 3 4 5 6 7 8 9 10 11 12 13 14 15 16 17 18 19 **20** 21 22 23 24 25 26 27 28 29 30 31

תשרי | א ב ג ד ה ו ז ח ט י יא יב יג יד טו טז **יז** יח יט כ כא כב כג כד כה כו כז כח כט ל

590

Bukhara *sukkah* reconstructed According to the tradition of Bukhara, Central Asia

The rich, colorful fabrics typical of the central Asian region of Bukhara, as well as the considerable height of the walls, gave this *sukkah* its magnificent appearance. The floor of the *sukkah* was covered with rugs and mattresses on which the family would sit to dine around low tables. Wreaths made from mint and basil leaves were suspended from the *sukkah* roof (*sekhakh*), and their fragrance would mingle with that from bunches of marigolds and cockscombs.

Textiles: late 19th century–
early 20th century
Ikat panels made of dyed silk fabrics
275 x 242 cm (Suzani embroideries)
165-110
Photograph: Israel Museum/
Avraham Hay

October | 1 2 3 4 5 6 7 8 9 10 11 12 13 14 15 16 17 18 19 20 **21** 22 23 24 25 26 27 28 29 30 31

תשרי | א ב ג ד ה ו ז ח ט י יא יב יג יד טו טז יז **יח** יט כ כא כב כג כד כה כו כז כח כט ל

Sukkah decorations
Szeged, Hungary,
late 19th–early 20th century

These *sukkah* panels are part of a set that decorated the *sukkah* of Rabbi Loew Immanuel of Szeged, Hungary (1854–1945), head of the neological community, a mainstream Hungarian faction loosely resembling Reform Judaism. Two of the panels are adorned with objects associated with the Temple, the seven-branched menorah and priestly laver, while the others are depicted with biblical characters of the patriarchs and other leaders. According to a tradition based on Kabbalistic sources, the *sukkah* is visited daily by one of these biblical figures as a special guest (*ushpizin*).

Oil on canvas
Photograph: Israel Museum/
Avraham Hay

October | 1 2 3 4 5 6 7 8 9 10 11 12 13 14 15 16 17 18 19 20 21 **22** 23 24 25 26 27 28 29 30 31

תשרי | א ב ג ד ה ו ז ח ט י יא יב יג יד טו טז יז יח **יט** כ כא כב כג כד כה כו כז כח כט ל

SHIVITI PLAQUE
GERMANY, 19TH CENTURY

Shiviti plaques, which serve as a reminder of God's presence, are usually hung near the Holy Ark in the synagogue, and some were put on the walls of the *sukkah*. The examples that feature chapters and verses from the Bible are sometimes called menorah plaques, as many feature the seven-branched candelabrum. Texts would include various versions and abbreviations of the names of God, blessings, prayers, names of angels, and various incantations commonly used in amulets. This *shiviti* features the commonly seen Kabbalistic prayer *Ana be-koah* and the verse from Psalms 16:8 "I have set the Lord always before me."

SCRIBE AND ILLUSTRATOR:
JOEL SOLOMON, WOHART, GERMANY
PEN AND INK ON PARCHMENT
14.5 X 11 CM
BEQUEST OF FELIX PERLA, LONDON
PHOTOGRAPH: ISRAEL MUSEUM

October | 1 2 3 4 5 6 7 8 9 10 11 12 13 14 15 16 17 18 19 20 21 22 **23** 24 25 26 27 28 29 30 31

תשרי | א ב ג ד ה ו ז ח ט י יא יב יג יד טו טז יז יח יט כ כא כב כג כד כה כו כז כח כט ל

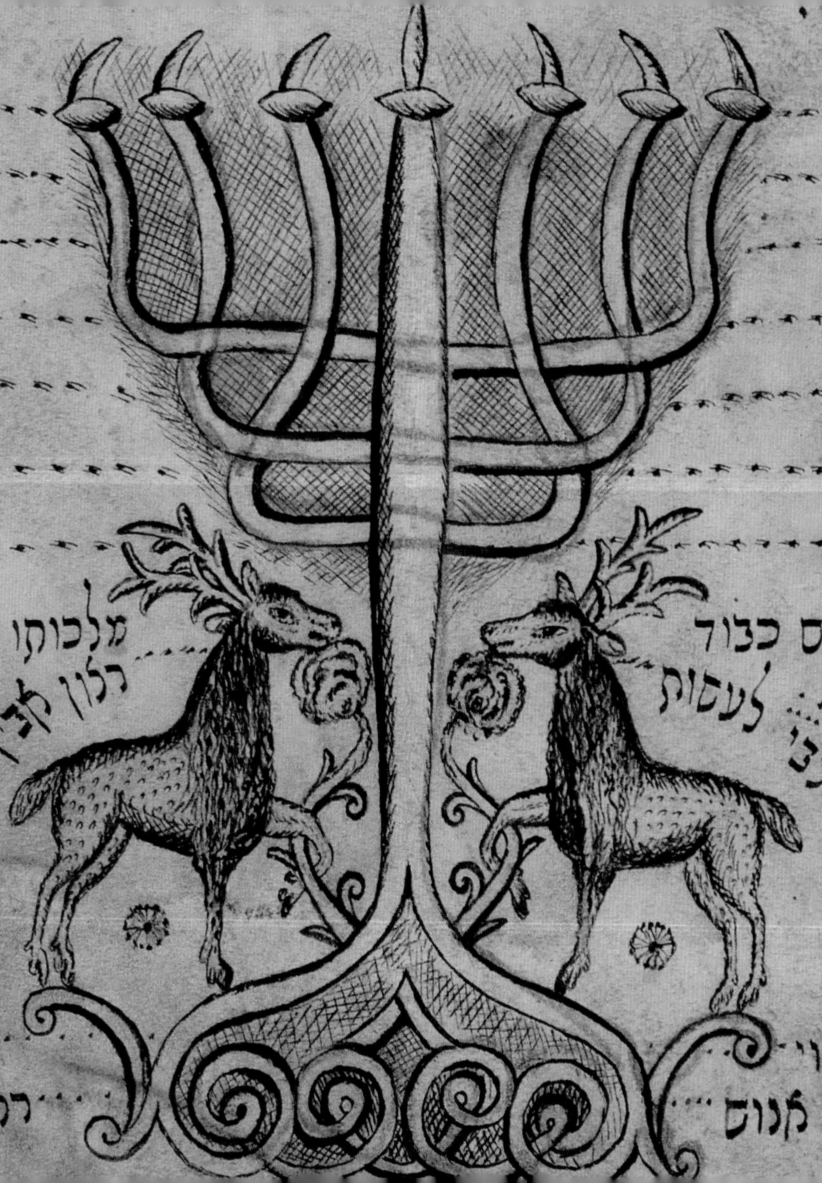
ברוך שם כבוד
מלכותו לעולם ועד
לעשות
רמה ותולעה

THE PROCESSION SEVEN TIMES ROUND THE DESK ON THE HOSANNA RABBA, 18TH CENTURY

ANONYMOUS ARTIST,
AFTER BERNARD PICART
(1673, FRANCE–1733),
ACTIVE HOLLAND
ETCHING ON PAPER
27.5 X 21 CM
PRINTED AND SOLD BY H. OVERTON
& J. HOOLE, LONDON
ISRAEL MUSEUM COLLECTION
768-6-44
PHOTOGRAPH: ISRAEL MUSEUM

It is customary to call the seventh and the last day of the Feast of Tabernacles (Sukkot) Hoshana Rabbah, "the great day of the call for help" (*Hoshana*="Save, I pray!"). It is a day for profound religious dedication and devotion, since it is considered the last day for atonement and forgiveness from God after Rosh Hashanah and Yom Kippur. This is the day of "signing the verdict." The suppliants hold the *lulav* (palm branch) and circle the *bimmah* at the synagogue, just as was done around the altar in the Temple. While all scrolls of Torah are taken out of the Ark, various *piyutim* (religious songs) are sung. Among the explanations for this ritual is that it is a commemoration for the seven times Joshua circled the walls of Jericho. In this print, the setting could be the great Portuguese Synagogue in Amsterdam. It is puzzling that in this English edition of Picart's book about Jewish religious ceremonies, the citation above the print is taken from the New Testament: "the great day of the Feast" (John 7:37).

October | 1 2 3 4 5 6 7 8 9 10 11 12 13 14 15 16 17 18 19 20 21 22 23 **24** 25 26 27 28 29 30 31

תשרי | א ב ג ד ה ו ז ח ט י יא יב יג יד טו טז יז יח יט כ **כא** כב כג כד כה כו כז כח כט ל

The PROCESSION seven times round the DESK on ÿ HOSANNA RABBA. or ÿ great day of ÿ Feast. John 7. 37.

Torah pointer
Amsterdam, Holland, 1990s

Torah pointers enable the reader of the Torah scroll to follow the correct reading of the text without touching the parchment, showing respect and protecting the scroll. These pointers are traditionally fashioned in the shape of a hand although this one is pointed. This Torah pointer (*yad*) is designed in a composition of straight lines whose elegant simplicity emphasizes the focus on the reading. The artist, Piet Cohen, was born in the Netherlands and produces ceremonial objects combining contemporary designs with ancient traditions.

DESIGNER: PIET COHEN
SILVER; SYNTHETIC STRING
ACQUIRED THROUGH THE
KATHARINE SONNENBORN FALK
FUND FOR MODERN JUDAICA
PHOTOGRAPH: ISRAEL MUSEUM

October | 1 2 3 4 5 6 7 8 9 10 11 12 13 14 15 16 17 18 19 20 21 22 23 24 **25** 26 27 28 29 30 31

תשרי | א ב ג ד ה ו ז ח ט י י״א י״ב י״ג י״ד ט״ו ט״ז י״ז י״ח י״ט כ כ״א **כב** כ״ג כ״ד כ״ה כ״ו כ״ז כ״ח כ״ט ל

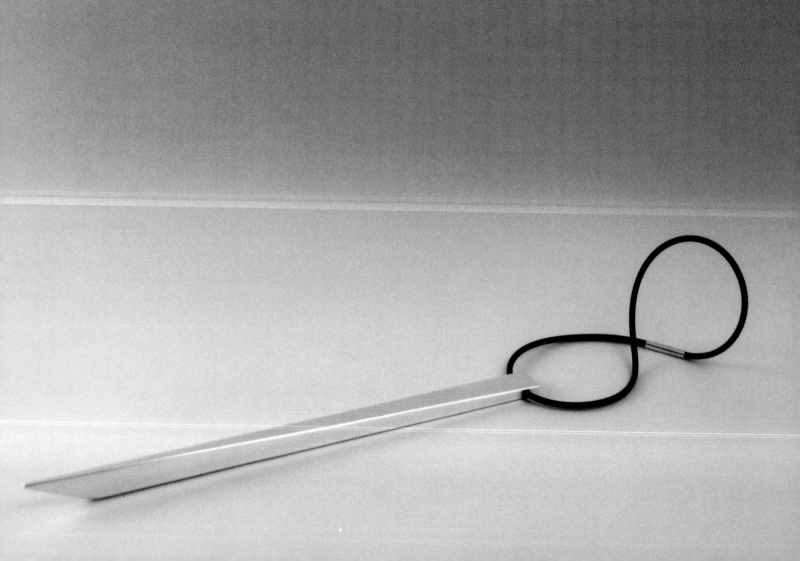

BOOK OF CUSTOMS (*SEFER HA-MINHAGIM*) AMSTERDAM, HOLLAND, 1713

Books describing customs and holidays for the whole year were written as illustrated guides to Jewish practice and reflect Jewish life in different places in Europe from the end of the Middle Ages to the beginning of the nineteenth century. This woodcut shows sweets traditionally given to children during the Simhat Torah holiday, which marks the beginning of the cycle of the Torah reading of the Five Books of Moses.

PRINT AND WOODCUTS ON PAPER
20.2 X 15.5
PHOTOGRAPH: ISRAEL MUSEUM

October | 1 2 3 4 5 6 7 8 9 10 11 12 13 14 15 16 17 18 19 20 21 22 23 24 25 **26** 27 28 29 30 31

תשרי | א ב ג ד ה ו ז ח ט י יא יב יג יד טו טז יז יח יט כ כא כב **כג** כד כה כו כז כח כט ל

BENEDICTION SHEET
NIKOLSBURG, MORAVIA, 1755

The single sheet contains various blessings recited after eating certain foods. On each side of the text are the figures of Moses and Aaron standing within two niches. From the artist's signature at the bottom of the page we learn that he was a native of Dreznitz (Strassnitz) in southern Moravia and active in Nikolsburg during the first half of the eighteenth century.

SCRIBE AND PAINTER:
SAMUEL DREZNITZ
PEN AND INK AND TEMPERA
ON PARCHMENT
61.3 X 52.2 CM
PHOTOGRAPH: ISRAEL MUSEUM/
RONY TERRY

October | 1 2 3 4 5 6 7 8 9 10 11 12 13 14 15 16 17 18 19 20 21 22 23 24 25 26 **27** 28 29 30 31

תשרי | א ב ג ד ה ו ז ח ט י יא יב יג יד טו טז יז יח יט כ כא כב כג **כד** כה כו כז כח כט ל

לכל ונורה הלך על הארץ ועל ... לכל ונורה הלך על

הארץ ועל פרי הגפן ... המחיה ועל הכלכלה בא

בא יעל הארץ ועל ... על המרוה ועל

... הגפן ועל פרי

... הגפן

על נהרות בבל שם ישבנו גם בכינו בזכרנו את

ציון על ערבים בתוכה תלינו

כנרותינו כי שם שאלונו שובינו דברי שיר

ותוללינו שמחה שירו לנו משיר ציון : **אך**

נשיר את שיר ייי על אדמת נכר : אם אשכחך ירושלים

תשכח ימיני : תדבק לשוני לחכי אם לא אזכרכי אם

לא אעלה את ירושלים על ראש שמחתי : זכר ייי לבני

אדום את יום ירושלים האומרים ערו ערו עד היסוד

בה : בת בבל השדודה אשרי שישלם לך את גמולך

שגמלת לנו : אשרי שיאחז ונפץ את עולליך אל הסלע :

להודות להלל לשבח לפאר לרומם

להדר ולנצח על כל דברי שירות

ותשבחות דוד בן ישי עבדך משיחך : בעצתך תנחני

ואחר כבוד תקחני : והוא רחום יכפר עון ולא ישחית

והרבה להשיב אפו ולא יעיר כל חמתו : אשרי הגבר

אשר תיסרנו יה ומתורתך תלמדנו : ואני בחסדך

בטחתי יגל לבי בישועתך אשירה לייי כי גמר עלי :

שוש אשיש בייי תגל נפשי באלהי כי הלבישני בגדי

ישע מעיל צדקה יעטני כחתן יכהן פאר וככלה תעדה

כליה : ויבטחו בך יודעי שמך כי לא עזבת דורשיך

ייי : שמחו בייי וגילו צדיקים והרנינו כל ישרי לב :

נר לרגלי דברך ואור לנתיבתי : אודך כי עניתני ותהי

לי לישועה :

שיר המעלות בשוב ייי את שיבת ציון היינו

כחלמים : אז ימלא שחוק פינו ולשוננו

נשא משך הזרע

בא יבא ברנה נשא אלומתיו

הריני מוכן ומזומן לקיים

מצות עשה של ברכת

המזון שנאמר ואכלת ושבעת וברכת את ייי

אלהיך על הארץ הטובה אשר נתן לך : לשם יחוד

קב ה ושכינתיה על ידי ההוא טמיר ונעלם

אברכה את ייי בכל עת תמיד תהלתו

בפי : סוד דבר הכל נשמע

את האלהים ירא ואת מצותיו שמור כי זה כל האדם :

תהלת ייי ידבר פי ויברך כל בשר שם קדשו לעולם

ועד : ואנחנו נברך יה מעתה ועד עולם הללויה :

מה שאכלנו יהיה לשובע : וכה ששתינו יהיה

לרפואה : ומה שהותרנו יהיה לברכה

ככתוב ויתן לפניהם ויאכלו ויותירו כדבר

ייי : ברוכים אתם לייי עושה שמים וארץ : **ברוך**

הגבר אשר יבטח בייי והיה ייי מבטחו : ייי עז לעמו

יתן ייי יברך את עמו בשלום :

והיה כעץ שתול על פלגי מים ועל יובל ישלח

שרשיו ולא יראה כי יבא חום והיה

עליהו רענן ובשנת בצרת לא ידאי ...

ברוך אתה ייי אלהינו מלך העולם אשר

קדשנו במצותיו וצונו על ... עירוב

פרי הא שראלנא לאפוי ...

Curtain (fragment)
Rabat, Morocco, early 20th century

This curtain was a wall hanging or room divider. Similar embroideries were used in various ceremonies, for example to cover the feet of the bride at the henna ceremony held the evening before the wedding.

Reversible silk thread
embroidery on cotton
87.5 x 52.5 cm
Gift of Baroness Alix
de Rothschild and the French
Friends of the Israel Museum
Photograph: Israel Museum/
Chanan Sadeh

October | 1 2 3 4 5 6 7 8 9 10 11 12 13 14 15 16 17 18 19 20 21 22 23 24 25 26 27 **28** 29 30 31

תשרי | א ב ג ד ה ו ז ח ט י י״א י״ב י״ג י״ד ט״ו ט״ז י״ז י״ח י״ט כ כ״א כ״ב כ״ג כ״ד **כה** כו כז כח כט ל

PEN AND INK, TEMPERA, AND
SILVER LEAF ON PARCHMENT
SCRIBES: LEVI BEN DAVID HALEVI
AND NETANEL (BEN) DANIEL
46 X 31 CM
ACQUIRED ON THE ADVICE OF
JOSEPH AND CAROLINE GRUSS AND
WITH THE ASSISTANCE OF FRIENDS
OF THE ISRAEL MUSEUM AT THE
SASSOON COLLECTION AUCTION,
ZURICH, 1978
PHOTOGRAPH: ISRAEL MUSEUM/
DAVID HARRIS

DE CASTRO PENTATEUCH, *HAFTAROT*, AND FIVE *MEGILLOT* MANUSCRIPT GERMANY, 1344

This decorated and illuminated Pentateuch is a fine example of a medieval Jewish manuscript. While the Torah scroll read publicly in the synagogue is never decorated, as prescribed in Jewish law, books such as these for personal use were often illustrated liberally. Written in square Ashkenazi script, the exact date of its completion is noted on the final page of the manuscript by Levi ben David HaLevi, as is the name of the intended owner, Joseph ben Ephraim, who commissioned and paid for its preparation. The initial word in each book is colorfully illustrated, some with silver leaf, as this example, *Bereishit*, illustrating the first word of Genesis. It is read on this day, called Shabbat Bereishit. Since Hebrew script lacks capital letters, decorating initial words became characteristic of Hebrew illuminated manuscripts, as this page illustrates. The manuscript was in the possession of David Henriques de Castro of Amsterdam until 1899 when it was acquired by David Solomon Sassoon.

October | 1 2 3 4 5 6 7 8 9 10 11 12 13 14 15 16 17 18 19 20 21 22 23 24 25 26 27 28 **29** 30 31

תשרי | א ב ג ד ה ו ז ח ט י יא יב יג יד טו טז יז יח יט כ כא כב כג כד כה **כו** כז כח כט ל

MAP OF THE PROMISED LAND DIVIDED AMONG THE TWELVE TRIBES, CA. 1690

ALEXIS-HUBERT JAILLOT, FRENCH
(1632–1712)
GUILLAME SANSON, FRENCH
(1633–1703)
HAND-COLORED ENGRAVING
ON PAPER, BY CORDIER
57.8 x 85.8 CM
FROM: ALEXIS-HUBERT JAILLOT,
ATLAS NOUVEAU, PIERRE MORTIER,
AMSTERDAM, CA. 1690
NORMAN BIER SECTION FOR
MAPS OF THE HOLY LAND
GIFT OF NORMAN AND
FRIEDA BIER, LONDON
B95.0679
PHOTOGRAPH: ISRAEL MUSEUM/
ILAN STZULMAN

In this map, which traces the shoreline between Sidon and Gaza, the twelve tribes of Israel are aligned on both banks of the river Jordan. Its prototype was a small unadorned map made in 1662 by Nicolas Sanson, whose family were pioneer cartographers in France. They established a unique French style of meticulous detail and typography. Jaillot (Nicolas' pupil) and Nicolas' son Guillame produced this larger, more decorated map based on their mentor's 1681 prototype, which for decades influenced cartographers in France and elsewhere. This map is adorned with large, informative cartouches; in the upper left the royal coat-of-arms of the Bourbon dynasty is held by angels hovering above garlands of flowers and leaves in the Baroque style. At the center stands Moses holding the Tablets of the Law, opposite Aaron the high priest; below, a vignette depicts the brazen serpent that saved the Israelites (Numbers 21:6–10). At the lower right, a cartouche tells the story of Adam and Eve and the serpent at the Tree of Knowledge. Two cornucopias and beasts of the Garden of Eden also decorate the cartouche.

October | 1 2 3 4 5 6 7 8 9 10 11 12 13 14 15 16 17 18 19 20 21 22 23 24 25 26 27 28 29 **30** 31

תשרי | א ב ג ד ה ו ז ח ט י יא יב יג יד טו טז יז יח יט כ כא כב כג כד כה כו **כז** כח כט ל

...DÆA seu TERRA SANCTA, quæ HEBRÆORUM, sive ISRAELITARUM TERRA, IN SUAS DUODECIM TRIBUS DIVISA, EÆ VERO SUNT CIS IORDANEM
...BUS IUDA, TRIBUS BENIAMIN, TRIBUS SIMEON, TRIBUS DAN, TRIBUS EPHRAIM, DIMIDIA TRIBUS MANASSE, TRIBUS ISACHAR, TRIBUS ZABULON, TRIBUS NEPTALIM, TRIBUS ASER, AC TRANS IORDANEM, TRIBUS RUBEN, TRIBUS GAD,
ALTERA DIMIDIA TRIBUS MANASSE, SECRETIS AB INVICEM, REGNIS IUDA ET ISRAEL, EXPRESSIS INSUPER SEX ULTIMI TEMPORIS EJUSDEM TERRÆ PROVINCIIS ex Conatibus Geographicis GULIELMI SANSON Nicolai Filij, Christianissimi Galliarum Regis Geographi, Cum Privilegio ad Vicennium

IUDÆA seu TERRA SANCTA
quæ HEBRÆORUM sive ISRAELITARUM
in suas duodecim Tribus divisa;
secretis ab invicem Regnis
IUDA, et ISRAEL
expressis insuper Sex ultimi temporis ejusdem Terræ Provincijs,
ex Conatibus Geographicis
GULIELMI SANSON Christianissimi Galliarum Regis Geographi.

SERENISSIMO PRINCIPI DELPHINO
Offerebat humillimus, Obsequentissimus, ac fidelissimus Servus
HUBERTUS IAILLOT
Avec Privilege du Roy,
Se Vend A AMSTERDAM chez P. MORTIER, et Compagnie. Aux Grand...

MARE MAGNUM quodet OCCIDENTALE

MARE MAGNUM

DESERTUM

EDOM quæ et IDUMÆA

EMATH

SOBA.

ARABIA DESERTA

AMMITARUM REGIO

TRIBUS ZABULON

DIMIDIA TRIBUS MANASSE

ISACHAR

DIMIDIA TRIBUS MANASSE trans Iordanem

SAMARIA

TRIBUS EPHRAIM

TRIBUS GAD

ITURÆA

TRIBUS DAN

TRIBUS BENIAMIN

IERUSALEM

TRIBUS SIMEON

TRIBUS IUDA

REGNUM IUDA

TRIBUS RUBEN

PERÆA

MOABITARUM REGIO

DESERTUM

MARE MORTUUM sive ASPHALTITES

DESERTUM SIN sive IUDÆÆ DESERTUM.

Terra Hus

Gessuri

TRACONITIS

MARE CENERETH sive GALILÆÆ JERUSALEM

Notarum Explicatio
Urbs Regia
Urbs Levitica
Urbs Refugij
Scala

THE SOWER, 1920S

To create one of his most famous images, Ben-Dov shot directly into the sun, casting the figure of the sower into silhouette. His camera was held very low, turning the lone man into a monumental figure. The composition of this photograph lies in an art-historical tradition that echoes paintings by Van Gogh *(Sower with Setting Sun)* and Jean-François Millet.

YAACOV BEN-DOV
(1882, RUSSIA–1968, ISRAEL),
IMMIGRATED TO ERETZ ISRAEL, 1908
GELATIN SILVER PRINT
PURCHASED WITH THE HELP OF
RENA (FISCH) AND ROBERT LEWIN,
LONDON

October | 1 2 3 4 5 6 7 8 9 10 11 12 13 14 15 16 17 18 19 20 21 22 23 24 25 26 27 28 29 30 **31**

תשרי | א ב ג ד ה ו ז ח ט י י״א י״ב י״ג י״ד ט״ו ט״ז י״ז י״ח י״ט כ כ״א כ״ב כ״ג כ״ד כ״ה כ״ו כ״ז **כ״ח** כ״ט ל

SHMUEL SCHULMAN, BORN RUSSIA,
ACTIVE ERETZ-YISRAEL
(PALESTINE), (1843–1900)
MICROGRAPHY, COLOR PRINT
ON PAPER, WARSCHAU, 1895
46.8 X 55.6 CM
969.1936
PHOTOGRAPH: ISRAEL MUSEUM/
ILAN STZULMAN

THE WESTERN WALL AND ITS SURROUNDINGS, JERUSALEM, 1895

Micrography is the art of using almost microscopic writing to create pictures. It was a technique perfected by many Jewish scribes. The work here stems from a long tradition of "Depictions of Holy Places"—a Jewish folk art bordering on cartography. As distinct from a topographical map with its standard scale, this is rather a topological map that recalls a medieval schema because of its lack of scale, which compresses and extends sites according to the artist's desire rather than factual evidence. The Western Wall stands at the center, flanked by the Dome of the Rock on the left, and the Al-Aqsa Mosque on the right. In the background, at the foot of the Mount of Olives, stand Zechariah's tomb, the family tomb of Bnei Hezir, and Absalom's tomb. The imaginary row of cypresses above the Western Wall may symbolize the cedars that were used to build the Holy Temple. In the frame are the words "And it shall come to pass in the last days... Come ye, let us go up to the mountain of the Lord" (Isaiah 2:2–3). In this picture, the contours are drawn in minuscule letters. In Judaism the written letter possesses mystical meaning, and here the connection between the drawings and the verses that delineate them bears a powerful message.

November | I 2 3 4 5 6 7 8 9 10 11 12 13 14 15 16 17 18 19 20 21 22 23 24 25 26 27 28 29 30

תשרי | א ב ג ד ה ו ז ח ט י יא יב יג יד טו טז יז יח יט כ כא כב כג כד כה כו כז כח **כט** ל

ועמדו רגליו ביום ההוא על הר הזתים אשר עלפני ירושלם מקדם.

Jewelry box
Nuremberg, Germany, 1540

This box, probably commissioned as a gift for a bride, bears the Hebrew inscription: "Her mouth is full of wisdom, her tongue with kindly teaching. She oversees the activities of her household and never eats the bread of idleness" from "Woman of Valor" (Proverbs 31:10–31). The hunting scenes engraved on the box are a popular motif frequently appearing in medieval Jewish manuscripts of this time.

Etched steel, partly gilt
66 x 73 x 110 cm
The Stieglitz Collection was donated to the Israel Museum, Jerusalem with the contribution of Erica and Ludwig Jesselson, New York, through the American Friends of the Israel Museum
Photograph: Israel Museum/ Avi Ganor

November | 1 **2** 3 4 5 6 7 8 9 10 11 12 13 14 15 16 17 18 19 20 21 22 23 24 25 26 27 28 29 30

תשרי | א ב ג ד ה ו ז ח ט י י׳א י׳ב י׳ג י׳ד ט׳ו ט׳ז י׳ז י׳ח י׳ט כ כ׳א כ׳ב כ׳ג כ׳ד כ׳ה כ׳ו כ׳ז כ׳ח כ׳ט ל

COFFIN
EIN GEDI, DEAD SEA SHORE,
SECOND TEMPLE PERIOD, 1ST CENTURY BCE

Ornamented marble sarcophagi, stone ossuaries, and lead coffins are common finds in tombs. Most people, however, could not afford such costly coffins and were buried in the ground in simple shrouds or wooden coffins, which do not usually survive the passage of time. This wooden coffin is a rare exception. It was preserved thanks to the dry climate of the Dead Sea region.

SYCAMORE WOOD
120 CM (LENGTH)
ISRAEL ANTIQUITIES AUTHORITY
PHOTOGRAPH: ISRAEL MUSEUM/
NAHUM SLAPAK

November | 1 2 **3** 4 5 6 7 8 9 10 11 12 13 14 15 16 17 18 19 20 21 22 23 24 25 26 27 28 29 30

חשון‎ א‎ ב ג ד ה ו ז ח ט י יא יב יג יד טו טז יז יח יט כ כא כב כג כד כה כו כז כח כט

Fragment of a synagogue screen
Synagogue at Ashkelon, Mediterranean coast, Byzantine period, 6th–7th century

Decorated on both sides with the same design, this marble fragment formed the upper part of the waist-high screen that separated the *bimmah* from the rest of the synagogue hall. The decoration combines rosettes, flowers, and interlaced circles with a menorah flanked by a *lulav*, *etrog*, and shofar.

Marble
47 cm (length)
Collection of the Deutsches
Evangelisches Institute für
Altertums wissenschaft
des Heiligen Lands

November | 1 2 3 **4** 5 6 7 8 9 10 11 12 13 14 15 16 17 18 19 20 21 22 23 24 25 26 27 28 29 30

חשון | א **ב** ג ד ה ו ז ח ט י יא יב יג יד טו טז יז יח יט כ כא כב כג כד כה כו כז כח כט

Jug and basin for priests (*COHANIM*)
United States, 1960

The *cohanim* (priests) and Levites form a special group among the Jewish people. In Temple times, they were the custodians and public servants of Israel in the Temple service. Today at synagogue services, the *cohanim* bestow the priestly blessing *birkat ha-cohanim* on the congregation after their hands are washed by Levites using a laver and basin for the ritual. This laver and basin was designed by Ludwig Yehuda Wolpert, who was influenced by the Bauhaus in Germany and used stylized calligraphy, a signature of his work.

ARTIST: LUDWIG YEHUDA WOLPERT
(1900–1981)
BRASS AND SILVER
21 CM (JUG AND BASIN HEIGHT);
32.8 CM (BASIN DIAMETER)
PHOTOGRAPH: ISRAEL MUSEUM/
DAVID HARRIS

November | 1 2 3 4 **5** 6 7 8 9 10 11 12 13 14 15 16 17 18 19 20 21 22 23 24 25 26 27 28 29 30

א ב **ג** ד ה ו ז ח ט י י״א י״ב י״ג י״ד ט״ו ט״ז י״ז י״ח י״ט כ כ״א כ״ב כ״ג כ״ד כ״ה כ״ו כ״ז כ״ח כ״ט | חשון

Ostracon
Mesad Hashavyahu, Iron Age,
Late 7th Century BCE

This ostracon (inscribed pottery shard) bears a letter of complaint addressed to the local authority, accusing a certain officer of unfairly confiscating someone's garment. The letter is interesting in light of the biblical injunction: "If you take your neighbor's garment in pledge, you must return it to him before the sun sets" (Exodus 22:25).

INK ON POTTERY
21 CM (HEIGHT)
ISRAEL ANTIQUITIES AUTHORITY
PHOTOGRAPH: ISRAEL MUSEUM/
AVSHALOM AVITAL

November | 1 2 3 4 5 **6** 7 8 9 10 11 12 13 14 15 16 17 18 19 20 21 22 23 24 25 26 27 28 29 30

חשון | א ב ג **ד** ה ו ז ח ט י י״א י״ב י״ג י״ד ט״ו ט״ז י״ז י״ח י״ט כ כ״א כ״ב כ״ג כ״ד כ״ה כ״ו כ״ז כ״ח כ״ט

AMULET CASES
ITALY, 17TH AND 18TH CENTURY

These amulet cases, called *Shaddai* (the name of the Almighty), were hung above a baby's cradle for protection against the evil eye. They would originally have contained an amuletic inscription on paper or parchment made for a particular user; this inscription would later be replaced by another as the case was handed from owner to owner. Both cases are decorated with the utensils of the Tabernacle.

CAST AND REPOUSSÉ SILVER; AGATE
LEFT TO RIGHT: 12.3 X 8.6 CM;
14.2 X 9.5 CM
THE STIEGLITZ COLLECTION WAS
DONATED TO THE ISRAEL MUSEUM,
JERUSALEM WITH THE CONTRIBUTION
OF ERICA AND LUDWIG JESSELSON,
NEW YORK, THROUGH THE
AMERICAN FRIENDS OF
THE ISRAEL MUSEUM
PHOTOGRAPH: ISRAEL MUSEUM/
AVI GANOR

November | 1 2 3 4 5 6 **7** 8 9 10 11 12 13 14 15 16 17 18 19 20 21 22 23 24 25 26 27 28 29 30

חשון | א ב ג ד ה ו ז ח ט י יא יב יג יד טו טז יז יח יט כ כא כב כג כד כה כו כז כח כט

The Wanderings and Life of Abraham, the Patriarch, ca. 1603

Abraham Ortelius, Flemish
(1527–1598)
Hand-colored engraving on paper
by Frans Hogenberg
36 x 47 cm (plate)
From: Abraham Ortelius,
Theatrum orbis terrarum,
Johannes Baptista Vrients,
Antwerp, 1603
Norman Bier Section for
Maps of the Holy Land
Gift of Norman and Frieda Bier,
London
B 95.0693
Photograph: Israel Museum/
Ilan Stzulman

This map of Canaan and part of Egypt, from the Dan to the Nile delta, is decorated with twenty-two medallions depicting scenes from the life of the patriarch Abraham, from his departure from Ur of the Chaldees, up to his death. At the upper left is a map of the Middle East, showing the route Abraham followed from Mesopotamia to Shechem. Above and below the map is the inscription "Get thee out of thy country, and from thy kindred, and from thy father's house, unto a land that I will show thee" (Genesis 12:1–2). Ortelius was the first cartographer to collect maps of uniform size together in a book with explanatory texts, creating a kind of atlas. He dedicated himself to the study of geography, and was tutored by Gerardus Mercator, the greatest geographer of his time. The map exemplifies the growing interest in the sixteenth century in historical as well as modern maps, and especially in biblical themes. It also illustrates vividly Ortelius's delicate touch as an engraver.

November | 1 2 3 4 5 6 7 **8** 9 10 11 12 13 14 15 16 17 18 19 20 21 22 23 24 25 26 27 28 29 30

א ב ג ד ה ו ז ח ט י יא יב יג יד טו טז יז יח יט כ כא כב כג כד כה כו כז כח כט | חשון

ABRAHAMI PATRIAR-
CHAE PEREGRINATIO,
ET VITA.

Abrahamo Ortelio Antverpiano auctore.

ABRAHAM EGREDERE DE TERRA TVA, ET DE COGNATIONE TVA, ET VENI IN TERRAM QVAM MONSTRAVERO TIBI.

Septemtrio.

Occidens

Oriens

Meridies.

Dño Ioanni Moflinio,
Montis S.Winoci ab-
bati reverendo, viro
humanitate & can-
dore eximio, multi-
pliciq; rerum cog-
nitione nobili. Ab.
Ortelius in perpetuæ
amicitiæ pignus DD.

AEGYP-
TVS.

Leucæ
Mill. Ger.
Mille Paſ.

10   20   30   40   50

ET DABO TIBI, ET SEMINI TVO POST TE, TERRAM PEREGRINATIONIS TVAE, OMNEM TERRAM CHANAAN, IN POSSESSIONEM AETERNAM.

Synagogue exterior
Hamburg, Germany, 1906

This postcard shows the inauguration of the Synagoge der Deutsch-Israelitischen Gemeinde in Hamburg, on the thirteenth of September, 1906. This huge Neo-Gothic building was typical of large urban synagogues in Germany. The Jewish congregation of Hamburg was the fourth largest in Germany. The synagogue was destroyed on Kristallnacht, the night of November 9, 1938, when many synagogues were looted and destroyed. Approximately 7,800 Jews from Hamburg and the area lost their lives during the Nazi period.

Black-and-white postcard
9 x 14 cm
Gift of Julian and
Serena Gecelter, South Africa

November | 1 2 3 4 5 6 7 8 **9** 10 11 12 13 14 15 16 17 18 19 20 21 22 23 24 25 26 27 28 29 30

חשון | א ב ג ד ה ו **ז** ח ט י יא יב יג יד טו טז יז יח יט כ כא כב כג כד כה כו כז כח כט

Synagoge der Deutsch-Israelitischen Gemeinde
in Hamburg am Bornplatz
Eingeweiht den 13. Sept. 1906.

Marriage contract (*KETUBBAH*)
Meshed, Iran, 1901

In 1839 the entire Jewish community of Meshed was forced to convert to Islam. Still, the Jews continued to observe their faith in secret. Although weddings were openly carried out in the Muslim fashion and confirmed by the Muslim deed of marriage, each family would also create and secretly preserve a traditional Jewish *ketubbah* written in Hebrew as well. This *ketubbah* records a wedding that took place on the eighth of Heshvan.

GOUACHE AND INK ON PAPER
220 X 140 CM
THE FEUCHTWANGER COLLECTION
PURCHASED AND DONATED TO THE
ISRAEL MUSEUM BY BARUCH AND
RUTH RAPPAPORT OF GENEVA
PHOTOGRAPH: ISRAEL MUSEUM/
DAVID HARRIS

November | 1 2 3 4 5 6 7 8 9 **10** 11 12 13 14 15 16 17 18 19 20 21 22 23 24 25 26 27 28 29 30

חשון ‏| א ב ג ד ה ו ז **ח** ט י יא יב יג יד טו טז יז יח יט כ כא כב כג כד כה כו כז כח כט

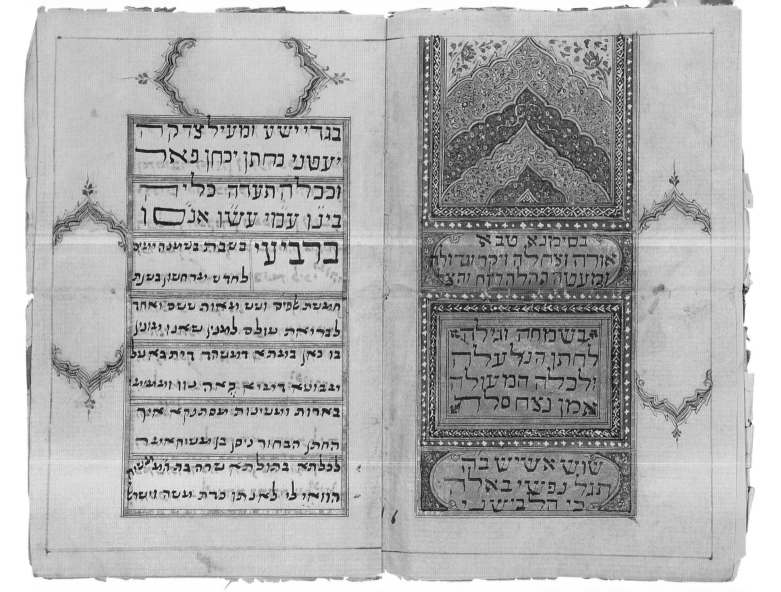

[Right page]

בסימנא טבא

אורה וצהלה ויקר וגדולה
ומעטה תהלה הדוח וה...

ובשמחה וגילה
לחתן הנעלה
ולכלה המעולה
אמן נצח סלה

שוש אשיש בה'
תגל נפשי באלה
כי הלבישני

[Left page]

בגרייש ומעיל צדקה
יעטני נחתן יכהן פאר
וככלה תעדה כליה
בינו עמי עשו אנשם ו
ברביעי בשבת בשמנה ימי
לחדש מרחשון בענת

תמצת שפיר וטע ונאוה עשכ ואחר
לבריאת עולם למנין שאנו מונין
בו כאן בעגתא דנעשהר דיתבא עב
ובבועא דיבוא כאה כון ונבובו
בארות ועעינות עסתנקא איך
החתן הבחור ניסן בן עשוק אוצר
לכבתא בהולתא שרה בת הגלשות
הואיל לי לאנתן כרת עשה ושש

Wedding box

This wedding box was made by the American Jewish artist Ilya Schor on the occasion of the wedding of his friend the Jewish painter Mane Katz. On the cover of the box is a depiction of a wedding ceremony, showing the bride and groom under a bridal canopy surrounded by guests. Inside the bottom of the box is the Yiddish inscription: "Ilya (Israel) Schor made this little box for the painter Mane Katz in the year (5)718 [= 1958] in New York."

New York, 1958
Artist: Ilya Schor
Pierced and engraved
gold and silver
36 x 90 x 62 x 61 cm
The Stieglitz Collection was
donated to the Israel Museum,
Jerusalem with the contribution
of Erica and Ludwig Jesselson,
New York, through the
American Friends of
the Israel Museum
Photograph: Israel Museum/
Avi Ganor

November | 1 2 3 4 5 6 7 8 9 10 **11** 12 13 14 15 16 17 18 19 20 21 22 23 24 25 26 27 28 29 30

חשון | ט ח ז ו ה ד ג ב א י יא יב יג יד טו טז יז יח יט כ כא כב כג כד כה כו כז כח כט

Interior of Centerville Station Synagogue New York, 1935

The somber atmosphere of this photograph reflects the silence of the place of prayer, located in hectic surroundings. The colored stained-glass windows shed soft light on the wooden interior, reminiscent of European synagogues. Above the Torah Ark is a round window with the Star of David, emphasizing the Jewish identity of the building.

Color postcard
9 x 14 cm
Gift of Julian and
Serena Gecelter, South Africa

November | 1 2 3 4 5 6 7 8 9 10 11 **12** 13 14 15 16 17 18 19 20 21 22 23 24 25 26 27 28 29 30

א ב ג ד ה ו ז ח ט 'י יא יב יג יד טו טז יז יח יט כ כא כב כג כד כה כו כז כח כט | חשון

INTERIOR OF SYNAGOGUE, CENTERVILLE STATION, N.Y.

MODERN MAP OF PALESTINE, 1486

AFTER MARINO SANUTO
(CA. 1260–1368) AND
PETRUS VESCONTE (D. CA. 1350)
HAND-COLORED WOODCUT ON
PAPER, BY JOHANNES SCHNITZER
FROM ARNHEM
39.7 X 58 CM
FROM: CLAUDIUS PTOLEMAEUS,
COSMOGRAPHIA, PUBLISHED BY
LEONARDUS HOLLE, ULM, 1486
NORMAN BIER SECTION FOR
MAPS OF THE HOLY LAND
GIFT OF NORMAN AND
FRIEDA BIER, LONDON
B 95.0700
PHOTOGRAPH: ISRAEL MUSEUM/
ILAN STZULMAN

This rare map, with its original coloring, is oriented to the east. It shows the division of the Holy Land into the patrimonies of the twelve tribes. The coastline extends from Sidon to Gaza. Although the map was originally made by Vesconte and Sanuto, Nicolaus Germanus, a fifteenth-century monk, added five "modern" maps including this one to a group of twenty-seven based on Ptolemaeus's drawings. Since then, it has been associated with Claudius Ptolemaeus, known in English as Ptolemy. One hundred and fifty years earlier, in September 1321, this map had been included in a book presented to Pope John XXII in Avignon, with the aim of rousing the European powers to launch a new crusade to conquer the holy sites in the Land of Israel. This map is of decisive importance in the development of the cartography of the Holy Land. Despite some inaccuracies, it is much more precise than other medieval maps in topographical detail and its indication of longitude and latitude. Its influence was felt until the end of the seventeenth century.

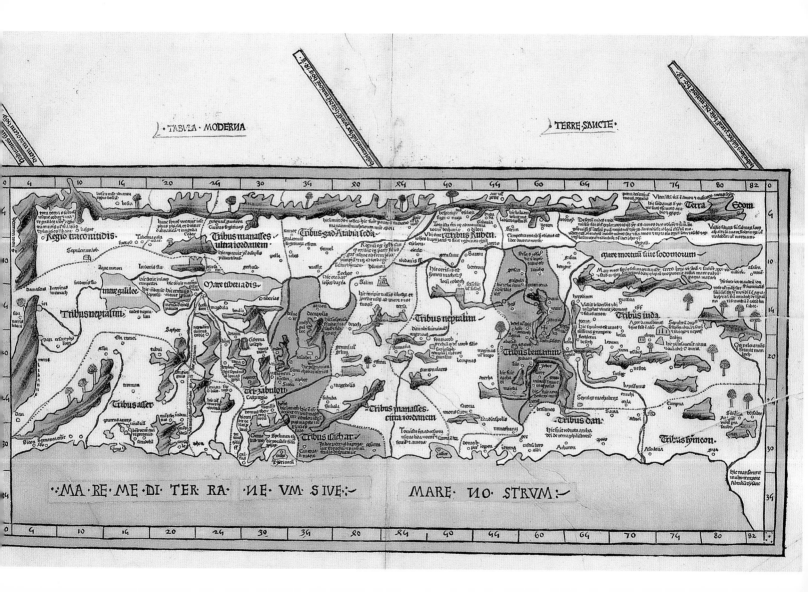

Prayers at Rachel's Tomb
Eretz Israel, early 20th century

The photograph shows the interior of the tomb of the biblical matriarch Rachel in Bethlehem, whose memorial day is in the month of Heshvan. On her tomb is a Hebrew sign inscribed with part of the quotation from Genesis 35:20: "Over her grave Jacob set up a pillar, it is the pillar at Rachel's grave to this day." The German and Hebrew writing on the postcard describe the elderly men from a Jerusalem old-age home who come to pray at the Tomb of Rachel for the well-being of friends, donors, and the nation of Israel in the Diaspora.

Sepia postcard
9 x 14 cm
Gift of Dr. Carl Wilhelm
Jakobonsky, Sweden, 1975
Photograph: Israel Museum

November | 1 2 3 4 5 6 7 8 9 10 11 12 13 **14** 15 16 17 18 19 20 21 22 23 24 25 26 27 28 29 30

חשון‎ | א ב ג ד ה ו ז ח ט י י"א י"ב י"ג י"ד ט"ו ט"ז י"ז י"ח י"ט כ כ"א כ"ב כ"ג כ"ד כ"ה כ"ו כ"ז כ"ח כ"ט

Gebetverrichtung am Grabe
Rahel's v. Greisen des Altenhauses
„Mosehab-et-Sekenim"
Jerusalem für das Wohl d. Mitglieder
und Spender desselben.

מצבת קברת הרחל

מצבת קבורת
רחל עד היום

שלשה מנינים זקנים מחוסי בית מושב הזקנים שבירושלם בהתפללם בעד שלום החברים
והנריבים ושאר אחב"י שבגולה על יד מצבת קבורת רחל אמנו זי"ע

THE FOURTH PART OF THE MAP OF ASIA, 1618-19

GERARDUS MERCATOR,
FLEMISH (1512–1594)
AFTER PTOLEMAEUS,
CA. 87–CA. 150 CE
HAND-COLORED ENGRAVING
ON PAPER
(ORIGINAL PLATE ENGRAVED IN 1578)
35.3 X 47.8 CM
FROM: PTOLEMAEUS-MERCATOR'S
GEOGRAPHIA, ISAAC ELZEVIR,
LEYDEN, 1618/19,
PUBLISHED BY JODOCUS HONDIUS,
EDITED BY PETRUS BERITUS
NORMAN BIER SECTION FOR
MAPS OF THE HOLY LAND
GIFT OF NORMAN AND FRIEDA BIER,
LONDON
M795-3-55
PHOTOGRAPH: ISRAEL MUSEUM/
ILAN STZULMAN

The Greek astronomer and geographer Ptolemaeus (Ptolemy) of Alexandria was considered the last of the great scholars of antiquity. His book *Geographia*, which saw forty-six editions between the fifteenth and eighteenth centuries, lists some eight thousand place names with their latitudes and longitudes. Ptolemaeus's maps laid the foundations for the transformation of cartography into a science. Mercator faithfully copied this map, one of the two most influential maps in the history of Holy Land cartography up to the eighteenth century. Oriented to the north, it includes the Mediterranean lands, from Babylonia (Iraq) to Cyprus. The Land of Israel is divided into Galilee, Samaria, Judea, and Edom, shown as the most densely populated area in the region. Mercator invented a projection from a sphere to a plane that is used in cartography to this day.

November | 1 2 3 4 5 6 7 8 9 10 11 12 13 14 **15** 16 17 18 19 20 21 22 23 24 25 26 27 28 29 30

חשון | א ב ג ד ה ו ז ח ט י יא יב **יג** יד טו טז יז יח יט כ כא כב כג כד כה כו כז כח כט

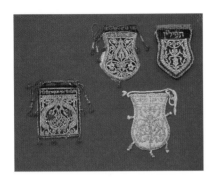

TEFILLIN BAGS
MOROCCO, 20TH CENTURY

These bags made of velvet or satin silk were used for keeping the phylacteries. Highly decorated, they were embroidered with the names of the bar mitzvah boy, the tree of life (sometimes in the shape of a lotus), birds, and *hamsa* (hand shapes) to ensure protection from the evil eye. Sometimes they were decorated with fine silver openwork.

VELVET; SILK;
GOLD-THREAD EMBROIDERY
24 X 16 CM
PHOTOGRAPH: ISRAEL MUSEUM/
CHANAN SADEH

November | 1 2 3 4 5 6 7 8 9 10 11 12 13 14 15 **16** 17 18 19 20 21 22 23 24 25 26 27 28 29 30

חשון | א ב ג ד ה ו ז ח ט י א י ב י ג **י״ד** ט ו ט ז י ז י ח י ט כ כא כב כג כד כה כו כז כח כט

Women's and children's socks
Iraqi and Iranian Kurdistan,
early–mid 20th century

Men and women both wore socks, but different designs were used by each sex. Children's socks, short and sometimes with a leather sole, were also worn in the house as slippers. They were gaily colored and decorated and show the influence of kelim patterns. They were knitted with pointed needles made from pomegranate wood or bone.

Hand-knit wool
20–30 cm (length)
Photograph: Israel Museum/
Yoram Lehmann

November ⏐ 1 2 3 4 5 6 7 8 9 10 11 12 13 14 15 16 **17** 18 19 20 21 22 23 24 25 26 27 28 29 30

א ב ג ד ה ו ז ח ט י יא יב יג יד **טו** טז יז יח יט כ כא כב כג כד כה כו כז כח כט ⏐ חשון

Seashore, Jaffa, 1920s

Ben-Dov faced into the sun to shoot this photograph, so the sea seems dark and stormy. This gives the image a dramatic, painterly quality that brings to mind the Romantic seascapes of artists such as Turner. The solitary figure standing on the shore, possibly a new immigrant, looks out to sea, toward the past and the place she left behind. Jaffa, the only active port in Eretz Israel during the period of the pre-State Zionist *aliyahs*, was the point of entry for all immigrants at this time.

חוף יפו

SABBATH CLOTH
ERETZ ISRAEL, 19TH CENTURY

This cloth was designed in the Old City of Jerusalem in the late nineteenth century by craftsman Simche Janower, who was born in Grodno, Lithuania, and came to live in the Old City of Jerusalem in 1853. Women of Jerusalem would order embroidery designs from him for different objects including phylactery (*tefillin*) bags, Sabbath aprons, and tablecloths. This richly embroidered special Sabbath tablecloth depicts holy sites with the Temple and Western Wall in the center and the tombs of Kings of the House of David, Rachel, Samuel, and Hulda in the four corners. Around the border is embroidered the song "Shalom Aleikhem," welcoming the Sabbath.

EMBROIDERY;
WOOL THREAD ON COTTON
114 X 130 CM
GIFT OF BORIS SCHATZ
PHOTOGRAPH: ISRAEL MUSEUM/
DAVID HARRIS

November | 1 2 3 4 5 6 7 8 9 10 11 12 13 14 15 16 17 18 **19** 20 21 22 23 24 25 26 27 28 29 30

חשון | א ב ג ד ה ו ז ח ט י יא יב יג יד טו טז **יז** יח יט כ כא כב כג כד כה כו כז כח כט

Mizrah
Germany, 1818

The *mizrah* (literally: east) is a single sheet or plaque, hung on an eastern wall in a Jewish home. It was meant to indicate the direction to face during prayers, toward Jerusalem. Over the years the *mizrah* became a typical ornament in Jewish homes often presented as a wedding gift. It was customary to decorate the *mizrah* sheet with drawings or papercuts. This papercut bears a Hebrew inscription mentioning the name of the maker, Shim'on Pfaumloch, butcher and inspector of kosher meat, as well as the married couple to whom the sheet is dedicated, and the Hebrew date of the eighteenth of Heshvan.

November | 1 2 3 4 5 6 7 8 9 10 11 12 13 14 15 16 17 18 19 **20** 21 22 23 24 25 26 27 28 29 30

א ב ג ד ה ו ז ח ט י יא יב יג יד טו טז יז **יח** יט כ כא כב כג כד כה כו כז כח כט | חשון

נעשה ונגמר ביום שנכפל בו כי טוב ח' טוב ח' מרחשון תקס"ט כפ"ק ט' הצעיר הנזכר למטה

וישוע

מצד זה רוח חיים

אייזק וואלה מן הצעיר שמעון פפלוינלאר ולעת עתה ש"ץ ושו"ב בעיר ד"ינסבאר

Packing at the Petah Tikva Orchards, 1920s

The citrus industry was one of the most important in the formative years of Israel, especially in the pre-State years. Apart from the groves where the fruit was grown, a whole infrastructure grew to support the agriculture and facilitate its sale and export: packinghouses, crate builders, sales operations, preserves and juice factories, and shipping companies were all a necessary part of the industry. The Petah Tikva packinghouse was one of the largest and most developed, and for many years all official visitors to Eretz Israel were taken to see it.

Yaacov Ben-Dov
(1882, Russia–1968, Israel),
immigrated to Eretz Israel, 1908
Gelatin silver print
Gift of Rena (Fisch) and
Robert Lewin, London

November | 1 2 3 4 5 6 7 8 9 10 11 12 13 14 15 16 17 18 19 20 **21** 22 23 24 25 26 27 28 29 30

א ב ג ד ה ו ז ח ט י יא יב יג יד טו טז יז יח **יט** כ כא כב כג כד כה כו כז כח כט | חשון

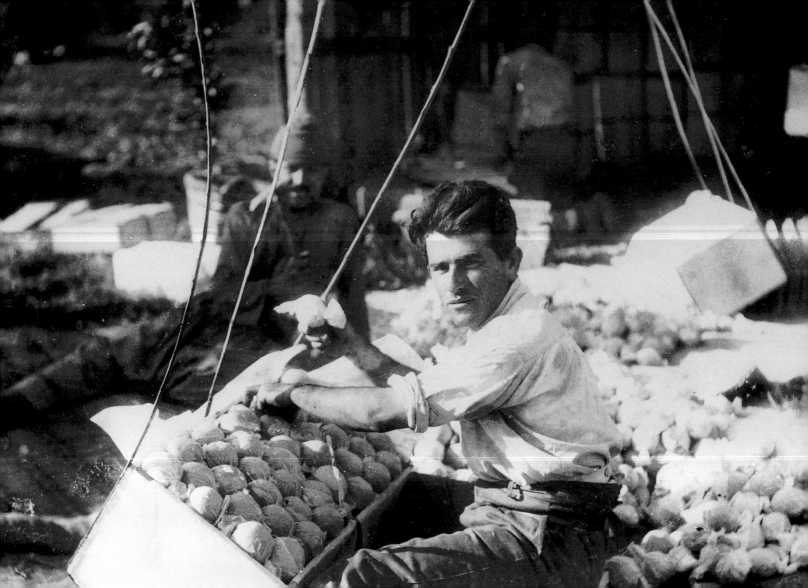

Hanukkah lamp
Ifrane, Morocco,
late 19th–mid 20th century

Hanukkah lamps made of stone or earthenware were to be found mostly in the small towns and villages of southern Morocco. These lamps generally take the form of boxes carved from a single stone block. It is interesting to note the similarities between Yemenite and southern Moroccan Hanukkah lamps, seeming to point to a long-ago common origin.

Steatite (soapstone)
15.8 x 14.5 x 3.2 cm
Gift of the Zeyde
Schulmann Collection
Photograph: Israel Museum/
Avraham Hay

November | 1 2 3 4 5 6 7 8 9 10 11 12 13 14 15 16 17 18 19 20 21 **22** 23 24 25 26 27 28 29 30

חשון‎ | א ב ג ד ה ו ז ח ט י יא יב יג יד טו טז יז יח יט כ כא כב כג כד כה כו כז כח כט

Marriage contract (*ketubbah*)
Isfahan, Iran, 1898

The *ketubbah* is a written contract of marriage between husband and wife. In the presence of two witnesses, the groom undertakes to guarantee the wife's sustenance should the marriage be dissolved. This prominent motif in the Isfahan *ketubbah*, a pair of facing lions, each with a sun with a human face on its back, is the symbol of Iranian royalty from antiquity; it was also frequently adopted by the Jewish community.

GROOM: ABRAHAM, SON OF ELIJAH
BRIDE: BRURIA, DAUGHTER OF JOSEPH
WATERCOLOR AND PEN AND INK ON
PAPER; COLORED PAPER BAND FRAME
97.5 X 79.3 CM
PHOTOGRAPH: ISRAEL MUSEUM/
DAVID HARRIS

November | 1 2 3 4 5 6 7 8 9 10 11 12 13 14 15 16 17 18 19 20 21 22 **23** 24 25 26 27 28 29 30

א ב ג ד ה ו ז ח ט י יא יב יג יד טו טז יז יח יט כ **כא** כב כג כד כה כו כז כח כט | חשון

Wrapper, towels, and other items for the ritual bath (MIKVEH)
Ottoman Empire, 19th century

Prior to her wedding, the bride was required to purify herself by immersion in a ritual bath *(mikveh)*. A gift of a set of bath accessories *(bógo do bányo)* was sent to her from the bridegroom. The bride wore the high-heeled clogs, an integral part of this gift, to avoid slipping on wet floors.

Silk linen and cotton wrap:
Silk, metal thread
Washing bowl: silver
Clogs: wood, inlaid mother of pearl
60 x 125–27 x 205 cm
Gift of Mazal-Tov Amon through
Eda Amon, Joseph Soustiel Paris,
Mrs. Bitran, Izmir
Purchased by courtesy of
Jacques Levy Barcelona
Photograph: Israel Museum/
David Harris

November | 1 2 3 4 5 6 7 8 9 10 11 12 13 14 15 16 17 18 19 20 21 22 23 **24** 25 26 27 28 29 30

חשון | א ב ג ד ה ו ז ח ט י יא יב יג יד טו טז יז יח יט כ כא **כב** כג כד כה כו כז כח כט

Woman's head covering
Tiznit, Morocco, mid 20th century

This elaborate head covering *(mehdor)* was worn by Jewish women in southern Morocco in accordance with the precept that married women should cover their hair. It was composed of coils of silver thread interwoven with hair from a horse's mane, as well as decorative silver pieces inlaid with semiprecious stones and beads.

SILVER-THREAD EMBROIDERY;
HORSE-MANE HAIR ON COTTON;
SILVER; ENAMEL; INLAID GLASS; BEADS
20 CM (HEIGHT)
PHOTOGRAPH: ISRAEL MUSEUM/
DAVID HARRIS

November | 1 2 3 4 5 6 7 8 9 10 11 12 13 14 15 16 17 18 19 20 21 22 23 24 **25** 26 27 28 29 30

חשון | א ב ג ד ה ו ז ח ט י יא יב יג יד טו טז יז יח יט כ כא כב **כג** כד כה כו כז כח כט

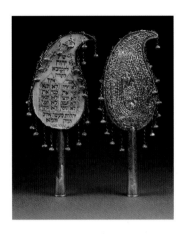

Torah finials
Yazd, Iran, 1927

These unusual flat Torah finials, called crowns, are different in form from the usual Torah finials. They were placed on top of the Torah scroll case. Their *boteh* shape, resembling a pear or pinecone, is influenced by Persian art and seen on rugs and other objects; it is known in the West as the paisley pattern. These finials are inscribed on one side with the Ten Commandments written on paper protected by glass; the other side is engraved in silver with floral patterns.

SILVER AND PEN AND INK
ON PAPER; GLASS
30 X 9.5 CM
GIFT OF ELIEZER BEN DOV, TEHRAN
PHOTOGRAPH: ISRAEL MUSEUM

November | 1 2 3 4 5 6 7 8 9 10 11 12 13 14 15 16 17 18 19 20 21 22 23 24 25 **26** 27 28 29 30

חשון | א ב ג ד ה ו ז ח ט י י״א י״ב י״ג י״ד ט״ו ט״ז י״ז י״ח י״ט כ כ״א כ״ב כ״ג **כד** כה כו כז כח כט

Hexagonal bottle
Provenance unknown, Byzantine Period, late 6th–7th century ce

This bottle, which was blown in a mold, is decorated with Jewish symbols in relief. Similar bottles bearing Christian symbols are also known. Such containers were used by pilgrims to carry souvenirs of water or oil from Jerusalem and other holy sites.

Glass
7.8 cm (height)
Dobkin Collection
Photograph: Israel Museum/
Avshalom Avital

November | 1 2 3 4 5 6 7 8 9 10 11 12 13 14 15 16 17 18 19 20 21 22 23 24 25 26 **27** 28 29 30

א ב ג ד ה ו ז ח ט י יא יב יג יד טו טז יז יח יט כ כא כב כג כד **כה** כו כז כח כט | חשון

Set of bathing accessories for the bridegroom
Herat, Afghanistan,
early to mid 20th century

Early in the morning the day before the wedding, the bridegroom went to a ceremonial bath with the male members of the family. This ceremony involved singing and dancing, and refreshments were served. The groom was given a massage, and his body was smeared with perfumed gel, among other beauty treatments.

Photograph: Israel Museum/
David Harris

November | 1 2 3 4 5 6 7 8 9 10 11 12 13 14 15 16 17 18 19 20 21 22 23 24 25 26 27 **28** 29 30

א ב ג ד ה ו ז ח ט י יא יב יג יד טו טז יז יח יט כ כא כב כג כד כה **כו** כז כח כט | חשון

Hanukkah lamp
Marrakesh, Morocco, 20th century

Eretz Israel (the Land of Israel) and Yerushalayim (Jerusalem) always aroused a
deep sense of yearning in Jews wherever they lived. The close connection to the
Zionist movement is clearly seen in the national emblems in this Hanukkah lamp.

Cast brass
13 x 10.5 cm
Gift of the Zeyde Schulmann
Collection
Photograph: Israel Museum/
Avraham Hay

November | 1 2 3 4 5 6 7 8 9 10 11 12 13 14 15 16 17 18 19 20 21 22 23 24 25 26 27 28 **29** 30

א ב ג ד ה ו ז ח ט י יא יב יג יד טו טז יז יח יט כ כא כב כג כד כה כו כז כח כט | חשון

Baking flatbread in the tradition of Kurdistan
Israel, 1979

There were two kinds of breads in Iraqi Kurdistan, both made from sourdough. The more common kind, *lahma reqiqa*, was very thin, flat, and dry, baked once a month on a convex iron plate. The dough was flattened into a very thin leaf and then baked on both sides. It was easy to store and was sprinkled with water before serving. When folded and filled with sugar, cheese, or nuts, it could be turned into a sweet cake.

Israel Museum
Ethnography Archive
Photograph: Israel Museum/
Ora Shwartz-Be'eri

November | 1 2 3 4 5 6 7 8 9 10 11 12 13 14 15 16 17 18 19 20 21 22 23 24 25 26 27 28 29 **30**

א ב ג ד ה ו ז ח ט י יא יב יג יד טו טז יז יח יט כ כא כב כג כד כה כו כז **כח** כט | חשון

ETHIOPIAN EMBROIDERY
BEERSHEBA, ISRAEL, 1991

The Jews of Ethiopia expressed their longing for Zion-Jerusalem in their handicrafts, a tradition that did not come to an end after emigration. Although embroidery was traditionally the domain of women in Ethiopia, Yazazo Aklum was one of the few men who took up the craft, among his other occupations. He embroidered pictures of his dreams, such as the Temple in the form of a traditional Ethiopian house, incorporating the Ten Commandments. The picture also represents members of the craftsman's extended family, with the names of the most important men in his family embroidered in Hebrew and Tigrina.

EMBROIDERER: YAZAZO AKLUM
IN THE TRADITION OF
DABAGUNA VILLAGE,
TIGRE PROVINCE OF ETHIOPIA
PHOTOGRAPH: ISRAEL MUSEUM/
ORA SHWARTZ BE'ERI

December ❘ I 2 3 4 5 6 7 8 9 10 11 12 13 14 15 16 17 18 19 20 21 22 23 24 25 26 27 28 29 30 31

חשון ‖ א ב ג ד ה ו ז ח ט י יא יב יג יד טו טז יז יח יט כ כא כב כג כד כה כו כז כח **כט**

Bags for the marriage contract (*KETUBBAH*)
Herat, Afghanistan, 1920

A bride's mother would make two bags as part of her daughter's trousseau, one for the *ketubbah* and one attesting to the bride's virginity. The mother would keep both bags after the wedding ceremonies. The marriage took place in the bride's home at noon, and that evening a joyful feast was held at the home of the groom, where the couple would live.

Cotton and silk trimmed
with ribbons
8–22 cm (length)
Gift of Leah Yekutiel
Photograph: Israel Museum/
David Harris

December │ 1 **2** 3 4 5 6 7 8 9 10 11 12 13 14 15 16 17 18 19 20 21 22 23 24 25 26 27 28 29 30 31

ב ג ד ה ו ז ח ט י יא יב יג יד טו טז יז יח יט כ כא כב כג כד כה כו כז כח כט ל **א** │ כסלו

Torah Ark curtain
Izmir, Ottoman Empire, 1907

In most Sephardi synagogues in Turkey it was customary to hang one curtain in front of the Ark and another inside. The Ark curtains were often made out of large hangings and bridal covers that had once been part of a dowry; this one was sewn together from cushion covers and parts of richly embroidered garments. The Hebrew dedication in memory of Rivkele by her husband, Eliahu Gabai, was added on its consecration to the synagogue.

December | 1 2 **3** 4 5 6 7 8 9 10 11 12 13 14 15 16 17 18 19 20 21 22 23 24 25 26 27 28 29 30 31

כסלו | א **ב** ג ד ה ו ז ח ט י יא יב יג יד טו טז יז יח יט כ כא כב כג כד כה כו כז כח כט ל

Prayer shawl bag
Rhodes, 20th century

The practice of reusing everyday objects and converting them into ritual objects was well known among Jews in the Ottoman Empire. Embroidered material perhaps once part of a dowry would be reused to form other objects such as this bag (in Ladino: *taléga koráča*), which was used to hold a prayer shawl *(tallith)*. It was probably given as a gift to a bridegroom or to a boy on his bar mitzvah.

Satin; couched metal thread
embroidery
20 x 25 cm
Gift of Clara Menasce, Brussels
Photograph: Israel Museum/
Nahum Slapak

December | 1 2 3 **4** 5 6 7 8 9 10 11 12 13 14 15 16 17 18 19 20 21 22 23 24 25 26 27 28 29 30 31

כסלו | א ב **ג** ד ה ו ז ח ט י יא יב יג יד טו טז יז יח יט כ כא כב כג כד כה כו כז כח כט ל

MIRROR WITH DEPICTION OF JACOB AND RACHEL JERUSALEM, EARLY 20TH CENTURY

This mirror was produced in the Bezalel workshop in Jerusalem. The cornerstone of Bezalel design was the creation of a habitat and lifestyle with symbolic Zionist meaning through the use of images that served the Zionist worldview, as well as an aspiration to link the "new" Jew with beauty and physicality. The story of Jacob and Rachel is one of sensual love and is therefore appropriate for the decoration of an object intended for a woman's toilet. It is also linked to the pastoral atmosphere of the biblical shepherd's life, which, in comparison to the difficulties of life in a modern European city or a poor Jewish shtetl, was filled with romantic charm. The combination of rich materials, a biblical subject, sensuality and romance, and a design that fuses the influence of Western art nouveau with Eastern formal motifs transforms this object into the representation of a secular Zionist worldview that correlated the ancient past with modern life. What is more appropriate than a mirror to reflect an independent ancient-modern identity?

December | 1 2 3 4 **5** 6 7 8 9 10 11 12 13 14 15 16 17 18 19 20 21 22 23 24 25 26 27 28 29 30 31

כסלו | א ב ג **ד** ה ו ז ח ט י יא יב יג יד טו טז יז יח יט כ כא כב כג כד כה כו כז כח כט ל

Hanukkah lamps
Morocco and Algeria,
18th–20th century

Celebrated for eight days, the Hanukkah festival commemorates the rededication of the Temple in Jerusalem by the Maccabees in 164 BCE. The structure and design of a Hanukkah lamp usually reflects the style typical of the area in which it was created. In these examples from North Africa, the influence of local Islamic architectural elements can be seen. The arabesque style with the combination of floral patterns and the architectural motif of the horseshoe arch recalls the influence of the thriving Hispano-Moorish tradition in those countries.

BRASS; COPPER
22–51 CM (HEIGHT)
PHOTOGRAPH: ISRAEL MUSEUM/
YORAM LEHMANN

December | 1 2 3 4 5 **6** 7 8 9 10 11 12 13 14 15 16 17 18 19 20 21 22 23 24 25 26 27 28 29 30 31

כסלו | א ב ג ד **ה** ו ז ח ט י יא יב יג יד טו טז יז יח יט כ כא כב כג כד כה כו כז כח כט ל

LEFT AND CENTER:
DOUBLE BEAKER, SEPARATED
REPOUSSÉ, ENGRAVED, AND
PARTLY GILT SILVER
VIENNA, AUSTRIA, 1707
137 X 74 CM (PART I), 137 X 72 CM (PART 2)

RIGHT: DOUBLE BEAKER
HALL (TIROL), AUSTRIA-HUNGARY, 1827
REPOUSSÉ, ENGRAVED, AND
PARTLY GILT SILVER
62 X 66 (PART I), 64 X 63 CM (PART 2)

CIRCUMCISION KNIVES, LEFT TO RIGHT:
GERMANY, 17TH CENTURY
PIERCED, ENGRAVED,
AND GILT SILVER; STEEL;
YELLOW AGATE
170 X 25 X 15 CM

GERMANY, 18TH CENTURY
PARTLY GILT SILVER
190 X 22 CM

DOUBLE BEAKERS AND KNIVES FOR CIRCUMCISION AUSTRIA AND GERMANY, 17TH–19TH CENTURY

The circumcision ceremony marks the entry of the male infant into the Covenant of Abraham, one of the central commandments in the Jewish faith. To perform the ritual the *mohel* (circumciser) uses a special set of implements including cups, knives, bottles, and shields.

THE STIEGLITZ COLLECTION WAS DONATED TO
THE ISRAEL MUSEUM, JERUSALEM WITH THE
CONTRIBUTION OF ERICA AND LUDWIG JESSELSON,
NEW YORK, THROUGH THE AMERICAN
FRIENDS OF THE ISRAEL MUSEUM
PHOTOGRAPH: ISRAEL MUSEUM/AVI GANOR

December | 1 2 3 4 5 6 **7** 8 9 10 11 12 13 14 15 16 17 18 19 20 21 22 23 24 25 26 27 28 29 30 31

כסלו | א ב ג ד ה ו ז ח ט י יא יב יג יד טו טז יז יח יט כ כא כב כג כד כה כו כז כח כט ל

COTTON SILK VELVET;
METAL-THREAD AND PEARL EMBROIDERY
TOP TO BOTTOM:
BAND: 91 X 3.5 CM
BAND: 45 X 3.5 CM
KERCHIEFS: 120 X 65 CM
GIFT OF ROBERT HASSON, TEL AVIV;
RACHEL COHEN; PERLA AMON, PARIS;
RACHEL KAMPEAS, ISRAEL
PHOTOGRAPH: ISRAEL MUSEUM/
NAHUM SLAPAK

AMULETIC BANDS AND KERCHIEFS FOR WOMAN IN CHILDBIRTH (*TOKADOR DE PARIDA*) RHODES AND IZMIR, LATE 19TH CENTURY

These amuletic bands and kerchiefs were important items used to protect the mother and newborn against the evil eye. The kerchiefs with a Hebrew inscription included one of the names for God as well as the names of angels who were believed to protect the new mother from Lilith, who was thought to threaten her life and that of the baby. Inscribed amuletic bands were also fastened across the mother's forehead.

December │ 1 2 3 4 5 6 7 **8** 9 10 11 12 13 14 15 16 17 18 19 20 21 22 23 24 25 26 27 28 29 30 31

כסלו │ א ב ג ד ה ו ז ח ט י יא יב יג יד טו טז יז יח יט כ כא כב כג כד כה כו כז כח כט ל

HANUKKAH LAMP
AUSTRIA-HUNGARY, LATE 18TH CENTURY

The main feature of the Hanukkah festival is the lighting of the Hanukkah lamp at home on each of the eight days of the festival. An additional light is added every evening. This lamp, in the shape of a bench with an unusual depiction of a gilt lion's head in the center, bears a Hebrew inscription with the blessings for lighting the candles and the name of its owner, Yehezkel R. M.

ARTIST: JOH. MATHER KIERMAYER (?)
(1767–1807)
REPOUSSÉ, ENGRAVED, AND CAST SILVER
17.8 X 23 X 6 CM
THE STIEGLITZ COLLECTION WAS
DONATED TO THE ISRAEL MUSEUM,
JERUSALEM WITH THE CONTRIBUTION OF
ERICA AND LUDWIG JESSELSON,
NEW YORK, THROUGH THE AMERICAN
FRIENDS OF THE ISRAEL MUSEUM
PHOTOGRAPH: ISRAEL MUSEUM/
AVI GANOR

December | 1 2 3 4 5 6 7 8 **9** 10 11 12 13 14 15 16 17 18 19 20 21 22 23 24 25 26 27 28 29 30 31

כסלו | א ב ג ד ה ו ז **ח** ט י יא יב יג יד טו טז יז יח יט כ כא כב כג כד כה כו כז כח כט ל

SABBATH SHEET
IRAQI KURDISTAN, MID 19TH CENTURY

This special sheet is decorated with blessings for the Sabbath Kiddush prayer and song composed by Isaac Luria, the sixteenth-century Kabbalist, for the Sabbath eve. The recurrent motif on this sheet is groups of circles representing the quince, a common local fruit; the central one is inscribed with verses from the Sabbath prayers.

INK ON PAPER
44 X 55 CM
DONATED BY ELIEZER BEN-DOV,
TEHRAN
PHOTOGRAPH: ISRAEL MUSEUM/
YORAM LEHMANN

December │ 1 2 3 4 5 6 7 8 9 **IO** 11 12 13 14 15 16 17 18 19 20 21 22 23 24 25 26 27 28 29 30 31

כסלו │ א ב ג ד ה ו ז ח **ט** י יא יב יג יד טו טז יז יח יט כ כא כב כג כד כה כו כז כח כט ל

אשת חיל מי ימצא ורחוק מפנינים
מכרה : בטח בה לב בעלה ושלל לא
יחסר : גמלתהו טוב ולא רע כל ימי חייה :
דרשה צמר ופשתים ותעש בחפץ כפיה :
היתה כאניות סוחר ממרחק תביא לחמה : ותקם
בעוד לילה ותתן טרף לביתה וחק לנערתיה :
זממה שדה ותקחהו מפרי כפיה נטעה כרם
חגרה בעוז מתניה ותאמץ זרועתיה : טעמה
כי טוב סחרה לא יכבה בלילה נרה : ידיה
שלחה בכישור וכפיה תמכו פלך : כפה פרשה
לעני וידיה שלחה לאביון : לא תירא לביתה
משלג כי כל ביתה לבוש שנים : מרבדים
עשתה לה שש וארגמן לבושה : נודע
בשערים בעלה בשבתו עם זקני ארץ : סדין
עשתה ותמכר וחגור נתנה לכנעני : עז
והדר לבושה ותשחק ליום אחרון : פיה
פתחה בחכמה ותורת חסד על לשונה :
צופיה הליכות ביתה ולחם עצלות לא תאכל :
קמו בניה ויאשרוה בעלה ויהללה : רבות
בנות עשו חיל ואת עלית על כלנה : שקר
החן והבל היפי אשה יראת ה' היא
תתהלל : תנו לה מפרי ידיה ויהללוה
בשערים מעשיה :

אתקינו סעודתא דמהימנותא
שלימתא חדותא דמלכא
קדישא : אתקינו סעודתא דמלכא דא היא
סעודתא דחקל תפוחין קדישין וזעיר אנפין
ועתיקא קדישא אתין לסעדה
אזמר בשבחין למיעל גו פתחין דבחקל
תפוחין דאינון קדישין :

Hanukkah lamp
Italy, 16th century

The Hanukkah lamp usually comprises eight lights and an additional light called a *shammash* (servant). The backplate of this lamp depicts two sea horses, their manes held by two mermaids placed above them, with a row of oil pans below. Sea horses and mermaids figure prominently in Italian early Renaissance art, so it is not surprising to find them integrated into Italian-Jewish art, including books, marriage contracts, Hanukkah lamps, and other artifacts.

December | 1 2 3 4 5 6 7 8 9 10 **11** 12 13 14 15 16 17 18 19 20 21 22 23 24 25 26 27 28 29 30 31

כסלו | א ב ג ד ה ו ז ח ט י יא יב יג יד טו טז יז יח יט כ כא כב כג כד כה כו כז כח כט ל

Henna ceremony
Moshav Bareket, Israel, 1980s

The Jewish Yemenite community in the rural Israeli village of Moshav Bareket retain the traditions they brought with them from their hometown of Habban in southeastern Yemen. Brides there have their hair done in many braids and their hands and feet decoratively painted with a reddish-brown paste made from the henna plant, which is believed to have protective powers. During the ceremony the bride is dressed in a traditional costume and wears lavish silver jewelry made by the community's silversmiths.

PHOTOGRAPH: ISRAEL MUSEUM/
DOUGLAS GUTHRY, JERUSALEM

December | 1 2 3 4 5 6 7 8 9 10 11 **12** 13 14 15 16 17 18 19 20 21 22 23 24 25 26 27 28 29 30 31

כסלו | א ב ג ד ה ו ז ח ט י **י'** י'ב י'ג י'ד ט'ו ט'ז י'ז י'ח י'ט כ כ'א כ'ב כ'ג כ'ד כ'ה כ'ו כ'ז כ'ח כ'ט ל

Hebrew-German primer, *Sefer Hinukh ha-Yeled* Rodelheim, Germany, 1828

This Hebrew-German primer contains pictures of animals with their Hebrew and German names, enabling the child to study Hebrew in an enjoyable and colorful way. Alphabet charts and books have long been a popular means of education in Jewish communities all over the world.

Letterpress, lithography, and
hand-coloring on paper
18.3 x 9.5 cm
The Feuchtwanger Collection,
purchased and donated by
Baruch and Ruth Rappaport,
Geneva
Photograph: Israel Museum

December | 1 2 3 4 5 6 7 8 9 10 11 12 **13** 14 15 16 17 18 19 20 21 22 23 24 25 26 27 28 29 30 31

כסלו | א ב ג ד ה ו ז ח ט י יא י**ב** יג יד טו טז יז יח יט כ כא כב כג כד כה כו כז כח כט ל

Storch. חֲסִידָה   Wolf. זְאֵב

SITE OF THE HOLY TEMPLE
JERUSALEM, 20TH CENTURY

The yearnings of Jews everywhere for the city of Jerusalem are manifested in many ceremonial and everyday objects. This glass painting of the site of the Holy Temple decorated in a folk style is attributed to Moses Shah, who moved to Jerusalem at the end of the nineteenth century. The building depicted here is the Dome of the Rock, the most commonly used image of Jerusalem (after the Holy Temple), along with the Hebrew inscription "If I forget thee let my right hand lose its cunning" (Psalms 167:5–6).

OIL PAINT ON GLASS; FOIL
46.5 x 63 CM
PHOTOGRAPH: ISRAEL MUSEUM

December | 1 2 3 4 5 6 7 8 9 10 11 12 13 **14** 15 16 17 18 19 20 21 22 23 24 25 26 27 28 29 30 31

כסלו | א ב ג ד ה ו ז ח ט י יא יב **יג** יד טו טז יז יח יט כ כא כב כג כד כה כו כז כח כט ל

Hanukkah lamp
Poland, 18th century

This Hanukkah lamp has two sockets on either side, indicating that it would also have been used to light the Sabbath lamps during Hanukkah. Jewish artists used sandcasting to produce brass Hanukkah lamps, which enabled them to make several pieces from one mold. This is probably why Polish lamps of this type were popular. Alongside brass lamps were more intricate lamps of silver made for wealthy families.

Cast brass
23 x 32 cm
Photograph: Israel Museum

December | 1 2 3 4 5 6 7 8 9 10 11 12 13 14 **15** 16 17 18 19 20 21 22 23 24 25 26 27 28 29 30 31

א ב ג ד ה ו ז ח ט י'א י'ב י'ג **י'ד** ט ו ט ז י ז י ח י ט כ כא כב כג כד כה כו כז כח כט ל | כסלו

Baking Indian bread
Bene Israel community, Thane, India, 1983

Jews, like other people in India, baked special breads called chapatis, which are
thin, round, and contain no yeast. They are baked over an open fire. Since chapatis
are tasty only when freshly made, women would get up early in the morning to
prepare them for breakfast.

PHOTOGRAPH: ISRAEL MUSEUM/
ORPA SLAPAK

December | 1 2 3 4 5 6 7 8 9 10 11 12 13 14 15 **16** 17 18 19 20 21 22 23 24 25 26 27 28 29 30 31

א ב ג ד ה ו ז ח ט י יא יב יג יד **טו** טז יז יח יט כ כא כב כג כד כה כו כז כח כט ל | כסלו

MIZRAH
LEUTERHAUSEN, GERMANY, 1833

The *mizrah* is a single sheet or plaque hung on an eastern wall facing Jerusalem to indicate the direction of prayer. This densely decorated sheet is covered with inscriptions including the *shiviti* verse from Psalms 16:8 "I have set the Lord always before me." It also features various benedictions, such as for wine, sustenance, and fruits of the fields.

PEN AND INK AND GOUACHE ON PAPER
32 X 41.4 CM
THE FEUCHTWANGER COLLECTION
PURCHASED AND DONATED TO THE
ISRAEL MUSEUM BY BARUCH AND
RUTH RAPPAPORT OF GENEVA
PHOTOGRAPH: ISRAEL MUSEUM/
PETER LENYI

December | 1 2 3 4 5 6 7 8 9 10 11 12 13 14 15 16 **17** 18 19 20 21 22 23 24 25 26 27 28 29 30 31

כסלו | א ב ג ד ה ו ז ח ט י י״א י״ב י״ג י״ד ט״ו **ט״ז** י״ז י״ח י״ט כ כ״א כ״ב כ״ג כ״ד כ״ה כ״ו כ״ז כ״ח כ״ט ל

Amuletic plaques
Sefrou, Morocco, 20th century

Eight silver triangles attached to a cord with loops bear initials engraved on both sides. This form of amulet was thought to protect against the effects of the evil eye.

Silver
3.5 cm (height)
Photograph: Israel Museum/
Zeev Radovan

December | 1 2 3 4 5 6 7 8 9 10 11 12 13 14 15 16 17 **18** 19 20 21 22 23 24 25 26 27 28 29 30 31

א ב ג ד ה ו ז ח ט י יא יב יג יד טו טז **יז** יח יט כ כא כב כג כד כה כו כז כח כט ל | כסלו

Hanukkah lamp
Bombay area, India, 20th century

This Hanukkah lamp from the Bene Israel, the largest of the three Jewish communities in India, was lit in the synagogue during the evening service. Later, after the lighting in the home, the family would celebrate by eating sweet dishes. Both the domestic Hanukkah lamps and those used in the synagogue had a back wall and a shelf into which arms with glass cups were fitted. The back wall assumed a variety of forms: Stars of David, hearts, birds' heads, triangles, polygons, or wavy outlines.

Wood; glass
40 x 46 cm
Photograph: Israel Museum/
Avraham Hay

December | 1 2 3 4 5 6 7 8 9 10 11 12 13 14 15 16 17 18 **19** 20 21 22 23 24 25 26 27 28 29 30 31

כסלו | א ב ג ד ה ו ז ח ט י יא יב יג יד טו טז יז **יח** יט כ כא כב כג כד כה כו כז כח כט ל

Hanukkah lamps
Yemen, late 19th–early 20th century

These Yemenite Hanukkah lamps are each carved from a single block of stone and have eight compartments for oil with no place for the additional *shammash* (servant light). They are similar to an early Hanukkah lamp found in the south of France from the twelfth century, and a contemporary type in the Anti-Atlas region of Morocco. Hanukkah lamps from the Talmudic period in the Holy Land were probably also made of stone and may therefore have been the source for the Yemenite stone lamps.

CARVED GRAY SOAPSTONE
21–30 X 15–17 X 5 CM
PERMANENT LOAN: SALMAN SCHOCKEN,
TEL AVIV
PHOTOGRAPH: ISRAEL MUSEUM/
DAVID HARRIS

December | 1 2 3 4 5 6 7 8 9 10 11 12 13 14 15 16 17 18 19 **20** 21 22 23 24 25 26 27 28 29 30 31

כסלו | א ב ג ד ה ו ז ח ט י יא יב יג יד טו טז יז יח **יט** כ כא כב כג כד כה כו כז כח כט ל

Hanukkah lamp
Leipzig, Germany, 1799

This Hanukkah lamp from Germany is richly ornamented in a triple-arched structure. The central gate is crowned by a two-headed eagle and flanked by two bears, beneath which are a crown and a seven-branched menorah motif guarded by the figures of Moses and Aaron. On the two gates are the blessings recited when kindling the Hanukkah lights, as well as the Hanukkah hymns. The figure of Judith holding the head of the Assyrian general Holofernes is seen to the left of the lamp; this story from the Apocrypha, in which Judith saved the Jewish nation, came to be connected with Hanukkah in medieval Jewish folklore. The style of this Hanukkah lamp is highly influenced by the rich decorative elements used in German silverwork of the eighteenth century.

REPOUSSÉ, ENGRAVED, CAST,
PARTLY GILT SILVER
27.5 X 30 X 10 CM
GIFT OF IGNAZIO BAUER,
MADRID 1950
PHOTOGRAPH: ISRAEL MUSEUM/
DAVID HARRIS

December | 1 2 3 4 5 6 7 8 9 10 11 12 13 14 15 16 17 18 19 20 **21** 22 23 24 25 26 27 28 29 30 31

כסלו | א ב ג ד ה ו ז ח ט י יא יב יג יד טו טז יז יח יט **כ** כא כב כג כד כה כו כז כח כט ל

HOLLEKREISCH
SWITZERLAND, 1950

In the ceremony for the naming of a girl, held in the home in Southern Germany, Alsace, and Switzerland, the cradle would be lifted and the word *hollekreisch* called out, as depicted in this naive folk art picture. This custom was known in the area as long ago as the twelfth century and was common among Jews well into the twentieth century. During the ceremony, children were invited to lift the cradle three times while calling out "*Hollekreisch*, what shall the baby be named?" Most probably the word derives from the French: "*haut la crèche*," meaning "raise the cradle."

ARTIST: ALIS GUGGENHEIM, 1950
OIL ON CANVAS
54 X 44 CM
GIFT OF SIEGMUND WIENER
AND EVA WIENER-KARO,
LUCERNE, SWITZERLAND
PHOTOGRAPH: ISRAEL MUSEUM

December | 1 2 3 4 5 6 7 8 9 10 11 12 13 14 15 16 17 18 19 20 21 **22** 23 24 25 26 27 28 29 30 31

א ב ג ד ה ו ז ח ט י יא יב יג יד טו טז יז יח יט כ **כא** כב כג כד כה כו כז כח כט ל | כסלו

Hanukkah Workshop in the Youth Wing, 2003

A seven-year-old girl concentrates on decorating her own dreidel, the four-sided spinning top traditionally played with during Hanukkah. During Jewish holidays the Youth Wing holds workshops for the whole family. Thousands of people come every day and enjoy the festive atmosphere. The children make art that is connected to the theme of the holy day and to the museums' collections.

Photograph: Israel Museum

December | 1 2 3 4 5 6 7 8 9 10 11 12 13 14 15 16 17 18 19 20 21 22 **23** 24 25 26 27 28 29 30 31

כסלו | א ב ג ד ה ו ז ח ט י יא יב יג יד טו טז יז יח יט כ כא **כב** כג כד כה כו כז כח כט ל

INTERIOR OF THE KADAVUMBAGAM SYNAGOGUE
COCHIN, INDIA
CONSTRUCTED 1539–1544,
DECORATED 16TH–18TH CENTURIES

The Kadavumbagam Synagogue in the town of Cochin in southwest India was one of eight synagogues in the area. According to local tradition, the Jewish community of Cochin is more than two thousand years old. The interior decoration and woodcarving of the synagogue and Torah Ark, with its lotus blossoms, birds, and cobras, was no doubt inspired by local elements and motifs. A characteristic feature of all the synagogues in this region was a semicircular balcony in front of the women's gallery, which provided an additional area for reading the Torah on Sabbath and festivals, along with the reader's desk (*tevah*) on the ground floor. This feature is rarely found in other synagogues.

CARVED AND PAINTED TEAK
8.8 X 5.2 X 5.5 M
GIFT OF DELLA AND FRED WORMS,
LONDON AND JERUSALEM
PHOTOGRAPH: ISRAEL MUSEUM/
NAHUM SLAPAK

December | 1 2 3 4 5 6 7 8 9 10 11 12 13 14 15 16 17 18 19 20 21 22 23 **24** 25 26 27 28 29 30 31

כסלו | א ב ג ד ה ו ז ח ט י יא יב יג יד טו טז יז יח יט כ כא כב **כג** כד כה כו כז כח כט ל

HANUKKAH LAMP
COCHIN, INDIA, LATE 19TH CENTURY

The Jews of Cochin, one of the three Jewish communities living in southwest India, celebrated Hanukkah with their own special ceremonies and traditions. On the Sabbath before the holiday they usually read from the Scroll of Antiochus, which briefly tells the story of the Hanukkah miracle. On Hanukkah itself, after the lights had been kindled at home, the whole family would walk to synagogue along a candlelit road often decorated on both sides with banana stalks.

December | 1 2 3 4 5 6 7 8 9 10 11 12 13 14 15 16 17 18 19 20 21 22 23 24 **25** 26 27 28 29 30 31

כסלו | א ב ג ד ה ו ז ח ט י יא יב יג יד טו טז יז יח יט כ כא כב כג **כד** כה כו כז כח כט ל

Hanukkah lamp
Gorodnitza (?), Ukraine, 19th century

This bench-shaped Hanukkah lamp is colorfully painted with illustrations of a rural scene near a river surrounded by trees. At the top of the back wall are two lions. Before porcelain was discovered, Hanukkah lamps were also made of faience produced by a flourishing Jewish industry in Galicia.

Painted porcelain;
decalcomania
146 x 269 x 110 cm
The Feuchtwanger Collection
purchased and donated to the
Israel Museum by Baruch and
Ruth Rappaport of Geneva.
Photograph: Israel Museum/
David Harris

December | 1 2 3 4 5 6 7 8 9 10 11 12 13 14 15 16 17 18 19 20 21 22 23 24 25 **26** 27 28 29 30 31

כסלו | א ב ג ד ה ו ז ח ט י י״א י״ב י״ג יד טו טז יז יח יט כ כא כב כג כד **כה** כו כז כח כט ל

Hanukkah lamp
Nuremberg, Germany, 1721

This Hanukkah lamp was crafted in Nuremberg, an important center of silver-smithing in the eighteenth century. The symbolic image of Judith appearing on this lamp has been connected to the festival since medieval times. Because of her act of heroism in killing the military leader Holofernes, she is often associated with the Hanukkah hero and soldier, Judah the Maccabee, who is also depicted on this lamp. The prayer recited after the blessing on the lights is engraved in Hebrew inside the medallion.

Repoussé, engraved, and partly gilt silver; semiprecious stones
Gift of Daniela Dror and Etienne Shwovacher, Tel Aviv
32.4 x 26.6 cm
Photograph: Israel Museum/ Yoram Lehmann

December | 1 2 3 4 5 6 7 8 9 10 11 12 13 14 15 16 17 18 19 20 21 22 23 24 25 26 **27** 28 29 30 31

כסלו | א ב ג ד ה ו ז ח ט י י"א י"ב י"ג י"ד ט"ו ט"ז י"ז י"ח י"ט כ כ"א כ"ב כ"ג כ"ד כ"ה **כ"ז** כ"ז כ"ח כ"ט ל

Hanukkah lamp
Germany, 1574

This rather early example of a Hanukkah lamp clearly shows the influence of Gothic architecture in the dragon heads and side panels fashioned in the shape of towers commonly found in European castles and city walls in the Middle Ages. The hymn recited after lighting the Hanukkah lights is inscribed on the back panel as well as the name of the artisan or the person who commissioned the lamp, Meir Heilprin, and the Hebrew year equivalent to 1574. Many Hanukkah lamps can be attributed to their country of origin on stylistic and architectural elements.

CAST AND CHASED BRONZE
22.3 X 34.4 X 10.4 CM
GIFT OF MR. AND MRS. A. A. HEN,
THE HAGUE, THE NETHERLANDS,
1948
PHOTOGRAPH: ISRAEL MUSEUM/
DAVID HARRIS

December | 1 2 3 4 5 6 7 8 9 10 11 12 13 14 15 16 17 18 19 20 21 22 23 24 25 26 27 **28** 29 30 31

כסלו | א ב ג ד ה ו ז ח ט י יא יב יג יד טו טז יז יח יט כ כא כב כג כד כה כו **כז** כח כט ל

HANUKKAH LAMP
MARRAKESH, MOROCCO,
LATE 19TH—MID 20TH CENTURY

The canopy roof of this Hanukkah lamp with its colorful glass windows, grid side panels, and arabesque decorations all conjure images of a legendary Oriental palace. The three-dimensional architectural elements of this lamp make it unusual and exceptional.

REPOUSSÉ, ENGRAVED, AND PIERCED
SHEET BRASS; COLORED GLASS
36 X 22 X 8.5 CM
GIFT OF THE ZEYDE SCHULMANN
COLLECTION
PHOTOGRAPH: ISRAEL MUSEUM/
AVRAHAM HAY

December | 1 2 3 4 5 6 7 8 9 10 11 12 13 14 15 16 17 18 19 20 21 22 23 24 25 26 27 28 **29** 30 31

כסלו | א ב ג ד ה ו ז ח ט י יא יב יג יד טו טז יז יח יט כ כא כב כג כד כה כו כז **כח** כט ל

Hanukkah lamps
Mazagan, Morocco, ca. 1950

The popular use of Hanukkah lamps leads to different forms and an innovative range of designs, sometimes incorporating cheap materials such as the metal meant for sardine tins, as can clearly be seen on the tin backplate. According to the maker, Meir Ben Ami, who later immigrated to Israel, this type of Hanukkah lamp was given to newlyweds as a wedding gift.

Maker: Meir Ben Ami
(b. Mazagan, 1910)
Sheet metal; cloth strips; glass
37.5 x 26
Gift of the Zeyde Schulmann
Collection
Photograph: Israel Museum/
Avraham Hay

December | 1 2 3 4 5 6 7 8 9 10 11 12 13 14 15 16 17 18 19 20 21 22 23 24 25 26 27 28 29 **30** 31

כסלו | א ב ג ד ה ו ז ח ט י יא יב יג יד טו טז יז יח יט כ כא כב כג כד כה כו כז כח **כט** ל

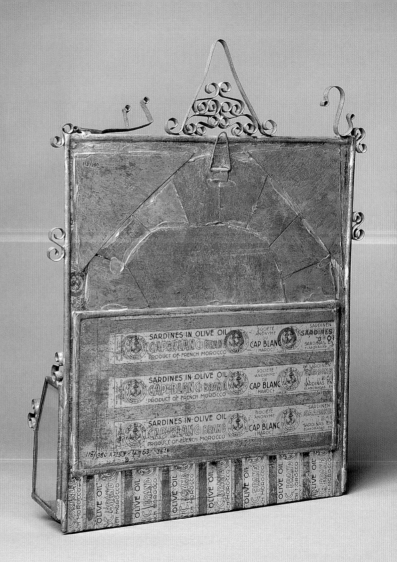

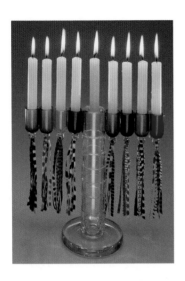

DESIGNER: LEO LIONNI
MAKER: GINO CENEDESE E FIGLIO,
VENICE, ITALY
GLASS; FABRIC RIBBONS
24 X 26 X 19 CM
PHOTOGRAPH: ISRAEL MUSEUM/
NAHUM SLAPAK

HANUKKAH LAMP
MURANO, ITALY, 1995

This modern, minimalistic Hanukkah lamp fashioned by the Italian designer
Leo Lionni is made from vividly colored ribbons and crystal from the prestigious
Murano glass factory, well known for its exceptional and unique products. It can
be assembled in a variety of ways, inviting users to exercise their own creativity.

December | 1 2 3 4 5 6 7 8 9 10 11 12 13 14 15 16 17 18 19 20 21 22 23 24 25 26 27 28 29 30 31

כסלו | א ב ג ד ה ו ז ח ט י יא יב יג יד טו טז יז יח יט כ כא כב כג כד כה כו כז כח כט ל

ABOUT THE JEWISH CALENDAR

The Jewish calendar is a combined solar/lunar calendar and consists of twelve lunar months. The months are calculated by the appearance of the new moon, and the beginning of the year by the earth's position in relation to the sun. In order to coordinate the lunar months with the solar year, a leap month was inserted seven times in every nineteen-year cycle. The first day of each month is called Rosh Hodesh, as is the thirtieth day (when it occurs) of the preceding month.

The Jewish day begins and ends at sundown. Thus, all holidays begin at sundown of the day preceding the date shown and end at sundown on the last day shown. The three main festivals—Passover, Shavuot, and Sukkot, also celebrated for historical reasons—reflect the changing seasons and correspond to the agricultural year. There is a difference between the length of holidays in Israel and in the Jewish Diaspora. Passover and Sukkot are celebrated for seven days in Israel and eight abroad, Shavuot for one day in Israel and two abroad.

The new year begins with Rosh Hashanah, at the start of the Hebrew month of Tishrei, which falls in September or October. As 2004/2005 is a leap year corresponding to the Hebrew year 5765, an extra month (Adar II) is added.

Wherever possible, the images in this book were chosen to match the calendar and holiday dates in the adjoining list.

Notable Dates	2005	5765/5766	Notable Dates	2005	5765/5766
Rosh Hodesh Shevat	Shevat 1	January 11	Rosh Hodesh Sivan	Sivan 1	June 8
Tu B'Shevat	Shevat 15	January 25	Shavuot	Sivan 6 (7)	June 13 (14)
Rosh Hodesh	Shevat 30	February 9	Rosh Hodesh	Sivan 30	July 7
Rosh Hodesh Adar	Adar 1	February 10	Rosh Hodesh Tammuz	Tammuz 1	July 8
Rosh Hodesh	Adar 30	March 11	Anniversary of the Death of Theodor Herzl	Tammuz 13	July 20
Rosh Hodesh Adar II	Adar II, 1	March 12	Fast of 17 Tammuz	Tammuz 17	July 24
Anniversary of the Death of Moses	Adar II, 7	March 18	Tish'ah beAv	Av 9	August 14
Fast of Esther	Adar II, 13	March 24	Rosh Hodesh	Av 30	September 4
Purim	Adar II, 14	March 25	Rosh Hodesh Elul	Elul 1	September 5
Shushan Purim	Adar II, 15	March 26	Rosh Hashanah	Tishrei 1 5766	October 4
Rosh Hodesh Nisan	Nisan 1	April 10	Rosh Hashanah	Tishrei 2	October 5
Passover	Nisan 14–21 (22)	April 23–30 (May 1)	Yom Kippur	Tishrei 10	October 13
Holocaust Memorial Day	Nisan 27	May 6	Sukkot	Tishrei 15–21 (22)	October 18–24 (25)
Rosh Hodesh	Nisan 30	May 9	Simhat Torah	Tishrei 22 (23)	October 25 (26)
Rosh Hodesh Iyyar	Iyyar 1	May 10	Rosh Hodesh	Tishrei 30	November 2
Memorial Day for Israel Defence Forces	Iyyar 2	May 11	Rosh Hodesh Heshvan	Heshvan 1	November 3
Israel Independence Day	Iyyar 3	May 12	Memorial day for the Matriarch Rachel	Heshvan 11	November 13
Lag B'Omer	Iyyar 18	May 27	Rosh Hodesh Kislev	Kislev 1	December 2
Jerusalem Day	Iyyar 28	June 6	Hanukkah	Kislev 25–Tevet 2	December 26–January 2, 2006

Contributors

Yigal Zalmona
Chief Curator-at-Large

Bronfman Archaeology Wing

Dr. Silvia Rozenberg
Tamar and Teddy Kollek Chief Curator

Michal Dayagi-Mendels
Frieder Burda Senior Curator of Israelite and Persian Periods

Haim Gitler
Curator of Numismatics

Yael Israeli
Senior Curator Emerita

David Mevorah
Curator of Hellenistic, Roman, and Byzantine Periods

Dr. Adolfo Roitman
Head of the Shrine of the Book and Curator of the Dead Sea Scrolls

Fine Arts Wing

Yudit Caplan
Associate Curator, Department of Photography

Meira Perry-Lehmann
Michael Bromberg Senior Curator of Prints and Drawings

Timna Seligman
Associate Curator, David Orgler Department of Israel Art

Shlomit Steinberg
Hans Dichand Curator of European Art

Ariel Tishby
Norman Bier Section for Maps of the Holy Land, Department of Prints and Drawings

Judaica and Jewish Ethnography Wing

Daisy Raccah-Djivre
Chief Curator, Curator of the Skirball Department of Judaica

Nurit Bank
Head of the Isidore and Anne Falk Information Center for Judaica and Jewish Ethnography

No'am Bar'am Ben-Yossef
Curator in the Julia and Leo Forchheimer Department of Jewish Ethnography

Chaya Benjamin
Curator in the Skirball Department of Judaica

Tania Coen-Uzzielli
Associate Curator in the Skirball Department of Judaica

Rosemary Eshel
Assistant Curator, Isidore and Anne Falk Information Center for Judaica and Jewish Ethnography

Ester Muchawsky-Schnapper
Curator in the Julia and Leo Forchheimer Department of Jewish Ethnography

The Ruth Youth Wing

Nurit Shilo-Cohen
Chief Curator

Publications Department

Nirit Zur
Head of Publications Department

Anna Barber
Senior Editor of English Publications

SELECTED BIBLIOGRAPHY

JUDAICA AND JEWISH ETHNOGRAPHY
Texts have been written and adapted from:

Bank, Nurit, and Allison Kupietzky, eds. *Cycles of Jewish Life: An Interactive Multimedia Virtual Exhibition from the Collections of the Israel Museum* (CD-ROM). Jerusalem: The Isidore and Anne Falk Information Center for Judaica and Jewish Ethnography, The Israel Museum, 2002.

Bar'am-Ben Yossef, No'am, ed. *Brides and Betrothals: Jewish Wedding Rituals in Afghanistan*. Jerusalem: The Israel Museum, 1998.

Ben-Ami, Alia, ed. *In All their Finery: Jewels from the Jewish World*. Jerusalem: The Israel Museum, 2002.

Benjamin, Chaya.. *North African Lights: HanukkahLamps from the Zeyde Schulmann Collection in the Israel Museum*. Jerusalem: The Israel Museum, 2003.

———. *The Stieglitz Collection: Masterpieces of Jewish Art*. Jerusalem: The Israel Museum, 1987.

Fishof, Iris, ed. *Jewish Art Masterpieces*. Westport, Conn.: Hugh Lauter Levin Associates, 1994.

Mikdash-Shamailov, Liya, ed. *Mountain Jews: Customs and Daily Life in the Caucasus*. Jerusalem: The Israel Museum, 2002.

Muchawsky-Schnapper, Ester. *The Yemenites: Two Thousand Years of Jewish Culture*. Jerusalem: The Israel Museum, 2000.

Müller-Lancet, Aviva, ed. *La Vie Juive au Maroc*. Jerusalem: The Israel Museum, 1983.

Sarfati, Rachel. *Sukkahs from Around the World*. Jerusalem: The Israel Museum, 2003.

Shahar, Isaiah. *Jewish Tradition in Art: The Feuchtwanger Collection*. Jerusalem: The Israel Museum, 1981.

Shwartz-Be'eri, Ora. *The Jews of Kurdistan: Daily Life, Customs, Arts and Crafts*. Jerusalem: The Israel Museum, 2000.

———. *"Jerusalem, the Homeland."* Israel Museum Journal 14 (1996): 17–34.

Slapak, Orpa, ed. *The Jews of India: A Story of Three Communities*. Jerusalem: The Israel Museum, 1995.

Yuhasz, Esther, ed. *Sephardi Jews of the Ottoman Empire: Aspects of Material Culture*. Jerusalem: The Israel Museum, 1990.

FINE ARTS

Chill, Abraham. *The Minhagim: The Customs and Ceremonies of Judaism, Their Origins and Rationale*. New York: Sepher-Hermon Press, 1989.

Laor, Eran, and Shoshana Klein. *Maps of the Holy Land: Cartobibliography of Printed Maps, 1475–1900*. New York: Meridian, 1986.

Nebenzahl, Kenneth. *Maps of the Holy Land, Images of Terra Sancta through Two Millennia*. Tel Aviv: Steimatzky, 1986.

Tishby, Ariel, ed. *Holy Land in Maps*. Jerusalem: The Israel Museum, 2001.

Wahrman, Nahum. *Israel's Holidays and Festivals, Customs and Symbols*. Jerusalem: Ahiyosef Publishing, 1964 (Hebrew).

Index

Harry N. Abrams, Inc.
EDITOR: Sharon AvRutick
DESIGNER: Helene Silverman
PRODUCTION MANAGERS: Stan Redfern/Norman Watkins

The Israel Museum, Jerusalem
CURATOR IN CHARGE OF PROJECT: Daisy Raccah-Djivre
PROJECT COORDINATOR: Rosemary Eshel
ARCHAEOLOGY COORDINATOR: Rotem Arieli
EDITOR FOR ARCHAEOLOGY: Nancy Benovitz
IMAGE RESEARCH FOR ARCHAEOLOGY: Bella Gershovich
COORDINATOR FOR FINE ARTS: Timna Seligman
IMAGE RESEARCH: Bella Zaichik

Israel Museum Products
GENERAL MANAGER: Rita Gans
PHOTO RESEARCH: Aliza Rosen
COORDINATOR: Ilana Frank
MARKETING MANAGER: Ronny Leviner

Library of Congress Cataloging-in-Publication Data

The Jewish world: 365 days: from the collections of the Israel Museum, Jerusalem
    p. cm.
Includes bibliographical references and index.
ISBN 0-8109-5579-2 (hardcover)
1. Art, Jewish. 2. Judaism—Liturgical objects. 3. Jewish art and symbolism.
4. Jews—Antiquities. 5. Art—Jerusalem. 6 Muze'on Yisra'el (Jerusalem)
7. Art calendars. 8. Jews—History.

N7414.8.I75J475 2004
704.9'4896'074569442—dc22
2004009024

Printed and bound in China

10 9 8 7 6 5 4 3 2 1

Harry N. Abrams, Inc.
100 Fifth Avenue
New York, N.Y. 10011
www.abramsbooks.com

Abrams is a subsidiary of

LA MARTINIÈRE

FRONT COVER TOP: Necklace, Sous region, Morocco, early 20th century (see July 26)

FRONT COVER BOTTOM: Shofar, Germany, 1681 (see October 4)

SPINE: Menorah, Synagogue at Ein Gedi, Byzantine Period, 6th century CE (see August 5)

BACK COVER: *Jerusalem, the Holy City, by far the most famous city of Judea and the East*, 1575 (see April 6)

PAGE 1: Gold glass base, Roman-Byzantine Period, Rome, 4th century CE (see February 22)